CompTIA.

Becoming a CompTIA Certified IT Professional is Easy

It's also the best way to reach greater professional opportunities and rewards.

Why Get CompTIA Certified?

Growing Demand

Labor estimates predict some technology fields will experience growth of over 20% by the year 2020.* CompTIA certification qualifies the skills required to join this workforce.

Higher Salaries

IT professionals with certifications on their resume command better jobs, earn higher salaries and have more doors open to new multi-industry opportunities.

Verified Strengths

91% of hiring managers indicate CompTIA certifications are valuable in validating IT expertise, making certification the best way to demonstrate your competency and knowledge to employers.**

Universal Skills

CompTIA certifications are vendor neutral—which means that certified professionals can proficiently work with an extensive variety of hardware and software found in most organizations.

Certify

Learn more about what the exam covers by reviewing the following:

- Exam objectives for key study points.
- Sample questions for a general overview of what to expect on the exam and examples of question format.
- Visit online forums, like LinkedIn, to see what other IT professionals say about CompTIA exams.

Purchase a voucher at a Pearson VUE testing center or at CompTIAstore.com.

- Register for your exam at a Pearson VUE testing center:
- Visit pearsonvue.com/CompTIA to find the closest testing center to you.
- Schedule the exam online. You will be required to enter your voucher number or provide payment information at registration.
- Take your certification exam.

Congratulations on your CompTIA certification!

- Make sure to add your certification to your resume.
- Check out the CompTIA Certification Roadmap to plan your next career move.

Learn more: **Certification.CompTIA.org/ITFundamentals**

* Source: CompTIA 9th Annual Information Security Trends study: 500 U.S. IT and Business Executives Responsible for Security
** Source: CompTIA Employer Perceptions of IT Training and Certification
*** Source: 2013 IT Skills and Salary Report by CompTIA Authorized Partner

CompTIA® IT Fundamentals™ (Exam FC0-U51 or FC0-Z51)

CompTIA® IT Fundamentals™ (Exam FC0-U51 or FC0-Z51)

Part Number: 093004
Course Edition: 1.1

Acknowledgements

We wish to thank the following project team for their contributions to the development of this certification study guide: Pamela J. Taylor, Laurie A. Perry, Gail Sandler, Jason Nufryk, Alex Tong, and Catherine M. Albano.

Notices

DISCLAIMER

TRADEMARK NOTICES

CompTIA® IT Fundamentals™ (Exam FC0-U51 or FC0-Z51)

About This Course

If you are a high-end computer user at home or college considering a career in information technology, or interested in furthering your knowledge about personal computers, the *CompTIA® IT Fundamentals™ (Exam FC0-U51 or FC0-Z51)* course is the first step in your preparation. In this course, you will identify PC components, work with files and folders, and conduct basic software installations. This course will provide you with the fundamental skills and concepts required to maintain, support, and work efficiently with personal computers. In addition, you will acquire the essential skills and information you need to set up, configure, maintain, troubleshoot, and perform preventative maintenance of the hardware and software components of a basic personal computer workstation and basic wireless devices. You will also implement basic security measures and implement basic computer and user support practices.

Whether you are a home user, an experienced knowledge worker, or someone new to the work force considering an information technology (IT) career, the *CompTIA® IT Fundamentals™ (Exam FC0-U51 or FC0-Z51)* course can benefit you in many ways. Having a basic foundational knowledge about personal computers and the skills required to work with them provides you with the starting point to build your career. If your existing job role is linked with personal computers, this course will provide you with the fundamental technical knowledge about personal computers that you need to work efficiently in your current role. It will also assist you if you are preparing to take the CompTIA® IT Fundamentals™ examination (Exam FC0-U51 or FC0-Z51).

Course Description

Target Student

This course is designed for individuals who are considering a career in information technology (IT) and who might be planning to pursue CompTIA IT Fundamentals certification, CompTIA A+™ certification, or other similar certifications.

Course Prerequisites

To ensure your success in your course you will need basic Windows end-user skills. You can obtain this level of skills and knowledge by taking either of the following CHOICE courses, or have equivalent experience:

- *Using Microsoft® Windows® 8.1*
- *Microsoft® Windows® 8.1 Transition from Windows 7*

Course Objectives

Upon successful completion of this course, you will be able to safely set up a basic workstation, including installing basic hardware and software and establishing basic network connectivity; identify and correct compatibility issues; identify and prevent basic security risks; and practice basic support techniques on computing devices.

You will:

- Identify hardware commonly found in or attached to computing devices.
- Identify software commonly installed on computing devices.
- Set up a basic workstation.
- Configure network access.
- Work with files, folders, and applications.
- Configure and use wireless devices.
- Secure computing devices.
- Support computers and users.

The CHOICE Home Screen

Logon and access information for your CHOICE environment will be provided with your class experience. The CHOICE platform is your entry point to the CHOICE learning experience, of which this course manual is only one part.

On the CHOICE Home screen, you can access the CHOICE Course screens for your specific courses. Visit the CHOICE Course screen both during and after class to make use of the world of support and instructional resources that make up the CHOICE experience.

Each CHOICE Course screen will give you access to the following resources:

- **Classroom**: A link to your training provider's classroom environment.
- **eBook**: An interactive electronic version of the printed book for your course.
- **Files**: Any course files available to download.
- **Checklists**: Step-by-step procedures and general guidelines you can use as a reference during and after class.
- **LearnTOs**: Brief animated videos that enhance and extend the classroom learning experience.
- **Assessment**: A course assessment for your self-assessment of the course content.
- Social media resources that enable you to collaborate with others in the learning community using professional communications sites such as LinkedIn or microblogging tools such as Twitter.

Depending on the nature of your course and the components chosen by your learning provider, the CHOICE Course screen may also include access to elements such as:

- LogicalLABS, a virtual technical environment for your course.
- Various partner resources related to the courseware.
- Related certifications or credentials.
- A link to your training provider's website.
- Notices from the CHOICE administrator.
- Newsletters and other communications from your learning provider.
- Mentoring services.

Visit your CHOICE Home screen often to connect, communicate, and extend your learning experience!

How to Use This Book

As You Learn

This book is divided into lessons and topics, covering a subject or a set of related subjects. In most cases, lessons are arranged in order of increasing proficiency.

The results-oriented topics include relevant and supporting information you need to master the content. Each topic has various types of activities designed to enable you to solidify your understanding of the informational material presented in the course. Information is provided for reference and reflection to facilitate understanding and practice.

Data files for various activities as well as other supporting files for the course are available by download from the CHOICE Course screen. In addition to sample data for the course exercises, the course files may contain media components to enhance your learning and additional reference materials for use both during and after the course.

Checklists of procedures and guidelines can be used during class and as after-class references when you're back on the job and need to refresh your understanding.

At the back of the book, you will find a glossary of the definitions of the terms and concepts used throughout the course. You will also find an index to assist in locating information within the instructional components of the book.

As You Review

Any method of instruction is only as effective as the time and effort you, the student, are willing to invest in it. In addition, some of the information that you learn in class may not be important to you immediately, but it may become important later. For this reason, we encourage you to spend some time reviewing the content of the course after your time in the classroom.

As a Reference

The organization and layout of this book make it an easy-to-use resource for future reference. Taking advantage of the glossary, index, and table of contents, you can use this book as a first source of definitions, background information, and summaries.

Course Icons

Watch throughout the material for the following visual cues.

Icon	*Description*
	A **Note** provides additional information, guidance, or hints about a topic or task.
	A **Caution** note makes you aware of places where you need to be particularly careful with your actions, settings, or decisions so that you can be sure to get the desired results of an activity or task.
	LearnTO notes show you where an associated LearnTO is particularly relevant to the content. Access LearnTOs from your CHOICE Course screen.
	Checklists provide job aids you can use after class as a reference to perform skills back on the job. Access checklists from your CHOICE Course screen.
	Social notes remind you to check your CHOICE Course screen for opportunities to interact with the CHOICE community using social media.

1 Identifying Computer Hardware

Lesson Time: 2 hours, 30 minutes

Lesson Objectives

In this lesson, you will identify computer hardware. You will:

- Identify various types of computing devices used in today's workplace.
- Identify internal computer components.
- Compare common computer connector types.
- Identify common peripheral devices.

Lesson Introduction

If you've worked with computers before, you know that they are useful and versatile machines that hold vast amounts of information and help you perform a wide range of tasks in a short amount of time. However, as a computer user, you may not know much about what goes on under the covers of the computers that you use every day.

In this lesson, you'll identify the hardware components commonly found in or attached to personal computers. By looking at the various types of computing devices that are available today, as well as the internal and external hardware that make up most computer systems, you'll be able to better describe their characteristics and functions.

TOPIC A

Identify Types of Computing Devices

There is a wide variety of computer types in use today. Some of these you won't interact with directly, others might be too small or underpowered for your needs, and some might be overpowered and too bulky for your needs. Somewhere out there, though, is just the right computing device to meet your needs. You might also have different needs at work or school than you do for home and recreation.

In this topic, you will explore a variety of computing devices from pocket-sized to room-sized and everything in between.

Computing Devices

A *computing device* is an electronic machine that uses binary data to automatically perform calculations. These calculations might be as simple as adding 1+1 and giving you the result of 2 or as complex as calculating the trajectory of an unmanned rocket into space or scanning your face to allow you into a locked room. These tools come in a variety of sizes and abilities. Some are small enough to fit in your pocket and some require a room to house them. In general, smaller devices contain fewer computing abilities.

Personal Computers

A *personal computer*, or PC, is a computing device designed to be used by one person at a time. These computing devices are found in offices, schools, and homes. PCs are used to run commercial software applications, access the Internet, communicate with other people over email, create new applications in any one of a number of programming languages, play games, do research, and much more. PCs are limited only by your imagination and your computer's computing power.

Desktop Computers

A *desktop computer* is a computing device designed to be placed on or near a user's desk. Its size and its need to be plugged in to a power source mean it typically needs to be placed where it will be used and not be moved. Desktop computers are usually tall, narrow rectangles that can be placed on or under the user's desk. The size varies greatly, but often is between 4 and 8 inches wide, about 10 to 16 inches tall, and about 14 to 20 inches front to back.

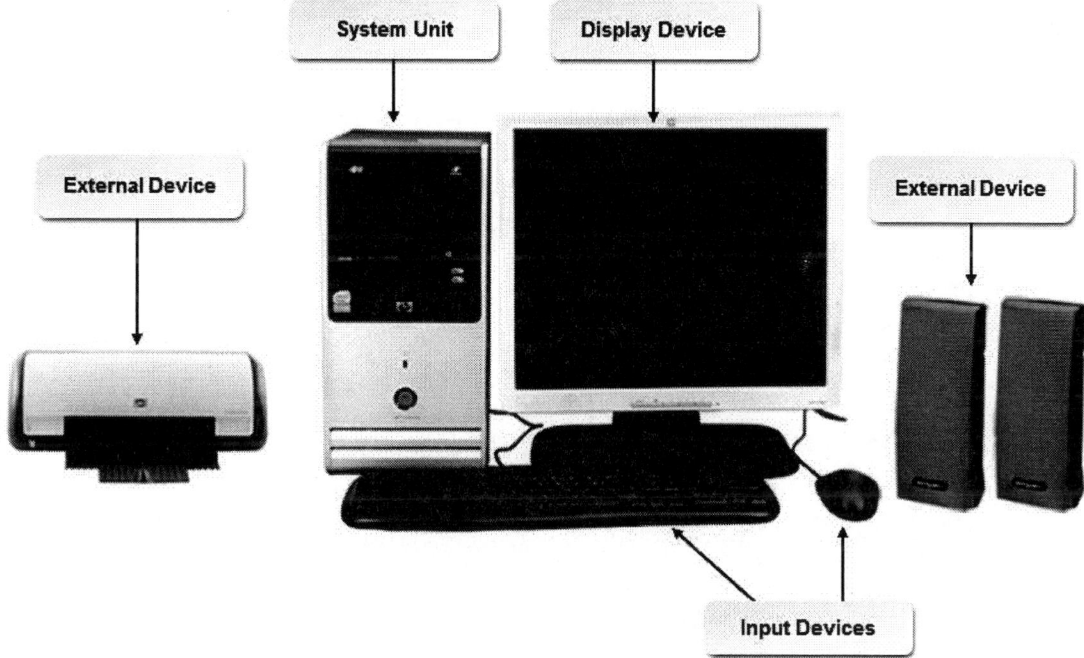

Figure 1-1: A desktop computer.

Desktop computers are composed of easily replaceable modular components inside the case. Peripherals are connected to the desktop computer to allow users to view and enter data or information. *Peripherals* are the computer components that can be attached to a computer. The peripherals typically attached to a desktop computer include a monitor, keyboard, mouse, and printer. Some of these components connect via wired connections to the computer and others use a transmitter and receiver to wirelessly connect to the computer.

All-in-One Desktop Computers

Some computers have the monitor and the computing components all in one physical device and are hence referred to as *all-in-one computers*. These computers take up less desk space than traditional desktop computers. The keyboard and mouse are separate peripherals, usually connected wirelessly to the computer.

Laptop Computers

A *laptop* is a complete computer system that is small, compact, lightweight, and portable. All laptops have specialized hardware designed especially for use in a smaller portable system, use standard operating systems, can run on battery or alternating current (AC) power, and can connect to other devices. Laptops and their components can vary by the following factors:

- Size of the device. Smaller models are referred to as *notebooks* or sub-notebooks and typically have fewer features.
- Display size, quality, and technology.
- Keyboard size, number of keys, and additional options.
- Pointing device used.
- Power supply type.
- Battery type used.
- Length of battery support time.
- How long it takes to recharge the battery.
- Power cord connection and power source options.
- Docking solutions.

- Connections for external peripherals.
- The power button can be located inside or outside of the closed case. It is more often located inside so that it is not accidentally turned on when it is in the user's briefcase or being transported in some other bag.
- Bays or connections for additional drives such as optical drives.

Figure 1-2: A laptop.

Tablets

Mobile devices that fall into the *tablet* PC category range in size from larger tablets that look like a traditional laptop but have a touchscreen to small notebook-sized mobile devices that operate similarly to a smartphone, but are a bit larger and have more computing power. Just like smartphones, tablet PCs can run a number of different operating systems depending on the manufacturer:

- Apple's iPad® and iPod touch® both run on iOS.
- The Android™ OS is used in a number of different tablet PCs including Amazon™ Kindle Fire™, Samsung™ Galaxy tablets, Toshiba Excite™.
- The Windows® 7 Home OS runs on Acer® ICONIA TAB, ASUS Eee Slate, and Samsung™ Series 7 tablet.
- Microsoft® Surface™ running the Windows RT OS, which is a tablet version of Windows 8.
- BlackBerry® PlayBook™ runs the BlackBerry OS.

For a complete and current list of tablets and operating systems, visit **www.tabletpccomparison.net**.

Tablets can connect to the Internet over wireless (Wi-Fi) connections. Some tablets can also connect to the Internet via cellular service just like a cell phone does.

Some laptops can be used as tablets. In some cases, the laptop hinges allow the keyboard to be folded behind the screen so the user can tap the surface of the display to make selections. On other laptops that convert into tablets, the keyboard is removed, leaving the user with just the display to use as a tablet.

Smartphones

Smartphones are high-end mobile devices that provide users with a wide range of functions, such as portable media players, video cameras, GPS, high-resolution touchscreens, high-speed Wi-Fi, web browsers, and mobile broadband, along with phone service. New smartphones are emerging almost every day. The market is expanding and demand for powerful mobile devices has never been higher. Although Android and iOS dominate the smartphone device marketplace, there are many other technologies and devices available.

It can be challenging for an IT technician to keep up with the mobile device market, as it is constantly changing and there are so many different smartphones all with unique features and functions. The most popular devices used in the marketplace are described in the following table.

Mobile Smartphone	Description
Apple iPhone	iPhones are a combination of phone, Internet gadget, and widescreen iPod, which runs on the iOS operating system. The common features of an iPhone include telephone, music player, camera, and games. The latest iPhone includes features such as video conferencing and Siri®—a voice-controlled software assistant to perform various tasks and run other applications through a multi-touch interface. iPhone applications utilize innovative iOS technology to facilitate Wi-Fi Internet connectivity with *General Packet Radio Service (GPRS),* an intuitive user interface, GPS, the accelerometer, audio, video and graphic capabilities, and other advanced features.
Android smartphones	Android-based smartphones have similar functions to the iPhone, except that the Android OS allows multiple applications to run simultaneously without interruption. Popular Android-based smartphones include: • Samsung Galaxy S® III • MOTOROLA® DROID RAZR M • HTC One™ X • HTC One™ S
BlackBerry smartphone	BlackBerry phones are primarily used by professionals to conduct business operations and tasks. The BlackBerry OS directly supports corporate business requirements with functions such as synchronizing with Microsoft® Exchange, IBM® Lotus® Domino®, or Novell® GroupWise® emails, contacts, and tasks by maintaining a high level of security.
Windows smartphone	Windows smartphones run on the Windows Phone OS, which is maintained and developed by Microsoft. Features include a suite of Microsoft® Office® applications, Outlook® Mobile, web browsing, Windows Media® Player, and other advanced features.

Servers

A *server* is a network computer that shares resources with and responds to requests from computers, devices, and other servers on the network. Servers provide centralized access and storage for resources that can include applications, files, printers, and other hardware as well as services, such as email. A server can be optimized and dedicated to one specific function, or it can serve general needs. Multiple servers of various types can coexist on the same network.

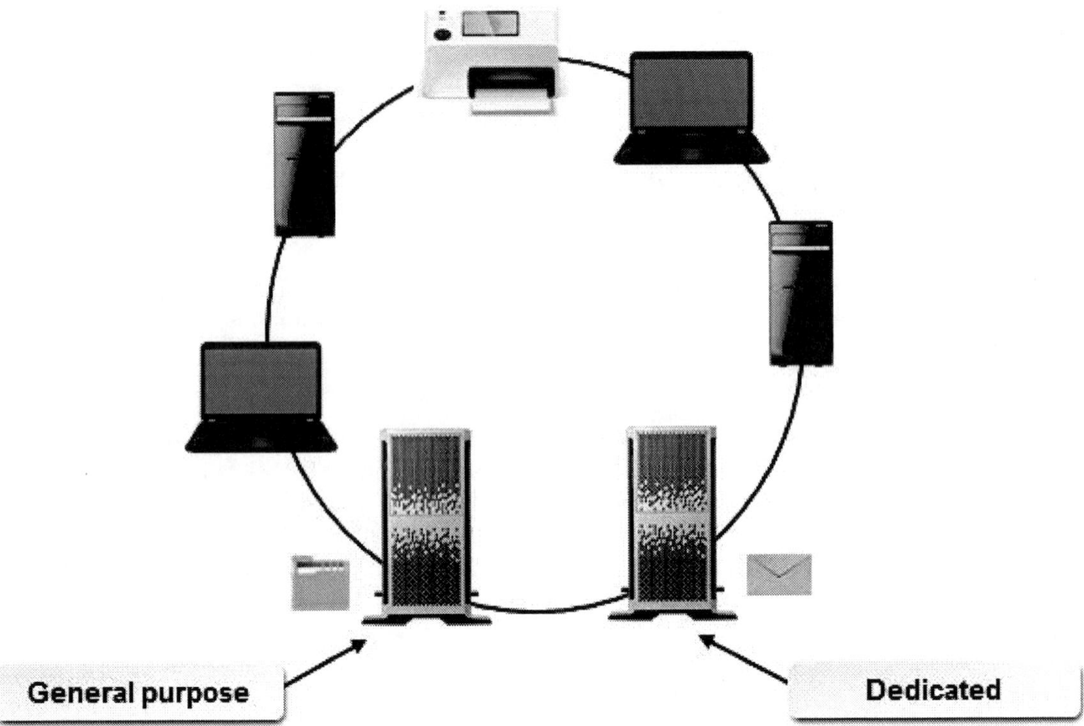

Figure 1-3: A server.

Other Computing Devices

You have seen the most commonly encountered computing devices that are currently in use by the majority of computer users. Other computing devices that you might encounter include supercomputers, mainframes, PDAs, and media players.

- A *supercomputer* is the fastest and the most expensive computer among all types of computers. Supercomputers are often used in research and simulations by hospitals, universities, and governments to accomplish a single, specialized task.
- A *mainframe* is a large computer that might serve a large organization. It is used to process and store information for many users at once; therefore, it requires much more processing power and storage capacity than other computers. Users access the mainframe through *terminals*. A terminal consists of a typewriter-style keyboard and a display screen, or monitor. Mainframe computers cost hundreds of thousands of dollars.
- An *eBook reader* is a device used to read electronic books, or eBooks. Some of these devices do nothing besides allow you to download and read eBooks. Other eBook readers include a browser to access the World Wide Web and to read email.
- A *personal digital assistant* (PDA) is a mobile hand-held device that provides computing, information storage, and information retrieval capabilities for personal or business use. PDAs are primarily used for keeping schedules, calendars, and address book information handy. Many people now use their smartphones in place of the more traditional PDA.
- A *multimedia player* is a handheld device that enables you to play digitally recorded audio, video, and combination audio/video files. Most players provide synchronization and transfer capabilities and some provide Wi-Fi connectivity as well.

ACTIVITY 1-1
Identifying Computing Devices

Before You Begin

Use the information from this topic and the Internet to research answers to the questions posed in this activity.

Scenario

You were recently hired as an intern for the IT department of Develetech Industries. Many employees are interested in getting a tablet for work. Some employees are also asking you for your advice for their home, personal use in deciding whether or not to purchase a tablet. In some cases, you believe the tablet would be a perfect fit, but in other cases you believe the person could be better served by using a desktop or laptop computer. Other employees want a tablet, but they will use it only for reading eBooks.

---

1. **Ariana is taking company sponsored training at the local college next semester. She has always used either work computers or public computers at the library. She sees the Windows® Surface™ advertisements everywhere and thinks this would be what she would like to get. The course she is taking uses Adobe® Photoshop® and some custom applications designed by the instructor. Ariana has saved up about $500 for her new computing device. What computing device would best meet her needs?**

2. **Stephanie is getting ready to retire. At work, she performed data entry, prepared management reports by using Microsoft Office applications, and responded to customer inquiries by using email. She will be traveling with her spouse for six months each year, visiting family and various parks across the country. They will reside at their beach-side home the other six months of the year. She has only ever used a standard desktop computer at work and would like to purchase a device that can be used in their RV to help with directions to their destinations. She wonders if she should also purchase a portable computer for accessing email, writing about their travels, and possibly creating a book about their experiences. What advice would you give her?**

3. **Douglas is a company sales rep. He travels about 75 percent of the time, traveling by air, train, and car. He needs to be able to show customers images of the new products he is promoting, maintain his contact database, find directions to the companies he is visiting, and reply to emails. What device would you recommend?**

TOPIC B

Identify Internal Computer Components

Inside every computing device, no matter the size and power, you will find many of the same components. The components vary by size, complexity, and computing power, but these components are what make the item function as a computing device.

Having a basic understanding of the components' features and functions will help you select the right device for the job.

Motherboards

The *motherboard* is the personal computer component that acts as the backbone for the entire computer system. Sometimes called the *system board* or mainboard, it consists of a large, flat circuit board with chips and other electrical components on it, with various connectors. Some components are *soldered* directly to the board, and some components connect to the board by using slots or sockets.

Figure 1-4: A motherboard.

CPUs

The *central processing unit* (CPU) is a computer chip where most of the computing calculations take place. On most computers, the CPU is housed in a single microprocessor module that is installed on the system board in a slot or a socket.

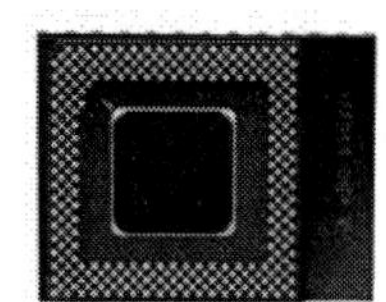
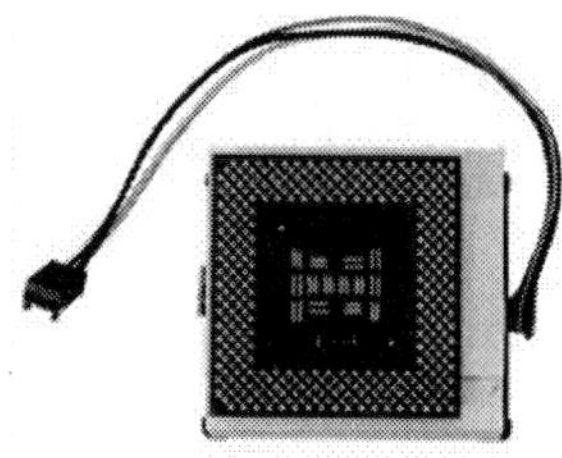

Figure 1-5: CPUs.

Most current processors are built with two or more individual CPUs mounted in a single chip, working in parallel. Multiple individual processors can share the workload more efficiently than a single processor. Dual-core and quad-core processors are engineered to include two to four cores on a single chip, while hexa- and octa-core processors include six and eight cores, respectively.

Before *multicore processors* were available, some hardware manufacturers provided additional processing power by using motherboards with sockets for additional CPUs. These are rarely used in personal computers anymore, but you will find them in server class computers.

Power Supplies

A *power supply* is an internal computer component that converts line voltage AC power from an electrical outlet to the low-voltage direct current (DC) power needed by system components. The power supply is a metal box in the rear of the system unit that is attached to the computer chassis and to the system board. Although the power supply is not itself a component of the system board, it is required in order for system components to receive power. The power supply contains the power cord plug and a fan for cooling because it generates a great deal of heat. Some power supplies have a voltage selector switch that enables you to set them to the voltage configurations used in different countries. AC adapters are generally built into the power supply for desktop systems and are external for laptops and other mobile systems power supplies.

Note: Another commonly used term for the power supply is the power supply unit (PSU).

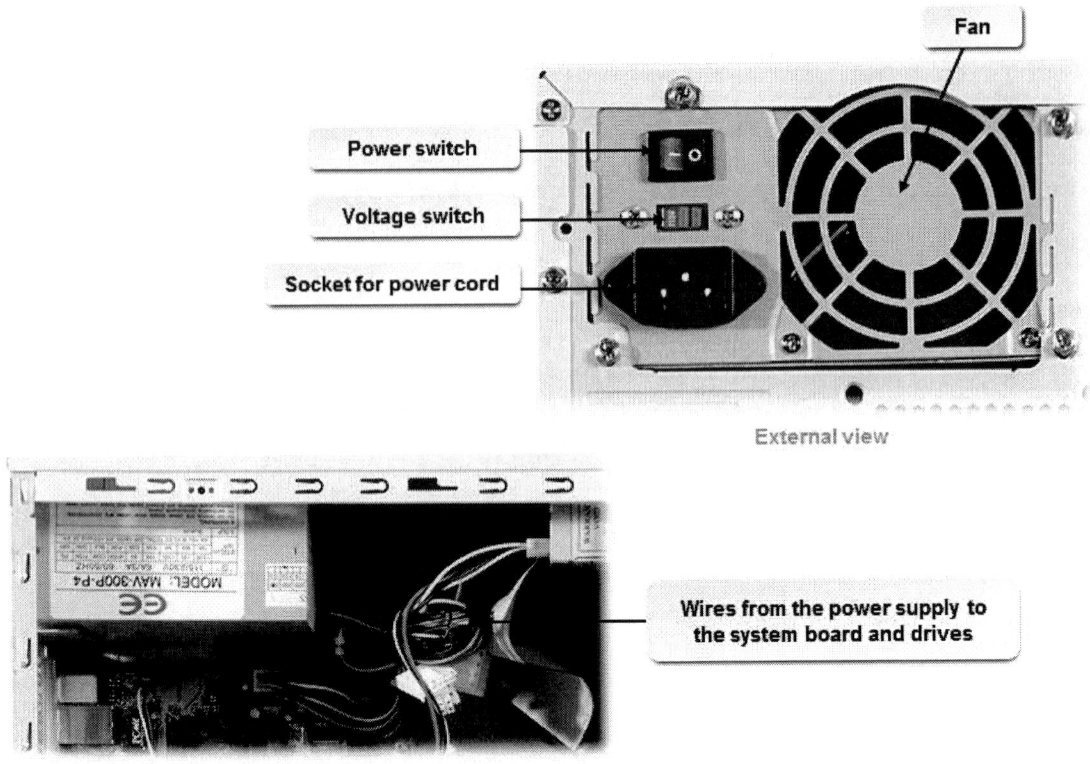

Figure 1-6: The power supply unit of a desktop computer.

RAM

Memory is the component that provides the workspace for a processor. *Random access memory* (RAM) is volatile memory. RAM requires a constant source of electricity to keep track of the data stored in it. When the power is no longer available, the data stored in RAM is lost. The computer can both read the data stored in RAM and write different data into the same RAM. Any byte of data can be accessed without disturbing other data, so the computer has random access to the data in RAM.

RAM is measured in small groups of data called bytes. A *byte* is the fundamental unit of measure for computer data. One typed character is about one byte. Each byte consists of eight *bits,* which are individual ones and zeros.

Because each byte is very tiny, other terms are often used to measure larger amounts of memory.

Memory Unit	*Description*
Byte	One character (a letter, number, space, or punctuation mark). A byte consists of 8 bits.
Kilobyte (KB)	1,024 bytes or 8,192 bits constitute 1 KB.
Megabyte (MB, Meg, or M)	1,048,576 bytes or 1,024 KB constitute 1 MB.
Gigabyte (GB)	1,073,741,824 bytes or 1,024 MB constitute 1 GB.
Terabyte (TB)	1,099,511,627,776 bytes or 1,024 GB constitute 1 TB.

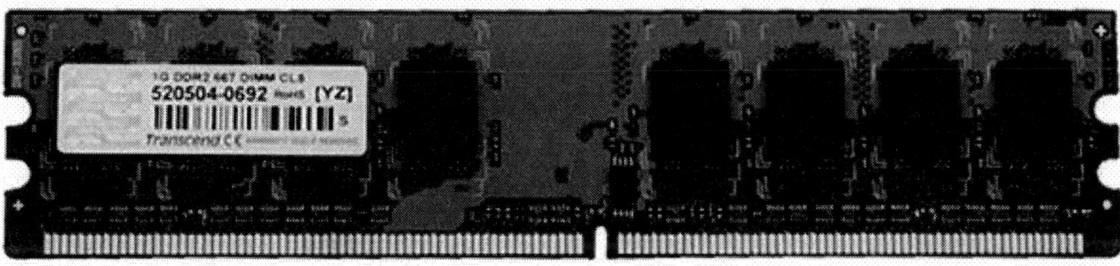

Figure 1-7: A sample memory module.

DIMM vs. SODIMM

Dual in-line memory modules (DIMMs) are found in many systems, and they have a 64-bit data path. DIMMs generally have 16 or 32 chips per module.

Small outline dual in-line memory modules (SODIMMs) are half the size of DIMMs and therefore cannot fit into a DIMM slot. SODIMMs are most often seen in laptops, small networking devices (such as routers), and PCs with smaller system boards. They have either 32- or 64-bit data paths.

Storage

Information and data in RAM is stored only as long as power is applied to the memory. If you turn off the device, then the information in RAM is lost. If you want to keep the information and data you have been working with, you need to save it to some type of storage device. The information previously saved to a storage device can be retrieved (or read) into computer memory.

There are many types of storage devices you can use to store your information. Identifying the types of storage devices will help you choose the best device based on your needs.

Storage Type	*Description*
Hard drive 	*Hard disk drives (HDDs)* are common storage devices. They are generally non-removable disks. Almost all computers use hard disk drives to store data. Hard disks store data digitally on circular platters. A platter's surface is highly polished and is magnetically charged. Digital data is stored on these platters in small magnetic domains. A computer's storage capacity can be expanded by adding additional hard disks. Today, the storage capacity of hard disk drives is expressed in gigabytes (GBs) and terabytes (TBs). The speed at which the disk in a hard drive rotates is measured in rotations per minute (RPM).

Storage Type	Description
Solid state drive 	*Solid state storage* is a personal computer storage device that stores data in special types of memory instead of on disks or tape. Common types of solid state storage include the USB devices that are commonly known as jump drives or thumb drives; flash memory cards; and secure digital (SD) memory cards. Solid state storage uses non-volatile memory to emulate mechanical storage devices, but solid state storage is much faster and more reliable than mechanical storage because there are no moving parts.
Optical drive 	*Optical disks* are personal computer storage devices, such as CDs, DVDs, or Blu-ray™ discs, that store data optically rather than magnetically. The removable plastic discs have a reflective coating and require an optical drive to be read. In optical storage, data is written by either pressing or burning with a laser to create pits (recessed areas) or lands (raised areas) in the reflective surface of the disc. A laser in the optical drive then reads the data off the disc. Optical drives can be internal or external, and they generally have a 5.25-inch form factor.

Types of Optical Discs

The following table describes the various types of optical discs.

Optical Disc Type	Description
CD-ROM	Compact Disc Read-Only Memory. Data is permanently burned onto the disc during its manufacture.
CD-R	CD-Recordable. Data can be written to the disc only once.
CD-RW	CD-Rewritable. Data can be written to the disc multiple times.
DVD-ROM	Digital Versatile Disc Read-Only Memory. Data is permanently burned onto the disc during its manufacture.
DVD-R	DVD-Recordable. Data can be written to the disc only once.
DVD+R	Another format of DVD Recordable. Data can be written to the disc only once.
DVD+R DL	DVD Recordable Double Layer. A higher-capacity double-layer format to which data can be written only once.
DVD-RW	DVD-Rewritable. Data can be written to the disc multiple times.
DVD+RW	Another format of DVD Rewritable. Data can be written to the disc multiple times.
DVD-RAM	DVD-Random Access Memory. Data can be written to the disc multiple times.

Optical Disc Type	Description
BD-ROM	Blu-ray discs are intended for high-density storage of high-definition video as well as data storage. They use blue laser light to read and store data. The blue laser has a shorter wavelength than other CD and DVD laser technologies, which enables the system to store more data in the same amount of physical space. Current Blu-ray discs hold 50 GB total. However, companies such as Sony are testing experimental discs that have storage capacities of up to 200 GB.

Note: There are several competing DVD formats. DVD-ROM, DVD-R, DVD-RW, and DVD-RAM are approved by the DVD Forum, while DVD+R, DVD+R DL, DVD+RW are not. Because some of the competing formats are incompatible, many hybrid DVD drives have been developed. These hybrid drives are often labeled DVD±RW.

USB Drives

When people say they are using a *USB drive*, typically they are referring to small solid-state devices such as thumb drives. Other drives can also be connected to the computer by using a USB connection. Some *tape drives*, which use magnetic tape that can be accessed and written to sequentially only (rather than jumping directly to the storage location for the desired data) can be connected via a USB connection. Hard drives enclosed in a case or placed in a hard drive dock can also be connected via USB connections.

Multi-card Readers and Writers

A wide variety of solid state memory cards are used in various devices such as phones and cameras. The device can usually be connected via a cable or wirelessly to the computer. Some computers also contain one or more slots in which you can insert the memory card after it has been removed from the phone or camera. Some of these multi-card readers allow you to insert SD, microSD, CompactFlash, or MS/MS Duo (Sony's Memory Stick) memory card. The reader/writer might be internal or connected via a USB port on the computer.

Mobile Media Devices

Mobile media devices such as music players use memory cards or solid state memory to store data. These features are also incorporated into eReaders and smartphones.

Expansion Cards

An *expansion card* is a printed circuit board that you install into a slot on the computer's system board to expand the functionality of the computer. Each card has a connector that fits into a slot on a system board and circuitry to connect a specific device to the computer. Some expansion cards connect to the system bus instead of a peripheral bus, use different slot types, or are built into the system circuitry instead of being separate physical boards.

Note: An expansion card is also known as an *adapter card*, I/O card, add-in, add-on, or simply a board.

The following table describes the various types of expansion cards.

Expansion Card Type	Description
Video card	If your motherboard doesn't have a built-in video port, or if you want to use a better video adapter than what is on your motherboard, you can use a video card. *Video cards* typically have their own bank of memory to improve the rate at which the images on screen can be updated. Video cards can have a variety of connectors on them for connecting video display devices. Some of the video adapters include VGA, DVI, and HDMI. Most video cards also include their own cooling fan.
Audio card	Audio connections might be built into your motherboard, or they might be placed on an expansion card. An *audio card* typically includes ports to connect speakers, a microphone, and headphones.
Network card	A network adapter allows your computer to connect to other computers over a wired or wireless connection. The functionality might be contained on your motherboard or it might be on a separate *network card*. The Ethernet cable connects to a port on the network card, allowing you to access servers, other computers, and the Internet. A wireless network card might or might not have an external antenna.
Modem	A *modem* allows your computer to connect to other computers and the Internet by using an analog phone line. This feature used to be the only way a home user could connect to online services. With the advent of cable networks and DSL, the slower rates of phone lines fell out of favor. Modems are still included in some computers, but not all. If you find you need this feature, you might need to install a modem card in your system.

Cooling Systems

Computers get very hot when they are running. For this reason, there are a number of cooling strategies employed within a computing device. You are likely to find fans located on several devices within your computer.

- Fans are located on the power supply, on the video card, and on the CPU. In addition, you might have one or more fans built into the computer case. Be sure not to block air flow for these fans. If the computer cannot be properly cooled, it will overheat, causing damage to chips, components, and the motherboard.
- Some systems have a *liquid cooling system* inside the case. These cooling systems use tubes filled with a coolant, connected to a radiator, and a pump to circulate the liquid coolant through the inside of your computer case. Fans move the air as well. The thermal conductivity of the liquid is higher than that of air, so the heat can be moved away from components more quickly than just relying on fans to move the air, and thus the heat, away from components. The components to be cooled are connected to the tube with water blocks (a flat copper or aluminum piece) with thermal paste to help transfer the heat between the water block and the component.
- *Heat sinks* are employed throughout your computer as another method of keeping components cool. The heat sinks are metal, usually formed into ridges, and installed on components. The heat sink transfers the heated air from the component to the fan (or liquid cooling system), which then moves the heated air out of the computer case, keeping the inside of the case and the components cooler.

ACTIVITY 1-2

Identifying Internal Computer Components

Scenario

You are an advisor for a local student computer club. As the club kicks off a new season, you want to find out how much the club members know about the internal components in a desktop computer. This information will help you determine what activities you should plan for the next meeting.

For this activity, refer to the following graphic.

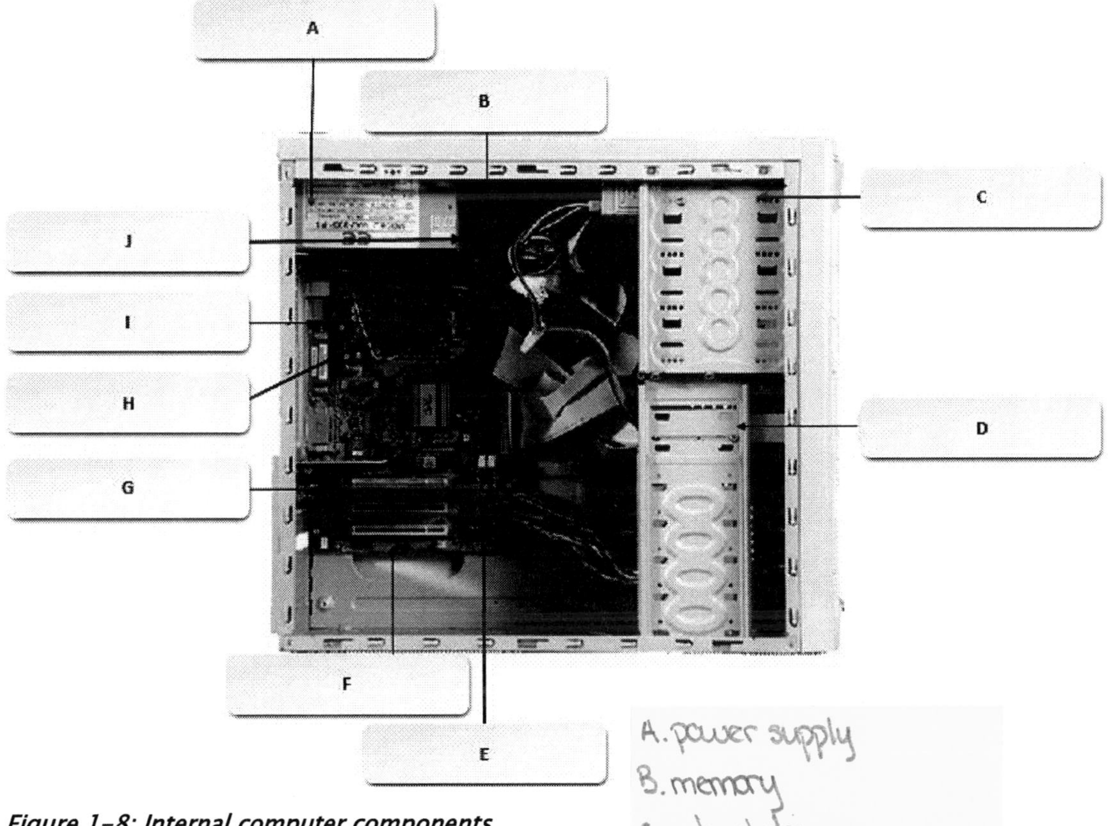

Figure 1-8: Internal computer components.

A. power supply
B. memory
C. optical drive
D. CD/DVD
E. motherboard

F. expansion slots
G.
H.
I.
J.

1. Locate the motherboard and the CPU.

2. Locate the power supply.

3. Identify the memory installed on the motherboard.

4. Identify the storage devices installed in the computer.

5. **Locate and identify each of the expansion cards installed in the computer.**

6. **Locate and identify each of the cooling strategies employed in the computer.**

TOPIC C

Common Computer Connector Types

You are now familiar with the common components that make up a personal computer. Next, you need to be able to identify how all the components are connected to form a complete personal computer system. In this topic, you will compare the connector types that are used to join hardware components together.

A personal computer is made up of many different components. All of these components need to be able to communicate with each other for the computer to function properly. As personal computers have evolved, many connection technologies have been implemented to provide communication among computer components. Identifying the different methods that are used to connect devices to a computer will enable you, a computer technician, to install, upgrade, and replace computer components quickly and effectively.

Ports

A *port* is a hardware interface that you can use to connect devices to a computer. The port transfers electronic signals between the device and the system unit. The port is either an electrically wired socket or plug, or it can be a wireless transmission device. Ports can vary by shape, by color according to the color coding standards, by the number and layout of the pins or connectors contained within the port, by the signals the port carries, and by the port's location. Ports exist for both internal and external devices. External ports often have a graphical representation of the type of device that should be connected to it, such as a small picture of a monitor adjacent to the video port.

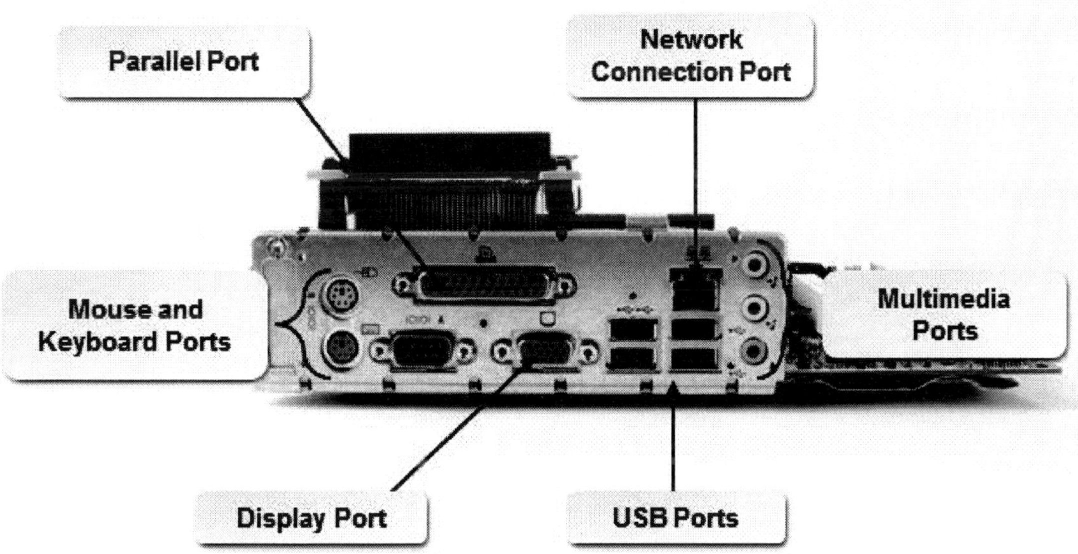

Figure 1-9: Ports on a personal computer.

Genders

Most ports and the cables that connect to them have genders. For example, most computer ports are jacks into which you plug in the matching cable. The computer jacks are most often the female connectors and the cable plug is most often the male connector. You can always look directly at the innermost electrical connections on the connectors to determine the gender. The one with the protruding pins is the male and the one with the holes to accept the pins is the female.

Port Shapes

Ports can have different physical shapes, such as round, rectangular, square, and oblong, although there is some standardization of physical properties and functions. Most connectors are keyed in some way to restrict connecting devices into the wrong port.

Connections

Computer connections are the physical access points that enable a computer to communicate with internal or external devices. They include the ports on both the computer and the connected devices, plus a transmission medium, which is either a cable with connectors at each end or a wireless technology. Personal computer connections can be categorized by the technology or standard that was used to develop the device.

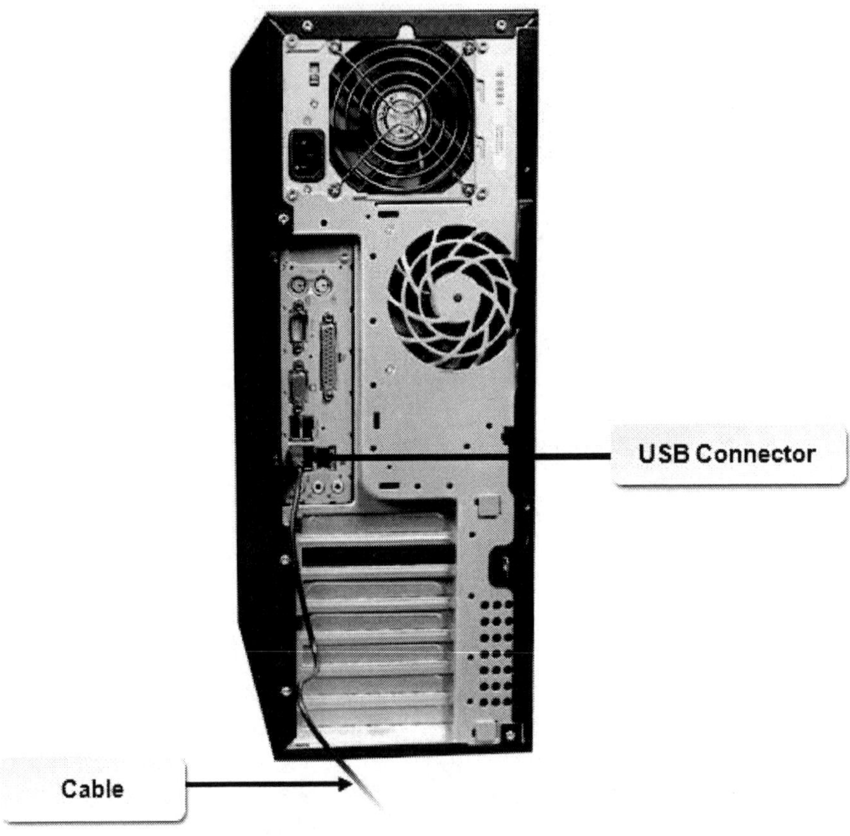

Figure 1-10: A personal computer connection.

PS/2 Ports and Connectors

The round 6-pin port, also referred to as a mini-Din connector or *PS/2 port*, is an interface located on the motherboard. The Din-6 port is the larger 13.2 mm port. Older keyboards and mice use PS/2 ports to connect to the motherboard. To avoid confusion between the identical-looking keyboard and mouse ports, PS/2 ports are often color-coded to match the end of the cable on the device: purple for the keyboard and green for the mouse. Or, there may be a sticker with a picture of a mouse and keyboard near the connectors.

Note: Newer mice and keyboards primarily use USB connectors, but some older systems may still use PS/2 technology.

Serial Ports and Connectors

A *serial connection* is a personal computer connection that transfers data one bit at a time over a single wire. Serial connections support two-way communications and were typically used for devices such as fax cards or external modems. These legacy serial ports have either 9-pin (DB-9) or 25-pin (DB-25) male connectors. A legacy serial cable ends with a female connector to plug into the male connector on the system unit. On system units that have color-coded ports, the serial port is teal-colored. Serial connections that are seen today are used to attach printers, scientific devices such as telescopes, networking hardware such as routers and switches, and industrial products. Because modern computers usually don't have serial ports, you'll need to connect a device with a serial connection through a serial-to-USB adapter.

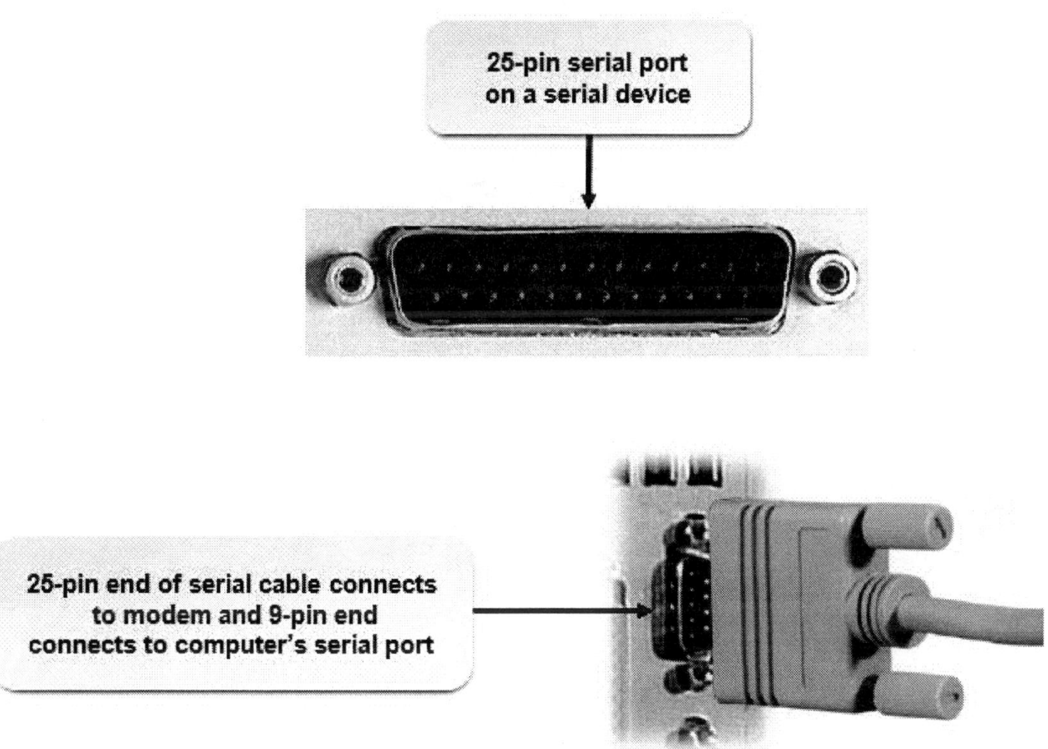

Figure 1-11: A serial connection.

Serial Port Naming

Serial ports are typically called COM1, COM2, COM3, and COM4, where "COM" is short for communications port. This port has been almost completely phased out in favor of USB. You'll probably find many systems with no serial ports at all.

Parallel Ports and Connectors

A *parallel connection* is a computer connection that transfers data eight or more bits at a time over eight or more wires. Any components connected by multiple data pathways may be considered to have a parallel connection. However, the term is generally used to refer to a standard legacy parallel port that uses eight data wires, and it is typically used to connect a printer to a system unit. Parallel connections in older personal computers support only one-way or unidirectional communications. Newer computers have parallel ports that support bidirectional communications. Standard parallel ports have 25-pin female connectors. A parallel cable has a 25-pin male connector to plug into the system unit and a 36-pin male Centronics connector at the other end to attach to the external device. On system units that have color-coded ports, the parallel port is burgundy or dark pink.

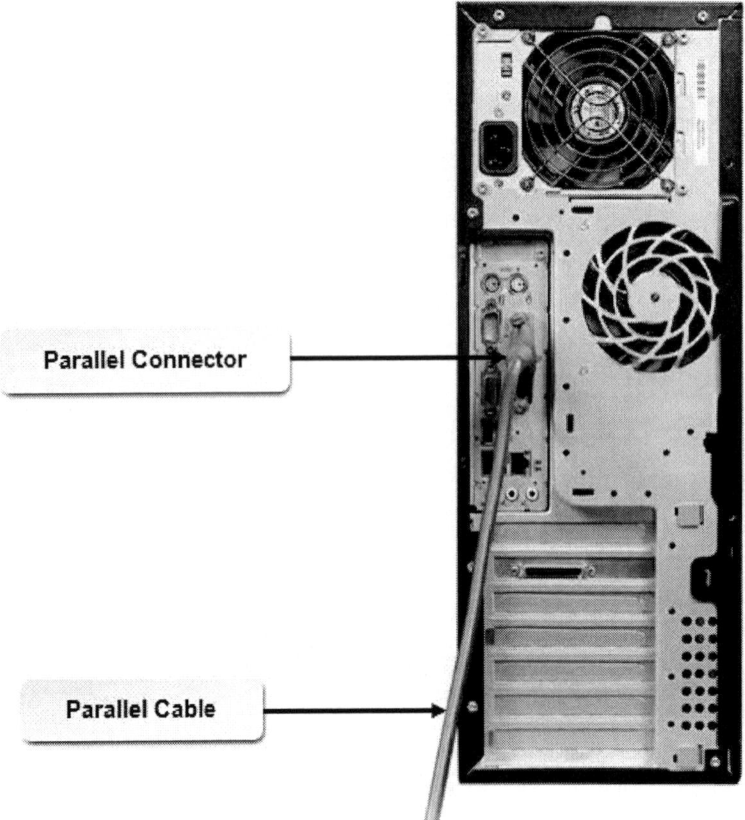

Figure 1-12: A parallel connection.

Note: The standard parallel port has been phased out in favor of USB, so you may find many systems with no parallel ports at all.

Power Connections and Connectors

Almost every device in a computer uses one of several types of power connectors to get electrical power from the computer's power supply.

Power Connector	Devices That Use It
Main power connector 	ATX connectors (20-pin or 24-pin) are used to supply power to the motherboard.
Berg 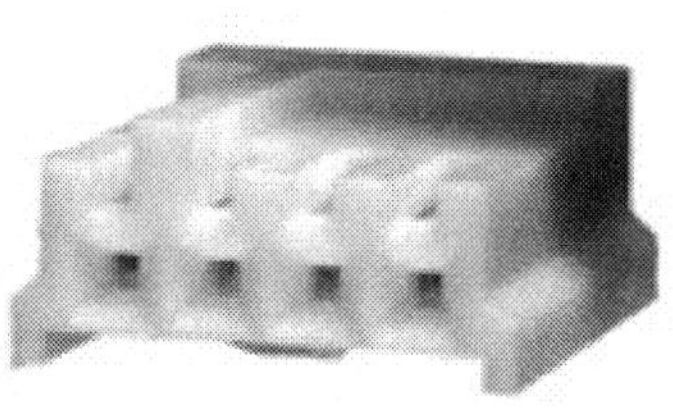	*Berg connectors* are used to supply power to floppy disk drives and some tape drives.
 Molex 	*Molex connectors* are used to supply power to Parallel Advanced Technology Attachment (PATA) drives, optical drives, and SCSI drives.
SATA power connector 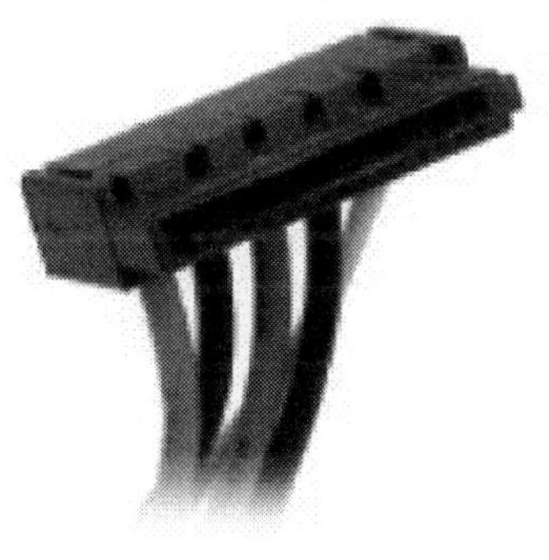	*Serial ATA (SATA) power connectors* are used to supply power to SATA drives.

USB Ports and Connectors

A *universal serial bus (USB) connection* is a computer connection that enables you to connect multiple peripherals to a single port with high performance and minimal device configuration. USB connections support two-way communications. All modern PC systems today have multiple USB ports and can, with the use of USB hubs, support up to 127 devices per port. USB cables may have different connectors at each end. The computer end of the cable ends in a Type A connector. The device end of the cable commonly ends in a Type B connector, or may also end in a Mini-A, Mini-B, Micro-AB, or Micro-B connector. The mini connectors are typically used for portable devices such as smartphones. The size of the connector varies depending on the device. USB connections transfer data serially, but at a much faster *throughput* than legacy serial connections. USB devices also incorporate Plug-and-Play technology that allows devices to self-configure as soon as a connection is made.

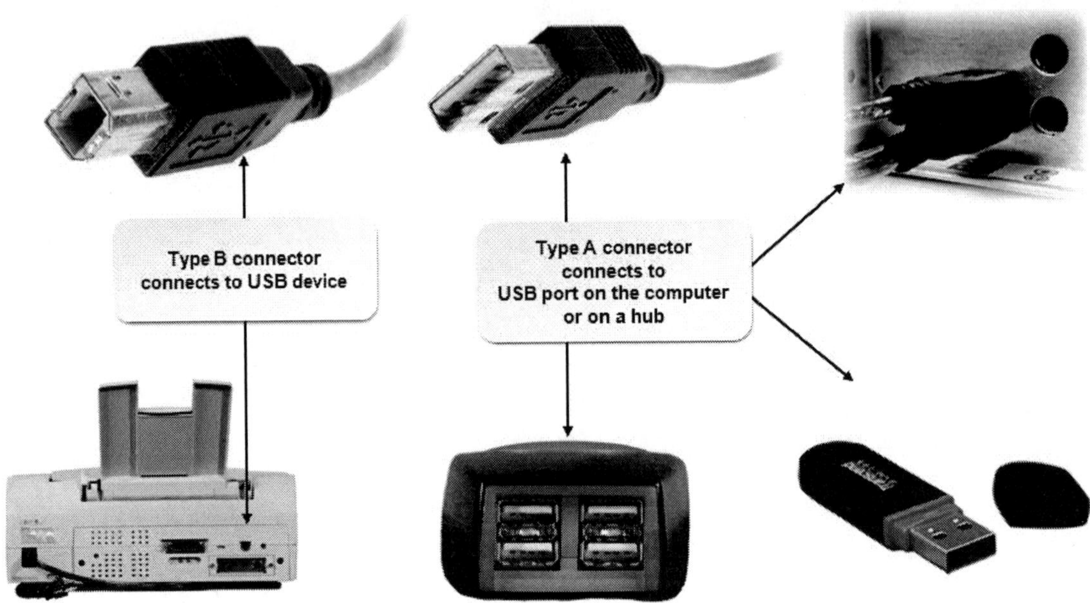

Figure 1-13: USB connections.

USB Standards

USB 2.0, released in April 2000, is the most commonly implemented standard. It can communicate at up to 480 Mbps. The original USB 1.1 standard is still commonly found in devices and systems. It can communicate at up to 12 Mbps. A USB 2.0 device connected to a USB 1.1 hub or port will communicate at only USB 1.1 speeds, even though it might be capable of faster speeds. Generally, the operating system will inform you of this when you connect the device.

USB 3.0, also called SuperSpeed USB, is the latest USB standard released in November 2008. It features a maximum transfer rate of 5.0 Gbps. It is 10 times faster than the USB 2.0 standard, has enhanced power efficiency, and is backward compatible with USB-enabled devices currently in use.

USB cables have a maximum distance before performance suffers. To work around this, one or more hubs can be used to create a chain to reach the necessary cable length. USB 1.1 has a maximum cable length of 3 meters, while USB 2.0's maximum length is 5 meters. In each case, a maximum of five hubs can be used to extend the cable length. The maximum cable length is not specified in the USB 3.0 specification.

FireWire Ports and Connectors

A *FireWire connection* is a computer connection that provides a high-speed interface for peripheral devices that are designed to use the *Institute of Electrical and Electronic Engineers (IEEE)* 1394 standard.

FireWire can support up to 63 devices on one FireWire port. FireWire 400 transmits at 400 Mbps and uses either a 6-pin, bullet-shaped, powered connector or a 4-pin square-shaped, unpowered connector. FireWire 800 transmits at 800 Mbps and uses a 9-pin connector.

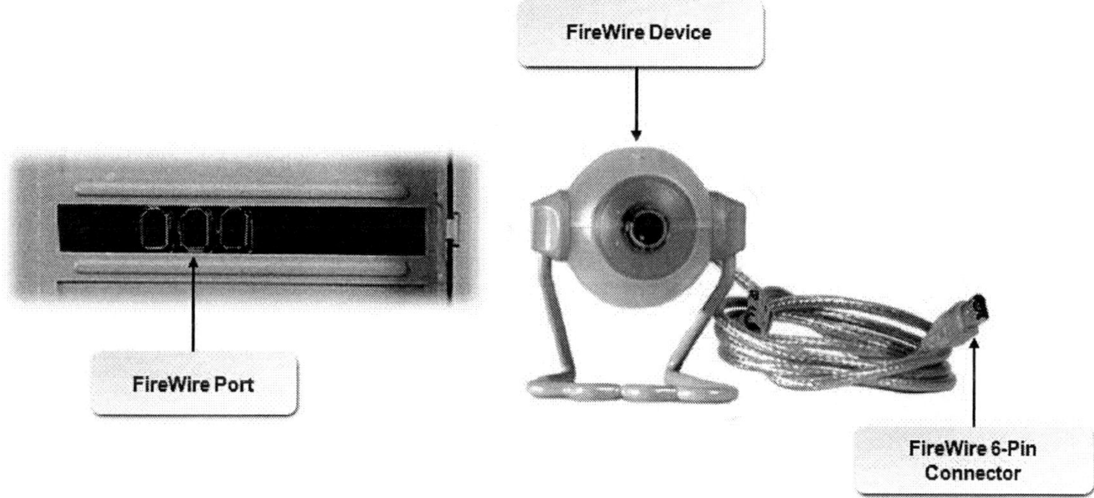

Figure 1-14: A FireWire connection.

FireWire Terminology

Apple was the primary vendor to promote the IEEE 1394 Standard and used the FireWire name as a trademark for the IEEE 1394 implementation included in its Macintosh® systems. FireWire has since become the common name for all IEEE 1394 devices.

FireWire vs. USB

FireWire predated USB and was faster than the original USB 1.1 standard. USB 2.0, with its increased speed, largely superseded FireWire. However, although USB 2.0 is faster by the numbers than FireWire, FireWire is actually faster on throughput, making it ideal for video/audio file transfers and external storage devices. A file transfer of 100 separate documents might be slightly faster on USB than FireWire, but a file transfer of a single 2 GB video file will be much faster in FireWire. Also, whereas USB provides a device up to 5 V power, FireWire provides up to 12 V power on the wire.

With the release of USB 3.0 and the latest FireWire S3200, the performance will still vary. USB 3.0 is 10 times faster than USB 2.0 and will remain the popular standard used for most devices. The FireWire S3200 standard, however, still has considerable advantages over USB. For example, FireWire uses much less CPU power and provides more power over a single cable connection.

Similar to USB, FireWire has maximum distance restrictions. However, FireWire's distances are greater than USB's. A FireWire chain, created with cables and repeaters, can reach up to 237 feet from device to host, whereas USB 2.0 can reach 30 meters (just under 100 feet).

Thunderbolt Ports and Connectors

Thunderbolt is an input/output connection developed by Apple and Intel. It carries data and display signals on a single cable. It also can be used to power peripherals with 10 watts of power. It is a dual-protocol technology that works with PCI Express and DisplayPort technologies. The data transfer rate of Thunderbolt is approximately 10 Gbps. Peripherals can be daisy-chained together so that multiple peripherals require only one port on the computer.

Thunderbolt was originally designed to use fiber-optic cabling, but is currently using multiple copper wires in the cable. Future plans include moving the technology to fiber-optic cabling, which provides the ability to have longer cables.

Audio Ports and Connectors

There are a number of audio/video connectors that are used to connect a wide variety of devices, including PCs, DVD and Blu-ray players, surround-sound systems, stereo equipment, projectors, and HDTVs. In addition to HDMI and DVI, common audio/video cable and connectors include those described in the following table.

Type	*Description*
Single-core/shielded cable 	The single core wire is the positive, and the shield is the negative. This type of cable is used for unbalanced audio signals. Generally, unbalanced audio cables are short, because noise is less of an issue.
One pair/shielded cable 	Uses a pair (white and red) of cores with one wire being the positive, and the other wire being the negative. The shield acts as a ground. This type of cable is used for balanced audio signals. Balanced audio is a method for minimizing noise and interference in audio cables.
TS and TRS connectors 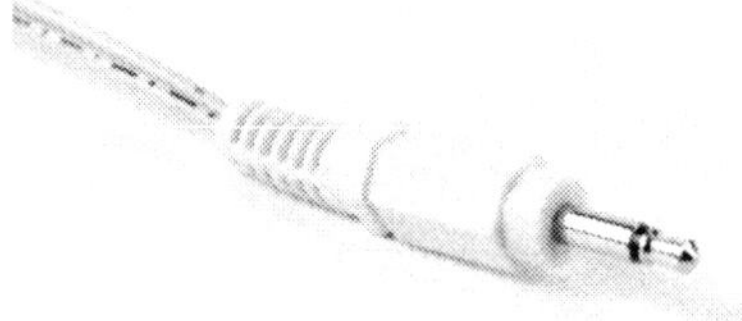	The most common connectors used in unbalanced audio cables are the 1/4-inch tip-sleeve (TS) or tip-ring-sleeve (TRS) and RCA connectors, which are typically used with high-end audio equipment. The 1/8-inch tip-sleeve is typically used with smaller audio devices such as Apple iPods. TS and TRS connectors are also referred to as phone jacks, phone plugs, audio jacks, and jack plugs. Traditionally, TS connectors are used for mono and TRS connectors are used for stereo. Some connectors can carry more signals; these are often used with camcorder, laptops, and other devices. Stereo connectors can also carry a single, balanced signal. Wiring configurations for TRS connectors include: • For unbalanced mono, the tip carries the signal, the ring is not connected, and the sleeve acts as ground. • For balanced mono, the tip is positive, the ring is negative, and the sleeve acts as ground. • For stereo, the tip carries the left channel, the ring carries the right channel, and the sleeve acts as ground.

Type	*Description*
3-pin XLR connectors 	The standard connector for balanced audio is the 3-pin XLR. The most common wiring configuration is: • Pin 1: Shield (ground) • Pin 2: Positive (hot) • Pin 3: Negative (cold)

Video Ports and Connectors

Display devices can use several different types of cables.

Cable Type	*Description*
Video Graphics Array (VGA)	The *DB-15* high-density VGA connector is the most common cable used for LCD monitors. It contains three rows of five pins. Pins 4, 11, 12, and 15 receive information from the device; pins 1, 2, 3, 13, and 14 send information to the display. Mini-VGA is used on smaller devices, such as laptops, in place of the standard full-sized cables.

Cable Type	Description
Digital Video Interface (DVI) 	DVI cables keep data in digital form from the computer to the display. There is no need to convert data from digital information to analog information. LCD monitors work in a digital mode and support the DVI format. • DVI-analog (DVI-A) is an analog-only format. It requires a DVI-A supported interface. The connector does not support dual link technology. It is commonly used to connect CRT or VGA devices to a computer by using a DVI-A adapter. • DVI-digital (DVI-D) is a digital-only format. It requires a video adapter with a DVI-D connection and a monitor with a DVI-D interface. The connector contains 24 pins/receptacles in three rows of eight above or below a flat blade, plus a grounding slot for dual-link support. For single-link support, the connector contains 18 pins/receptacles. • DVI-integrated (DVI-I) supports both digital and analog transmissions. This gives you the option to connect a monitor that accepts digital input or analog input. In addition to the pins/receptacles found on the DVI-D connector for digital support, a DVI-I connector has four additional pins/receptacles to carry an analog signal. For single-link support, the connector contains 18 pins/receptacles, and 4 additional pins for analog transmissions.
High Definition Multimedia Interface (HDMI) 	HDMI is the first industry-supported uncompressed, all-digital audio/video interface. HDMI uses a single cable composed of copper wires to provide an interface between any audio/video source, such as a set-top box, DVD player, or A/V receiver and an audio and/or video monitor, such as a digital television (DTV). The connector is made up of 19 pins and can support a number of modes such as High Definition TV (HDTV), Standard Definition TV (SDTV), and Enhanced Digital TV (EDTV) and can run to 50 feet or more in length. HDMI has largely superseded DVI and is compatible with the DVI standard. It can be used with PC systems that support DVI.

Cable Type	Description
Mini-High Definition Multimedia Interface (Mini-HDMI) 	Mini-HDMI is similar to the full size HDMI connector, except that it is specified for use with portable devices. The connector is a smaller version of the full size with same number of pins. The difference between the full size and the mini is that some of pins have different transmission functions.
Separate Video (S-Video) 	S-Video is an analog video signal that carries the video data as two separate signals (brightness and color). S-Video works in 480i or 576i resolution.  **Note:** Video resolution is sometimes noted in the format shown here, particularly when television signals are being discussed. A resolution of 480i indicates a vertical frame resolution of 480 interlaced lines that contain picture information, while a resolution of 576i indicates a vertical frame resolution of 576 interlaced lines that contain picture information.
Component/RGB 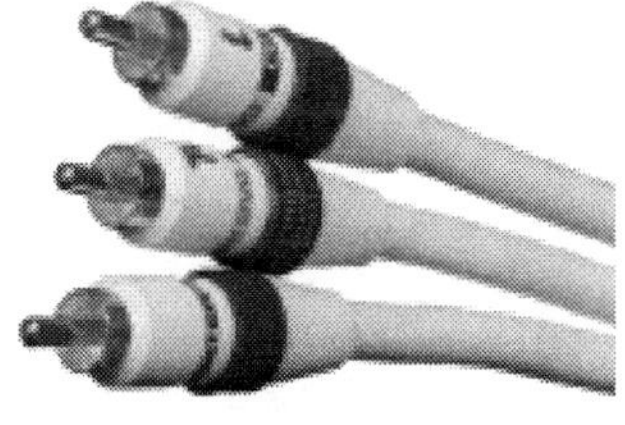	Component video is a type of analog video information that is transmitted or stored as two or more separate signals. Analog video signals (also called components) must provide information about the amount of red, green, and blue to create an image. The simplest type, RGB, consists of three discrete red, green, and blue signals sent down three coaxial cables.
Composite video 	Composite video is the format of an analog (picture only) signal before it is combined with a sound signal and modulated onto a radio frequency (RF) carrier.

Cable Type	Description
Coaxial 	A coaxial cable, or coax, is a type of copper cable that features a central conducting copper core surrounded by an insulator and braided or foil shielding. An insulator separates the conductor and shield, and the entire package is wrapped in an insulating layer called a jacket. The data signal is transmitted over the central conductor. The outer shielding serves to reduce electromagnetic interference.
DisplayPort 	DisplayPort is a digital display standard that aims to replace DVI and VGA standards. DisplayPort is not backward compatible with DVI and HDMI and is a royalty-free standard. However, by using special dual-mode ports and suitable adapters, it may be possible to use DVI and HDMI signals with DisplayPort. Similar to Peripheral Component Interconnect Express (PCIe), DisplayPort also supports high-quality gaming and other applications that use high-end graphics.
Radio Corporation of America (RCA) 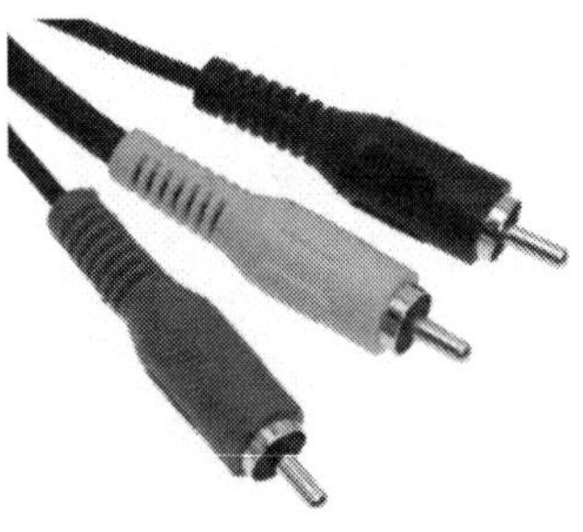	RCA cables and connectors are used to carry audio and video transmissions to and from a variety of devices such as TVs, digital cameras, and gaming systems. In some cases, the RCA cable may also be used as a power cable, a loudspeaker cable, and to carry digital audio. The female jacks on the devices are colored to provide a guide as to what type of connector can be attached. Common colors found are: • Yellow for various composite connections. • Red for the right channel of the audio transmission. • White or black for the left channel of audio transmission.
Bayonet Neill-Concelman (BNC) 	The BNC connector is used with coaxial cable to carry radio frequencies to and from devices. The BNC cable can be used to connect radio equipment, aviation electronics, and to carry video signals. The actual BNC connectors come in two versions. The connector will be either 50 or 75 ohms, depending on the specific cable that is attached.

Ethernet and Displays

Some display devices such as the Apple Thunderbolt display include an Ethernet port for connection directly to a network.

DVI Single Link vs. Dual Link

DVI cables use a technology called Transition Minimized Differential Signaling (TMDS) to transmit serial data over a high-speed connection. Single link cables use a single TMDS transmitter to carry data, while double-link uses two. Therefore, dual link cables can transmit larger images at higher speeds than single link.

Wireless A/V Connections

Wireless connections are being used in conference rooms to connect computers to display boards. This is not a common method of connection yet, but as more people want to avoid cluttering their work areas with wires, it might become more popular. A wireless audio/visual adapter needs to be attached to the display monitor in order for the display to receive a signal from the device that is projecting to it.

eSATA Connectors

External SATA (eSATA) is an external interface for SATA connections. Like USB and FireWire, it provides a connection for external storage devices. eSATA connections provide fast data transfers without having to translate data between the device and the host computer. eSATA interfaces do require an additional power connector to function. You can provide eSATA functionality by installing eSATA cards in systems.

The eSATA port shown in the following graphic also allows USB peripherals to connect to the same port. This combination port allows either eSATA or USB devices to be plugged in. It is technically an eSATAp port, or a powered eSATA port.

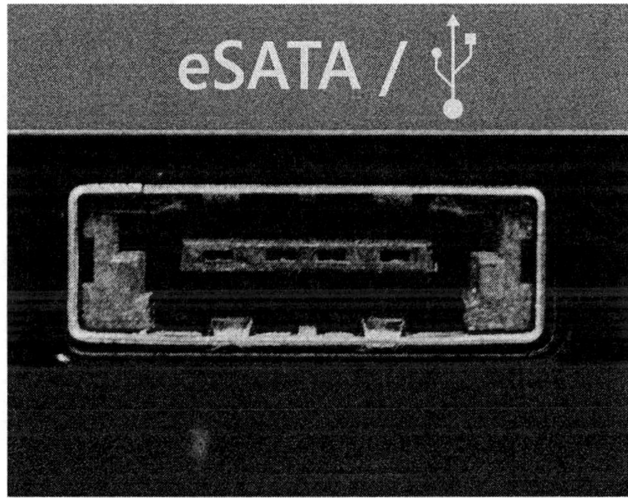

Figure 1-15: eSATA and USB port

RJ-45 Ports and Connectors

The *RJ-45 connector* is used on twisted pair cable. RJ-45 is an eight-position connector that uses all four pairs of wires. Be careful not to confuse the RJ-45 connector with the similar, but smaller, RJ-11 connector. The RJ-11 connector is a six-position connector that uses just one pair of wires. It is used in telephone system connections and is not suitable for network connectivity. The RJ in RJ-11 or RJ-45 is an abbreviation for "registered jack."

Figure 1-16: RJ-45 connector.

RJ-11 Ports and Connectors

The *RJ-11* connector is used with Category 1 cables in telephone system connections and is not suitable for network connectivity. However, because the RJ-11 connector is similar in appearance to the RJ-45 connector, they are sometimes confused. RJ-11 connectors are smaller than RJ-45 connectors and have either four or six pins.

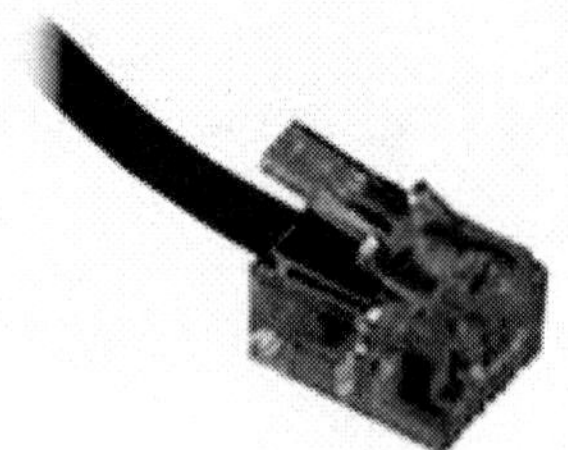

Figure 1-17: RJ-11 connector.

ACTIVITY 1-3
Comparing Connector Types

Before You Begin

Your instructor has a pile of cables that have not been labeled. You also have a computer you can examine to see which cables can be connected to it.

Scenario

While cleaning out a storage cabinet, you found lots of cables. You decided that you should see how many of these cables might work with your current computer. You want to neatly organize the cables you might use with your computer in one box and those that you won't need into another box. You also want to label each cable so that in the future you know which cables are which.

---

1. From the pile of cables provided, locate a cable for each port on your computer and connect it to the appropriate port.
2. Determine if any of the cables provided cannot be connected to your computer.
3. Place any cables that cannot be used with your computer in a box. Label each of the cables with the connector type and place back in the box.
4. Remove the cables you connected to your computer and label each connector type and place them in a second box.

TOPIC D

Identify Common Peripheral Devices

Much of the work that you will perform as a PC technician will involve installing and configuring various hardware and software components. As an IT professional, you will often find yourself setting up end-user workstations or helping those end users with the hardware they need to make their daily lives easier. Installing and configuring peripheral components—such as display devices, keyboards and mice, or even more specialized devices—are some of the more common tasks that you will perform. By identifying common peripheral devices, you will be better prepared when you are called on to install and configure them.

Peripheral Devices

A peripheral is a device that connects to a computer to expand the computer's functionality. This includes devices that enable the user to input, output, store, and share data.

You can enhance the functionality of practically any personal computer by connecting different types of external devices to the system unit. Also called peripheral devices, external devices can provide alternative input or output methods or additional data storage. You connect external devices to the system unit via cable or a wireless connection. Some devices have their own power source, whereas others draw power from the system. Common examples of external devices include keyboards, mice or other pointing devices, microphones, cameras, scanners, printers, and external drives.

Input Devices

Computers need user input, such as directions or commands, and user interaction with the programs that are included in order to produce something of use. Keyboards and pointing devices are the standard input devices for personal computers these days, but there is an ever-growing number of input devices available for the user to interact with in a variety of ways. As a technician, part of your responsibilities will include installing and configuring all types of input devices.

Types of Input Devices

Common input devices include mice and keyboards, but even these two components come in a variety of implementations. The following tables describe some of the keyboards and pointing devices available in the market. This first table describes keyboards.

Keyboard	Description
Standard keyboard 	Standard keyboards are rectangular in shape and have 84, 101, or 104 keys. • The original PC keyboard, the XT, has 84 keys. A numeric pad is integrated to the right of the alphabetical keys. Function keys are along the left side of the keyboard. • The AT keyboard also has 84 keys and is very similar to the original PC keyboard. However, on the AT keyboard, the numeric pad is separate from the alphabetical keys. • The AT Enhanced keyboard has 101 keys. The function keys are integrated across the top. Arrow keys have been added, as well as a set of six keys—**Insert, Delete, Home, End, Page Up,** and **Page Down**. There are also additional command keys such as **Esc** and **Ctrl**. • The Windows 104-key keyboard is similar to the AT Enhanced keyboard, but adds two **Windows** keys and a **Menu** key. The **Windows** keys are analogous to clicking the Windows **Start** button and the **Menu** key performs the same functions as right-clicking the mouse.
Ergonomic keyboard 	Natural or ergonomic keyboards usually split the keyboard in half so each hand can comfortably use its own set of keys. Built-in wrist rests are common, and some ergonomic keyboards also have an integrated pointing device such as a trackball or touch pad.
Dvorak keyboard 	Dvorak keyboards rearrange the keys into a more efficient arrangement that makes faster typing possible for users who have become familiar with it.

The following table lists the various pointing devices available.

Pointing Device	Description
Mouse 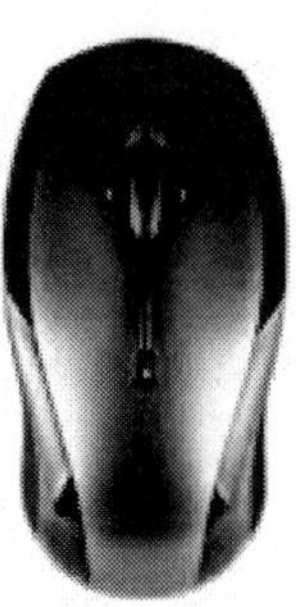	A *mouse* is a small object that runs across a flat surface and has at least one, but typically two or three, buttons that send electronic signals to the graphical user interface (GUI). Its name is derived from its appearance—a small rounded rectangle shape with a single cord attached at one end. Mice can be: • Mechanical—A ball on the underside runs along a flat surface. Mechanical rollers detect the direction the ball is rolling and move the screen pointer accordingly. • Optical—A laser detects the mouse's movement. Optical mice have no mechanical moving parts, and they respond more quickly and precisely than other types of mice.
Trackball mouse 	A *trackball* is basically an upside down mouse. The ball is mounted on the top of the case instead of the bottom and signals are sent to the computer by moving the ball with your thumb, fingers, or palm instead of by rolling the ball across a flat surface. Like a mouse, a trackball has at least one button that is used to send electronic signals to the computer.
Touch pad 	A *touch pad* is a small, touch-sensitive pad where you run your finger across the surface to send electronic signals to the computer to control the pointer on the screen. Touch pads can have buttons like a mouse or trackball, or the touch pad can be configured to detect finger taps on its surface and process those signals like button clicks.
Trackpoint 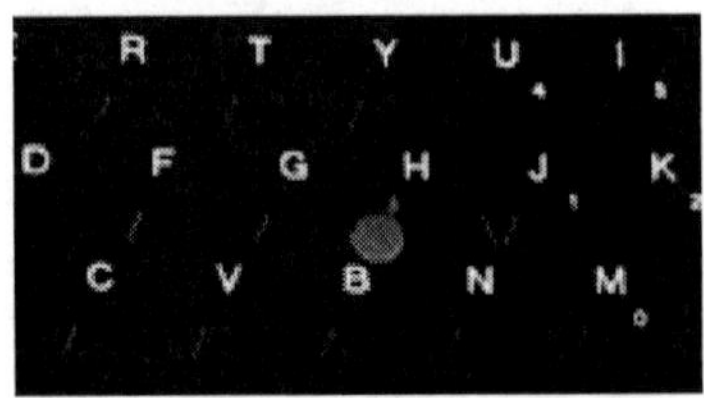	A *trackpoint*, or pointing stick, is most commonly found on laptops. Located in the center of the keyboard, the trackpoint is a small joystick-like button that responds to user force in all directions in order to move the mouse pointer on screen.

Pointing Device	Description
Stylus pen 	A stylus or *stylus pen* is most often used with tablets, or on a drawing tablet connected to a computer. The stylus might or might not have buttons that act as mouse buttons. Some styli are pressure sensitive, creating a broader, darker line when used for drawing. When used on a touch-sensitive display, the stylus is used to select text, buttons, and icons.
Joystick 	A *joystick* is a pivoting stick or lever attached to a base that is used to control movement on a device. It typically also includes push buttons, toggles, or switches that control other actions associated with the program or device that the input is controlling. The joystick inputs the angle and direction of a desired movement. Joysticks are most commonly used to control video games or other computer programs, but are also used to control machines and devices such as cranes and unmanned vehicles. Legacy joysticks connected to a computer via a game port, a device port designed specifically for connecting this input device. However, most modern joysticks connect to the device via a USB connection.

In addition to various keyboard and pointing devices, other input devices include graphics tablets, scanners, microphones, and webcams.

Input Device	Description
Scanner 	A *scanner* is used to take a photo-identical copy (scan) of a physical hard copy of any kind of document, such as a piece of paper or a photo, and create a digital-format copy of the document. A scanner is similar to a photocopy machine or copier but with a much smaller footprint. Scanners can be attached directly to a personal computer to import scanned copies of documents. With the proper software or program installed, scanned versions can be manipulated and edited once they have been imported. A scanner typically uses a USB or high-speed USB connection to connect between devices.
Microphone 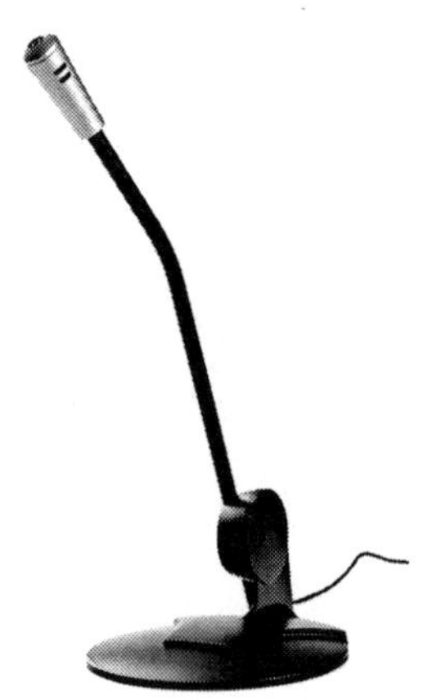	Microphones record any type of sound and convert it to electronic or digital format. Once in this format, the recorded sounds can be manipulated or edited, and used in a variety of ways. Microphones typically connect to a device through a MIC jack, although some connect with a USB connection. Some laptops may have a built-in microphone.
Webcam 	A web camera, or *webcam*, is used to send periodic images or continuous frames to a website for display. Webcam software usually captures the images as JPEG or MPEG files and uploads them to a web server. Webcam images can also be accessed by using some instant messaging software and by some video applications. Some corporations use webcams as a security measure. Webcams commonly use USB or FireWire cables and connectors.

Input Device	Description
Graphics tablet 	A *graphics or drawing tablet* is a tablet surface typically used by artists and computer-aided design (CAD) designers to draw image and pictures by using a stylus the same way you would draw the image on paper, but instead, you draw on the tablet. The image you create is displayed on your computer monitor. Some graphics tablets include a small screen within the tablet surface so you can see what you are drawing without needing to look up from your drawing surface.

Output Devices

Output devices enable the user to get information and data out of the computer. Typical examples include printers, speakers, and displays.

A *printer* is a device that produces text and images from electronic content onto physical media such as paper, photo paper, and labels. A printer is one of the most popular peripheral devices in use in most computing environments. Printers employ a range of technologies; the quality of the print output varies with the printer type and generally in proportion to the printer cost. A printer output of electronic documents is often referred to as "hard copy." Printers can connect to computers by using a variety of connection types, with the most popular methods being USB, networked, and wireless.

Speakers can be attached to the device to play the audio out loud, without the need for headphones. Speakers are connected to the line out port or jack on the sound card. Some speaker sets are permanently connected to each other. Other speaker sets are connected by the user to each other or to a subwoofer. A cable runs from one of the speakers to the line out port to connect both speakers to the computer. If the card is color-coded, the speaker port will be lime. The port might be labeled as Line Out, Out, Spkr, or Speaker, or it may have an image with an arrow indicating the direction of the audio (out). Speakers typically have a 1/8-inch phono plug built into the attached cable.

A display device allows you view content accessible through your computer. This is typically in the form of a monitor. As the technology has changed for home television, so too has monitor technology. Display devices have a variety of connection types, including HDMI, DVI, and DisplayPort.

Types of Output Devices

The following tables list various types of output devices. These include printers, displayers, and speakers.

There are many technologies used to produce printer output, but the three most often encountered are laser, inkjet, and thermal printers.

Printer Type	Description
Laser Printer	A *laser printer* is a printer that uses a laser beam to form images and toner to print the images on a printing medium, such as paper or photo paper.
Inkjet Printer	An *inkjet printer* is a printer that forms images by spraying liquid ink from an ink cartridge out of nozzles aimed carefully on the printer. Inkjet printers have a self-cleaning cycle and will park the printhead when not in use. The printer can use heat or vibrations to release the ink.

Printer Type	Description
Thermal Printers	A *thermal printer* is a general term for any printer that uses a heating element to create the image on the paper with dye, ink from ribbons, or directly with pins while the feed assembly moves the media through the printer. There are several types of thermal printers that use significantly different technologies and are intended for different uses. The most sophisticated types of thermal printers can produce professional photo-quality images. There are also thermal printers for everyday office use and for special-purpose applications. Most thermal printers will require special *thermal paper* that contain chemicals designed to react and change color as it is heated by the heating element within the printer to create images. These printers are commonly used with cash registers to print receipts.

There are several different types of display devices that you might be asked to install or configure.

Display Device	Description
CRT	*Cathode ray tube (CRT)* displays use electron beams within a vacuum tube to create images on a fluorescent screen. The intensity of three electron beams, one for each primary color (red, blue, and green), are manipulated to display the image on the screen. CRT monitors are larger, heavier, and boxier than their more modern counterparts due to the components used to build them, especially the thick glass used for the screen. The screen may be curved or flat, but CRTs are not considered flatscreen monitors. CRT monitors have for the most part been replaced by more modern and efficient displays like LCD, LED, or plasma screens, though many may still be in use in organizations who have yet to upgrade their devices.
LCD	*Liquid crystal display (LCD)* flatscreen displays are a compact, lightweight alternative to traditional CRT displays. LCDs consume much less energy than CRTs and do not emit nearly as much electromagnetic radiation as CRTs do. LCD monitors use a *cold cathode fluorescent lamp (CCFL)* as the backlight source. CCFLs use electrodes and mercury vapor to create ultraviolet light that is used as the light source. Depending on the LCD screen, the user may need to sit directly in front of the screen to see the display properly. A unique feature of LCD displays is that the screen auto centers. There is typically no center alignment needed.
LED	*Light-emitting diode (LED)* displays utilize the same screen as an LCD display, but use a different backlighting technique/technology. Instead of the CCFLs used in LCD, LED screens use one of two types of light emitting diodes as a backlighting source: dynamic RGB LEDs, which are located behind the panel; or white edge-LEDs, which are located around the edge of the screen and use a diffusion panel to evenly distribute the light source. LED displays consume even less power than LCD displays. However, LED displays are currently more expensive to purchase.

Display Device	Description
OLED	*Organic light emitting diode (OLED)* displays utilize the same technology as LED displays, but use organic compounds that emit light when subjected to an electric current as the light source. However, OLED screens can be used in a larger variety of dimensions than LED screens, and are currently utilized in computer monitors, television screens, tablets, and mobile phones.
Plasma	*Plasma displays* use xenon and neon rays and a flat panel of glass to provide visuals with high contrast, brightness, and vibrant colors that can be viewed from a multitude of angles. However, plasma displays can suffer from image burn-in from repeated, long-term use. They are currently available only in very large dimensions, typically 40 inches or more, and are mostly marketed and utilized as television displays. They can also be incredibly heavy and cumbersome due to the technology.
Projector	Video projectors are often used to display the video output onto a whiteboard or other surface so that a larger audience can see it.

Speakers can be attached to the device to play the audio out loud, without the need for headphones. Speakers are connected to the line out port or jack on the sound card. Some speaker sets are permanently connected to each other. Other speaker sets are connected by the user to each other or to a subwoofer. A cable runs from one of the speakers to the line out port to connect both speakers to the computer. If the card is color-coded, the speaker port will be lime green. The port might be labeled as Line Out, Out, Spkr, or Speaker, or it may have an image with an arrow indicating the direction of the audio (out). Speakers typically have a 1/8-inch phono plug built into the attached cable.

Devices that Perform Both Input and Output Functions

Some devices provide both input and output functionality. This includes devices such as fax devices, external storage devices, and touchscreen devices.

- Fax device functionality might be built into a card inserted in an expansion slot in your computer case, or it might be built into a printer. Printers with fax capabilities are referred to as multi-function devices. A *multi-function device (MFD)* is a piece of office equipment that performs the functions of a number of other specialized devices. MFDs typically include the functions of a printer, scanner, fax machine, and copier. However, there are MFDs that do not include fax functions. Although the multifunction device might not equal the performance or feature sets of the dedicated devices it replaces, multi-function devices are powerful, can perform most tasks adequately, and are an economical and popular choice for most home or small-office needs.
- There is a wide variety of external storage devices. Some are portable; others require access to network cabling.

External Storage Device	Description
Flash drive	A *flash drive* is portable, with most being about 1/2-inch wide, 1/4-inch deep, and 3-inches long. These typically connect to a USB port on your computer.
External hard drive	An external hard drive might connect to your computer via USB or FireWire. Some external hard drives come encased in an enclosure and others use an internal hard drive, placed in a docking unit.

External Storage Device	Description
Optical discs and drives	CD, DVD, and Blu-ray discs that are capable of being written to fall into the category of being both input and output devices. The drive can be internal to the system or connected via USB or FireWire. The disc can be written on one computer and then read by any other computer.
Network attached storage	A *network attached storage (NAS)* device is a hard drive that connects directly to the network cabling rather than to a specific computer. You can control which computers can access the NAS device.
Memory card	The memory card used in your music player, camera, or smartphone can be connected to your computer to read and transfer images and data from the portable device to your computer. You can also write to the memory card while it is in your computer and then access the images or data on your music player, camera, or smartphone.
Mobile media	In addition to having memory cards in cameras and smartphones, there is memory built into the device on which images and data can be stored. In order to transfer the images and data from the internal mobile media memory to your computer, you will need to be able to connect the mobile device to your computer by using either a cable or a wireless networking protocol such as Bluetooth®.
Smartphone	Smartphones typically use a USB connection to connect to a wall charger or to a computer. Connecting the smartphone to the computer allows you to read from and write to the internal memory or the memory card in the phone.

- *Touchscreen* monitors enable input by touching images on the screen. The screen also acts as the display for the computing device. This technology is used in bank ATMs, some point-of-sale terminals at fast food restaurants, and other situations in which a separate keyboard for input is not appropriate. Touchscreens are also found on many smartphones, tablets, and laptops sold for general public use.

ACTIVITY 1-4
Identifying Peripheral Devices

Before You Begin

Your instructor will provide you with a variety of input, output, and input/output devices, as well as locations in which to organize the devices.

Scenario

In clearing up the storage closet that you have been working on, you decide it would help if the devices were organized by type. On one set of shelves you want to organize all of the input devices. On another set of shelves you want to place all of the output devices. On a third set of shelves you want to put all of the devices that can be both input and output devices.

---

1. Locate all of the input devices.
    a) Locate and label each of the types of keyboards.
    b) Locate and label each of the types of pointing devices.
    c) Locate and label any scanners.
    d) Locate and label any webcams and microphones.
    e) Place like devices in the same box or on the same shelf or rack on the shelving unit for input devices.
2. Locate all of the output devices.
    a) Locate and label each of the types of printers.
    b) Locate and label each type of display.
    c) Locate and label each pair of speakers.
    d) Place like devices on the same shelf or rack on the shelving unit for output devices.
3. Locate all of the input/output devices.
    a) Locate and label any devices that include fax functionality.
    b) Locate and label all external storage devices. Be sure to include the type of external storage device and the connection type on the label.
    c) Locate and label any touchscreen devices.
    d) Place like devices on the same shelf or rack on the shelving unit for input/output devices.

Summary

In this lesson, you identified computer hardware. You identified various types of computing devices, internal computer components, various types of computer connections and ports, and common peripheral devices. Being familiar with the many types of computer hardware will help you determine which hardware components are appropriate for use in different situations.

How many of the personal computer components described in this lesson are familiar to you?

Which of the device connections discussed in this lesson have you worked with before? Which were new?

Note: Check your CHOICE Course screen for opportunities to interact with your classmates, peers, and the larger CHOICE online community about the topics covered in this course or other topics you are interested in. From the Course screen you can also access available resources for a more continuous learning experience.

2 Identifying Computer Software

Lesson Time: 2 hours

Lesson Objectives

In this lesson, you will identify computer software. You will:

- Compare the functions and features of common operating systems.
- Identify common applications and their purposes.

Lesson Introduction

In the previous lesson, you identified computer hardware. The other major element of a computing device is the software, which includes the operating system and the application software. In this lesson, you will identify computer software.

Operating system software provides the user interface for interacting with the hardware components, whereas application software enables you to accomplish specific tasks. By identifying the functions and features of common operating systems, as well as the various types of application software available, you can decide which computer software is best suited to your needs or to the needs of any users you need to support.

TOPIC A

Compare Functions and Features of Common Operating Systems

In the last topic, you identified computer hardware. You can buy the newest computer and the shiniest peripherals, but without operating system software to communicate with the hardware, you will never be able to benefit from your investment. In this topic, you will compare the functions and features of common operating systems.

As a professional IT support representative or PC service technician, your job will include installing, configuring, maintaining, and troubleshooting operating systems. Before you can perform any of these tasks, you need to understand the basics of what an operating system is, including the various versions, features, components, and technical capabilities. With this knowledge, you can provide effective support for all types of system environments.

Operating Systems

An *operating system (OS)* is a software package that enables a computer to function. It performs basic tasks, such as recognizing the input from a keyboard, sending the output to a display screen or monitor, and controlling peripheral devices such as disk drives and printers. It creates a user-friendly environment that enables users to use a computer efficiently without having to know the underlying technologies. Depending upon the version and manufacturer, the features of the user interface and functionality vary.

Figure 2-1: An operating system software package allows a computer to function.

Operating System Functions

The operating system provides the following functions:

- Provides the user-friendly environment to work with system features and applications.
- Converts a user's input and sends it to the monitor or other display device.
- Controls peripheral devices such as disk drives and printers.
- Provides the structure for files and folders.
- Monitors the operating system's health and functionality.

Licensing

A software license is a legal document used to control the distribution and use of software. There are five main types of software licenses.

Note: These license types apply to applications, operating systems, and all other forms of software.

License Type	Description
Open source	*Open source* software enables users to access its source code and gives them the right to modify it. Open source licensing ensures that free and legal redistribution of the software is possible.
Freeware	*Freeware* applications can be downloaded from the Internet directly and used without any restrictions.
Commercial	A *commercial* software application is sold to users. As the name suggests, it is intended to meet commercial needs. Many commercial software publishers ask their users to register their copies within a specified period of time. This type of software does not allow users to access the source code or modify it.
Copyleft	*Copyleft* is the method of ensuring that all original work, and all the derivative works created from it, are kept free and open. The term "copyleft" is used to define a concept that is essentially the opposite of "copyright." Software developer Richard Stallman proposed this concept to create a licensing arrangement under which software can be freely used, modified, and copied by others. The Free Software Foundation (FSF) recommends that all free software be copylefted and released under General Public License (GPL).
Shareware	*Shareware* applications are free applications that a user can download from the Internet directly. The only difference between a freeware and shareware application is that the shareware is usually provided on a trial basis. That is, the user will have to purchase the full version of the software once the trial period expires. Some shareware applications have restricted features. Users can use these features only once they purchase the full version.

Software Registration

It is always good practice to register the software you use. Registering your copy of a software application helps prevent software piracy. By registering the software, a user becomes eligible to receive regular updates, upgrades, and technical support.

Types of Operating Systems for Workstations

Operating system software is written to work in the background to create the working environment for a computer. The operating system software sets the rules for how a system and application work together, how security is handled, and in what format the data is stored in disk drives.

Operating System	Definition
Windows	Microsoft® Windows® is the single most popular and widely deployed operating system on both desktop computers and server systems in the world today. The various versions of Windows all feature a graphical user interface (GUI), support for a wide range of applications and devices, a minimum of 32-bit processing, native networking support, and a large suite of built-in applications and accessories such as the Internet Explorer® browser. Windows currently comes pre-installed on many personal computers sold commercially. There have been several versions of Windows since its inception. The most current version is often deployed on personal and professional computers.
Mac OS X	*OS X®* is the operating system developed by Apple Computing, Inc. OS X is a Linux® derivative, and consists of UNIX-based operating systems and GUIs. This proprietary operating system is included on all Macintosh computer systems. OS X features include: • Multiple user support. • Integrated Mac, Windows, and UNIX server, file, and printer browsing in the Finder. • The Safari® web browser. • Native TCP/IP networking. • Many file- and network-level security features. • Comprehensive hardware device support with a unique Macintosh computer system design.
Linux	*Linux* is an open-standards UNIX derivative originally developed and released by a Finnish computer science student named Linus Torvalds. The Linux source code was posted publicly on a computing newsgroup, and the code was developed and tested cooperatively all over the world. Because the source code is open, it can be downloaded, modified, and installed freely. However, many organizations prefer to purchase and implement a *Linux distribution.* A Linux distribution is a complete Linux implementation, including kernel, shell, applications, utilities, and installation media, that is packaged, distributed, and supported by a software vendor.
Chrome OS	Built on the open source Chromium OS, the Chrome operating system was developed by Google as its commercial OS. With manufacturing partners, the Chrome OS is installed on laptop computers that are known as *Chromebooks.*

Types of Operating Systems for Mobile Devices

Some operating systems are designed specifically to work with mobile devices such smartphones and tablets.

Operating System	Definition
Apple iOS	*iOS* is the base software that allows all other applications to run on an iPhone®, iPod touch®, or iPad®. The iOS user interface supports direct touch, multitouch, and using the *accelerometer.* Interface control elements consist of switches, buttons, and sliders. The response to user input is immediate and provides a fluid interface that includes swiping, tapping, pinching, and reverse pinching, all of which have specific definitions within the context of the iOS operating system and its multitouch interface.

Operating System	Definition
Android OS	*Android*™, on the other hand, is a layered environment built on the Linux kernel foundation that includes not only the operating system, but middleware, which provides additional software for the operating system and additional built-in applications. The Android OS was developed by the *Open Handset Alliance* and is owned by Google. It supports open-source–developed applications and functions and comes with basic operating system services, message passing, and so on. The major difference between Android and iOS is that iOS runs on Apple products only, whereas the Android OS is used by many different mobile device manufacturers and is more widespread across a number of different mobile devices. Android also enables manufacturers to overlay a suite of applications that they support.
BlackBerry OS	BlackBerry® phones are primarily used by professionals to conduct business operations and tasks. The BlackBerry OS directly supports corporate business requirements with functions such as synchronizing with Microsoft Exchange, IBM® Lotus® Domino®, or Novell® GroupWise® emails, contacts, and tasks by maintaining a high level of security.
Firefox OS	Developed by Mozilla, the Firefox OS is an open source operating system based on Linux.
Windows Phone OS	Windows smartphones run on the Windows Phone OS, which is maintained and developed by Microsoft. Features include a suite of Microsoft® Office® applications, Outlook® Mobile, web browsing, Windows Media® Player, and other advanced features.

Operating System Compatibility Issues

If you are upgrading an existing computer to a different version of Microsoft Windows, you will need to ensure that the existing computer hardware is compatible with the target operating system. To do so, you can either run the **Upgrade Assistant** tool available on Microsoft's website, or you can download a third party utility that will scan your computer and generate a compatibility report.

Note: The Windows Upgrade Assistant is available online at **http://windows.microsoft.com/en-us/windows-8/upgrade-assistant-download-online-faq.**

Another significant compatibility issue concerns the architecture of your OS and your computer. Modern operating systems are usually 64-bit. This means that they can take advantage of processors with larger memory addresses, which affords greater performance. However, older operating systems, and some still supported today, are 32-bit. The differences between these architectures can cause a number of conflicts, as described in the following table.

Compatibility Issue	Description
Hardware	The 32-bit and 64-bit OS architectures have different hardware requirements. The latter tends to require more random access memory (RAM) and storage space, or it may not function properly. Most important, however, is its processor. A 32-bit OS can usually run on a 64-bit processor, but a 64-bit OS cannot run on a 32-bit OS.

Compatibility Issue	Description
Applications	Applications designed to run on 64-bit operating systems are not compatible with 32-bit OSs. The reverse is not necessarily true, as 64-bit OSs can usually run 32-bit applications. However, there still may be compatibility issues, and the application may not run as intended. You may be able to select an appropriate application compatibility mode for the application after you have upgraded the operating system. For example, Windows 8.1 will allow you to emulate Windows 7 and earlier operating systems when you go to run an older application.
Drivers	A *driver* is specialized software that controls a device attached to a computer. A 64-bit driver will not work with a 32-bit OS, and this is also true vice versa.

ACTIVITY 2-1

Comparing Functions and Features of Operating Systems

Scenario

As an intern, you are being exposed to operating systems you had previously not encountered. You are creating a list to help you remember which operating system is used on which equipment. Your list also includes information about when it would be most appropriate to use the operating system.

---

1. **Identify the functions of operating system software. (Choose three.)**
   - ☐ Creates a working environment
   - ☐ Performs specific tasks
   - ☐ Sets rules for how a system and application work together
   - ☐ Specifies how security is handled
2. **Which operating system from Microsoft is available for desktop and server use?**
   - ○ Linux
   - ○ Mac OS X
   - ○ Windows
   - ○ Chrome
3. **Which operating system is freely available and comes in many distributions.**
   - ○ Linux
   - ○ Mac OS X
   - ○ Windows
   - ○ Chrome
4. **Which operating system distribution method is available by purchase only?**
   - ○ Open source
   - ○ Freeware
   - ○ Shareware
   - ○ Commercial
   - ○ Copyleft
5. **Which operating systems are for mobile devices, in particular, smartphones? (Choose two.)**
   - ☐ Linux
   - ☐ Chrome OS
   - ☐ Apple iOs
   - ☐ Mac OS X
   - ☐ Android OS

TOPIC B

Identify Application Software

In the last topic, you compared the features and functions of common operating systems. Although today's OSs do perform many helpful functions, there is still a need for additional software to ensure that you can perform your tasks as efficiently as possible. In this topic, you will identify application software.

Application software enable you to accomplish specific tasks, such as writing a letter, creating a slide presentation, or surfing the web. There are literally thousands of different applications out there to choose from, so being able to identify common types of application software, along with their uses, will help you to identify the specific software applications that will meet your needs or the needs of the users you are supporting.

Application Software

Application software is a program that provides specific functionality such as word processing, graphics creation, or database management. It is generally written to run on a specific operating system. This means that the word processor you purchased for a Microsoft Windows operating system may not work with a Macintosh operating system. Application programs may come pre-installed on a computer system or may need to be purchased and installed on the system.

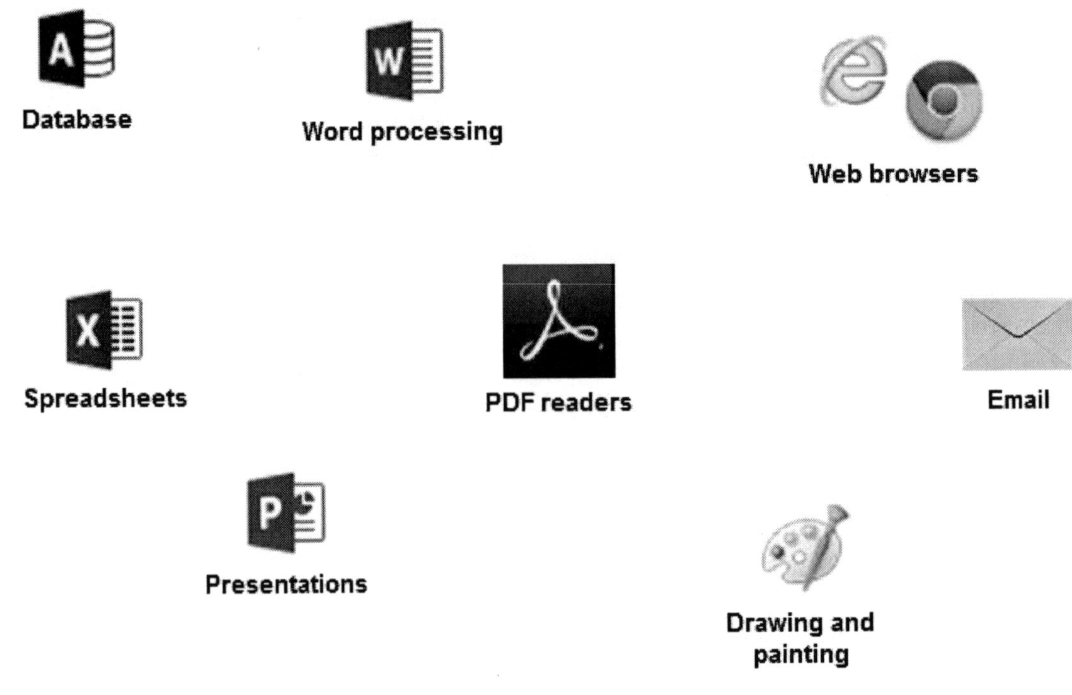

Figure 2-2: Software applications that run on a Windows operating system.

Application Platforms

Application software can be designed to run on multiple platforms. "Mobile" refers to the devices such as laptops, smartphones, iPads, and other tablet devices. "Desktop" is the traditional CPU and monitor with all the peripherals. Applications that users access and use through a *web browser* are known as "web-based."

Types of Productivity Software

Productivity software is a broad term that describes applications that range from those used to create documents to those used to manage your projects and organize your time. Some common examples include:

- **Word processing** software is used to create and work with typed documents. Examples include Microsoft Word and Apple iWork Pages.
- **Spreadsheet** software is used to calculate and analyze tables of numbers. Examples include Microsoft Excel and Apple iWork Numbers.
- **Email** software is used to communicate with others. Examples include Microsoft Outlook and Gmail.
- Basic **database** software is used to manage large volumes of lists and records. Examples include Microsoft Access and FileMaker Pro.
- **PDF** software is used to view, create, and work with PDF documents. Examples include Adobe Acrobat and Foxit PhantomPDF.
- **Presentation** software is used to create and work with slide shows. Examples include Microsoft PowerPoint and Apple iWork Keynote.
- **Desktop publishing** software is used to work with page layouts and typography in documents and publications. Examples include Adobe InDesign and Microsoft Publisher.
- **Personal information managers (PIM)** are used to manage your contacts and schedules. Examples include Windows Contacts and Google Calendar.
- **Remote desktop** software is used to access another desktop to provide troubleshooting assistance. Examples include Windows Remote Desktop Protocol (RDP) and Virtual Network Computing (VNC).

Types of Collaboration Software

Collaboration software is designed to facilitate sharing data and resources between users in a variety of locations and using a variety of computing devices. Common types of collaboration software include:

- **Online workspace** enables users to work with common files in a shared space on the web. Examples include Microsoft SharePoint.
- **Document storage/sharing** provides a repository to store and share files between users in various locations. Examples include OneDrive and Dropbox.
- **Screen sharing** software enables users to see each other's desktops from remote locations. Examples include Windows Remote Assistance and TeamViewer.
- **Video conferencing** software enables users to communicate with audio and video functionality from diverse locations. Examples include Skype and Google Hangouts.
- **Instant messaging** software enables users to exchange short notes, or chat, online in real time. Examples include Microsoft Lync and AOL Instant Messenger (AIM).
- **Email** software also allows users to share contact and calendar information.

Types of Utility Software

Every operating system comes with a host of utilities designed to help you diagnose and troubleshoot problems and simplify tasks. If you are considering an IT career in computer support, knowledge of these tools will help you maintain equipment and troubleshoot issues with the operating system.

- **Antimalware** detects and eliminates malicious software that resides on a computer. Examples include Windows Defender and Malwarebytes Anti-Malware.
- **Software firewalls** filter incoming or outgoing network traffic depending on how they are configured. Examples include ZoneAlarm and Comodo Internet Security (CIS).

- **Diagnostic/maintenance** software reports on any problems or issues that a computer may be experiencing. Examples include Windows Action Center and PC-Doctor.
- **Compression** software reduces the size of files so that they can be stored and transmitted more easily. Examples include WinZip and 7-Zip.

Types of Specialized Software

The specialized software category contains all of the other types that do not fit in the first three. Companies in architectural, engineering, medical, and financial fields require software applications that are specific for the documents and files that they need to create and use. Some common specialized software applications might include:

- **Computer-aided design (CAD)** software is used to create design specifications for electronics, mechanical objects, animation, and other products. Examples include AutoCAD and SketchUp.
- **Graphic design** software is used to create visual representations of concepts and ideas. Examples include Adobe Illustrator and CorelDRAW.
- **Medical** software that is used to collect, analyze, and present data related to medical information. Examples include Kareo and athenaCollector.
- **Scientific** software is used to collect, analyze, and present data used in experiments. Examples include LISREL and Sage.
- **Financial** software is used to keep track of expenses, maintain a budget, file taxes, and manage other financial information. Examples include Quicken and Microsoft Dynamics.
- **Gaming** software enables you to purchase, collect, and play video games on a computer. Examples include Steam and Origin.
- **Entertainment** software enables you to purchase, collect, and experience entertainment media such as music and movies on a computer. Examples include Google Play and iTunes.

Common File Types and Extensions

Standard file extensions that follow the names of files can indicate whether a particular file is a program file or a data file. If it is a data file, the extension can indicate the application category that might be used to edit the file. Many common file extensions are three characters long, although there is no longer a strict character limit for the file name or extension in most modern operating systems. A period separates the extension from the file name itself.

The following table lists a number of common file types and extensions.

Types of Files	*File Extensions*	*Description*
Documents	.txt	A plain text file that contains no formatting other than spaces and line breaks. You can open files that have a .txt extension in any text editing program, such as Notepad, or word processing programs, such as Microsoft Word.
	.rtf	Rich Text Format (RTF), or a text file that includes a limited amount of formatting such as bold and italic. You can open files that have the .rtf extension in various applications, such as common word processors or Microsoft's WordPad accessory.
	.doc/.docx	A data file created in a word processing program, such as Microsoft Word or WordPad. You might also see .docx, which is the Office 2007, 2010, and 2013 format.

Types of Files	File Extensions	Description
	.xls/.xlsx	Data files created in Microsoft Excel. Files® created in Office 2007, 2010, and 2013 are indicated by the .xlsx file extension.
	.ppt/.pptx	Data files created in Microsoft PowerPoint®. Files created in Office 2007, 2010, and 2013 are indicated by the .pptx file extension.
	.pdf	The versatile Portable Document Format (PDF) file format can be read by any computer with a free reader application, such as Adobe Reader.
Audio	.aac	The Advanced Audio Coding file format.
	.flac	The Free Lossless Audio Codec file format.
	.m4a	The Apple Lossless Audio Codec file format used for digital music files.
	.mp3	The Moving Picture Experts Group Layer 3 format used to store and play audio files in digital audio players.
	.wav	An audio file in the Waveform Audio File format that was developed by Microsoft and IBM.
Images	.bmp	The Microsoft Windows bitmap image file format.
	.gif	The Graphics Interchange Format image file format.
	.jpg/.jpeg	The Joint Photographic Experts Group image file format that is commonly used in photographs.
	.png	The Portable Network Graphic image file format.
	.tif/.tiff	The Tagged Image File format.
Video	.avi	The Microsoft Audio Video Interleaved file format that contains audio and video data.
	.flv	The Adobe Flash video file format used for delivering videos over the Internet.
	.mp4	The Moving Picture Experts Group Layer 4 (MP4) format used to store and play video files.
	.mpg/.mpeg	The Moving Picture Experts Group file format for audio and video files.
	.wmv	The Microsoft Windows Media video file format.
Executables	.app	The application program executable file format used by Apple.
	.bat	A batch file; a small text file containing a list of system commands that execute in a batch rather than requiring the user to enter each command in succession.
	.com	A command file or compiled application file.
	.exe	Windows executable file that launches programs and applications.

Types of Files	File Extensions	Description
	.msi	A Windows Installer package; a file that can specify installation parameters for an application.
	.scexe	A Linux self-extracting executable file.
Compression formats	.iso	An optical disc image of a file system that is commonly used for archiving.
	.dmg	A password-protected, compressed Apple Disk Image file format used by Mac OS X.
	.gzip/.gz	The free file compression file format developed for the GNU Project.
	.jar	A Java archive file format used to distribute Java class files and associated metadata files.
	.rar	Developed by Eugene Roshal, this archive file format supports compression, among other features.
	.7zip/.7z	The open archive file format that uses compression.
	.tar	A compressed file created with the XZ compression format.
	.zip	A file compression format that has built-in support in most operating systems.

Note: Because Windows uses the file extension to determine how the system will use a file, if you alter a file name extension, you might find that a program file will not execute properly or that a data file will not automatically open in the associated application.

ACTIVITY 2-2

Identifying Application Software

Scenario

You are going through some of the Help Desk tickets in the Application Software category. Some of the questions relate to which application the user should request to have installed on their computer to perform a specific task in their job. Other requests deal with which applications to use with which file types and extensions.

---

1. **Laura needs to use her personal computer to analyze tables of numbers. Which application software would you recommend?**
   - ○ Word processing
   - ○ Spreadsheet
   - ○ Database
   - ○ Web browsing

2. **Daniel needs to display a series of images and text in a meeting with the sales reps. Which application software would you recommend?**
   - ○ Word processing
   - ○ Database
   - ○ Presentation
   - ○ Spreadsheet

3. **Gary is creating a newsletter for his department. It will highlight many of the accomplishments achieved over the past quarter. He knows that some of the information is contained in an Access file and some is contained in Excel files. Some of the managers have given him Word documents containing information they would like him to include in the newsletter. He would like to send the newsletter electronically rather than printing it. Which types of applications will he need to access these files? What do you recommend that he use to create the newsletter?**

4. **Jordan works with an outside vendor that is constantly sending him files that have a .zip extension, or ZIP files. What type of application will he need to open these files?**
   - ○ File compression software
   - ○ Presentation software
   - ○ Graphic design software
   - ○ Spreadsheet software

5. Josie has a USB drive with XLSX files on it. Which of the following applications should she use to open them?

- ○ Microsoft Paint
- ○ Adobe Reader
- ○ Microsoft Excel
- ○ Microsoft WordPad

Summary

In this lesson, you identified computer software. By comparing functions and features of common operating systems and identifying common application software types and file types, you have prepared yourself to be more effective in selecting the operating system and application software that is most appropriate for a specific situation.

With which type of operating system (mobile, desktop, or web-based) do you have the most experience? Which do you have the least experience using?

List one software application that you use most frequently. Which of its features do you like the most?

Note: Check your CHOICE Course screen for opportunities to interact with your classmates, peers, and the larger CHOICE online community about the topics covered in this course or other topics you are interested in. From the Course screen you can also access available resources for a more continuous learning experience.

3 Setting Up a Basic Workstation

Lesson Time: 3 hours, 30 minutes

Lesson Objectives

In this lesson, you will set up a basic workstation. You will:

- Connect hardware.
- Install and configure operating systems.
- Install and configure applications.
- Configure accessibility options.

Lesson Introduction

So far in this course, you've identified computer hardware and software. Now it's time to put them together and configure a computing device. In this lesson, you will set up a basic workstation.

Setting up a basic workstation, whether it's a laptop or a desktop, is a fundamental skill that you will perform many times in your career as a PC support technician. There are many variables you will need to master, such as connecting hardware components, installing and configuring operating systems, installing and configuring application software, and configuring accessibility options, in order to ensure that you are meeting the needs of your users.

TOPIC A

Connect Hardware

In this lesson, you will set up a basic workstation. To start, you need to ensure that all of the physical components are properly attached to each other. In this topic, you will connect hardware.

Even the most basic workstation usually needs to have a few external components connected to it, and as user needs become more complex, the number and variety of hardware components required to build a workstation also increases. Connecting hardware together into a basic workstation enables you to meet the needs of your users.

Workstation Setup Process

To set up a basic workstation, you can follow this process:

1. Gather and connect hardware components. At a minimum, you will probably need to plug in cables for a monitor, keyboard, and mouse. But, if you have additional hardware—a printer, speakers, and a webcam, for example—you should connect them to the desktop computer, too.
2. Power on the computer.
3. If necessary, run the operating system setup utility.
4. If necessary, configure the peripherals. In some cases, this might be accomplished during the operating system installation.
5. Configure and verify the Internet connection. In some cases, this might be accomplished during the operating system installation.
6. Install security software.
7. Identify which applications should be on the workstation, and install or uninstall applications as necessary.
8. Update operating system, security, and application software as needed to ensure that all software is up to date.
9. Configure user accounts as needed.
10. Perform basic cable management to reduce clutter and enhance physical safety.

Cable Management

In office environments where there are many computers, there can be many cables and power cords. If these cords and cables are lying on the floor, they could possibly cause a tripping hazard. Even with only one or a few computers, the cables that connect peripherals to computers and computers to networks can quickly become disorganized and unsightly.

You can use some simple cable management techniques and tools to group and organize cables together to keep them out of the way and hidden from the general working space. Here are a few tips for managing cables:

- If cords and cables must traverse a floor area where people need to walk, it is recommended that cord protectors be used to shield the cords and cables from being damaged by pedestrian traffic, as well as to minimize the chance of someone tripping on the cords and cables.
- You can use Velcro® strips, twist ties, or even large binder clips to gather a computer's cables together so that they take up less space in your work area. Avoid using tie wraps, as they would need to be cut and replaced any time that you replace a cabled component.

Access the Checklist tile on your CHOICE Course screen for reference information and job aids on How to Connect Hardware.

ACTIVITY 3-1
Connecting Hardware

Before You Begin

You have a desktop computer equipped with a digital video interface and a 15-pin VGA-style monitor port, or you have a digital flat-panel LCD monitor that uses the 29-pin DVI connector or an HDMI connector. The computer is turned off, and a power cord, monitor, keyboard, and mouse are available. Other peripheral devices such as speakers, webcams, or USB hubs might also be available.

Scenario

You are a new computer support intern at Develetech Industries. Your first assignment is to build yourself a Windows 8.1 desktop computer to use during your internship.

---

1. Connect the monitor to the desktop computer.
   a) Verify that the computer is turned off.
   b) Locate the monitor cable and examine the connector.
   c) If you have a standard VGA CRT monitor, locate the VGA adapter port on the computer. If you have an LCD monitor, locate the VGA adapter, the 29–pin DVI adapter, the HDMI adapter, or the USB port on the computer.
   d) Insert the monitor connector into the appropriate port, making sure to align the pins carefully. If necessary, connect the other end of the video cable to the monitor. You might need to remove a plastic guard on the back of the monitor to access the port(s) on the monitor.
   e) Tighten the screws if the cable is equipped with screws. Do not over-tighten them.
   f) Plug the monitor's power cable into a free power source.
   g) If necessary, insert the other end of the power cable into the port on the monitor.

2. Connect the keyboard.
   a) Determine the connection type used by the available keyboard.
   b) Plug the keyboard into the appropriate PS/2 or USB port.
   If you are using a wireless keyboard, plug the receiver into the USB port and verify that the keyboard is turned on.

3. Connect the mouse.
   a) Determine the connection type used by the available mouse.
   b) Plug the mouse into the appropriate PS/2 or USB port.
   If you are using a wireless mouse, plug the receiver into the USB port and verify that the mouse is turned on.

4. If necessary, connect the speakers to the computer.
   a) Determine if you need to connect the speakers to each other and, if so, connect them to each other.
   b) Locate the speaker jack on the computer.
   c) Plug the speaker cable into the jack.
   d) If necessary, connect speakers to an external power source.

5. If necessary, connect the microphone to the MIC jack.
   a) Locate the MIC jack on the computer.
   b) Connect the microphone to the MIC jack.

6. If necessary, connect the digital camera to a USB port.

Note: If your digital camera uses a different connection type, use the appropriate cable and connect to the appropriate port.

   a) Locate a USB port on your computer.
   b) Insert the USB end of the cable into the appropriate port present in the computer.
   c) If necessary, insert the USB cable's connector into the port present in the camera.

7. If necessary, connect the network cable to the computer and the other end of the cable to a network connection.

8. Start the computer and verify that the peripherals are functional.
   a) If necessary, connect the computer power cable to the computer and the other end to an external power source.
   b) If necessary, turn on the power supply located next to the main power connector.
   c) Turn on the monitor and any other peripherals you connected.
   d) Press the power button on the computer to turn it on.
   e) After the system has started to boot, verify that the power light on the monitor is lit and is not flashing.
   f) Watch the monitor and verify that the display is clear.
   g) Verify that all other peripherals appear to be working properly.

      For some peripherals, you'll need to install the operating system before you can verify their functionality.

TOPIC B

Install and Configure Operating Systems

In the last topic, you connected hardware to make a basic workstation. For you to be able to use the workstation, it needs an operating system installed and configured on it. In this topic, you will install and configure the operating system.

One of the most basic tasks you will perform as IT support technician is installing and configuring operating systems on computers. By installing and configuring operating systems, you provide the basic functionality required to use the computer hardware.

Operating System Hardware Requirements

Each operating system (OS) requires specific minimum hardware. This is commonly referred to as the Hardware Compatibility List (HCL). This information can be found on the packaging for commercial OSs or by doing a search at the vendor's website. Open source OSs will list the minimum hardware requirements somewhere on the page for their distribution of the OS.

Information included in the HCL might include the minimum RAM, hard disk space, and monitor resolution needed. It might also list additional hardware required to use the OS.

Operating System Installation Programs

Depending on which operating system you plan to install, you might be required to run one of the following types of installation programs:

- A Windows setup wizard, which prompts you for various types of information to install and initially configure the operating system.
- A system image, which reflects the contents of an installation CD-ROM or DVD-ROM (ISO file), a virtual machine containing the installed OS, or a USB stick image containing the installed OS.

Common Operating System Configuration Parameters

No matter what type of OS you are installing, there are certain pieces of information that you'll need to supply to ensure that it operates properly after you install it.

- Date
- Time zone
- Language
- Keyboard type
- Screen resolution
- Audio settings

Note: Parameters such as date, time zone, and language are commonly referred to as localization settings.

In some cases, you might be asked for some or all of this information during the actual installation process; other times, you will need to configure the OS to provide this information.

Multiple User Accounts

A *user account* is an information profile that uniquely identifies a user on a computer. Every user account on a computer needs to have a unique *user name* and *password.* Users can set their own passwords. Different users on the same computer may have different *rights* and *permissions* that enable them to access resources and perform specific tasks such as printing or installing new applications.

User Account Information

The following table provides more information about some of the characteristics of user accounts.

User Account Characteristics	*Description*
User name	A unique name identifying a user on a computer.
Password	A case-sensitive string of alphanumeric characters that must be typed before a user can access a computer. A password acts as a key to log on to your computer. A strong password is a combination of both upper- and lowercase letters, numbers, and special characters.
Permissions and rights	A set of rules that determines what things a user is allowed to do on a computer and what resources the user can access; by limiting a user's permissions and rights, you can keep the person from opening files, installing unwanted software, or changing certain computer settings.

Peripheral Configuration

Some operating system utilities are designed to help you configure peripheral devices. For example, in Windows 8.1, you can use the following Control Panel utilities to configure peripheral devices.

- Use **Devices and Printers** to add devices, manage printers, configure the mouse, and access **Device Manager**, which enables you to scan for hardware changes.
- Use **Display** to configure display devices, including adjusting screen resolution, configuring a second monitor, and adjusting screen brightness.
- Use **Keyboard** to configure the keyboard properties including the device properties.
- Use **Mouse** to configure mouse and pointer properties, such as primary button, double-click speed, and pointer options.
- Use **Sound** to configure audio devices, such as speakers and microphones.
- Use **Speech Recognition** to configure the microphone and computer for voice input.

OS Updates

Software updates are software programs or code intended to address security flaws and performance issues in an existing version of software. Software updates are often available free of cost. Software updates may be released for an operating system or a software application.

Versioning provides information about the iteration of the software you are using. Software versions are changed every time the software is upgraded or newer features have been added to it.

Operating system updates can be classified into four categories.

Operating System Update Category	*Description*
Patch	*Patches* are small units of supplemental code meant to address either a security problem or a functionality flaw in a software package or operating system.
Hotfix	A *hotfix* is a patch that is often issued on an emergency basis to address a specific security flaw.

Operating System Update Category	*Description*
Service Pack	A *service pack* is a larger compilation of system updates that can include functionality enhancements, new features, and typically all patches, updates, and hotfixes issued up to the point of the service pack release.
Rollup	A *rollup* is a collection of previously issued patches and hotfixes, usually meant to be applied to one component of a system, such as the web browser or a particular service.

Automatic updates is a feature of an operating system or a software application that enables updates to be downloaded and installed automatically on a system at a scheduled time. After a manufacturer releases an update, it gets downloaded to your system the next time you connect to the Internet. You can configure the settings to allow for automatic installation of the updates the moment they are downloaded or to notify you of the downloaded update so that you can install it later. You can also disable automatic updates.

Access the Checklist tile on your CHOICE Course screen for reference information and job aids on How to Install and Configure Operating Systems.

ACTIVITY 3-2

Installing Windows 8.1

Before You Begin

You have connected a keyboard, mouse, and monitor to a desktop computer. You might also have connected speakers, a microphone, a webcam, or other peripheral devices to the desktop computer. All of these hardware components are compatible with installing Windows 8.1. Your instructor will provide you with a DVD or USB drive that contains the Windows 8.1 installation files, as well as a valid product key for installing the OS, and information related to a Microsoft account that has been created for you for this class.

Note: Activities may vary slightly if the software vendor has issued digital updates. Your instructor will notify you of any changes.

Scenario

The next stage of your assignment at Develetech Industries as a new computer support intern is to install the Windows 8.1 operating system on your newly built desktop computer.

---

1. Insert the Windows 8.1 installation media and restart the computer.
   a) Locate the DVD or USB drive that contains the Windows 8.1 installation files.
   b) Insert the DVD or USB drive into the desktop computer.
   c) Press and hold the power button until the computer shuts down.
   d) Press the power button again to restart the computer.

2. Start the Windows 8.1 installation wizard.

   Note: Depending on what was previously installed on the system and the manufacturer of the system, you might need to make a menu selection in order to boot from the installation media. Follow your instructor's directions if you are not prompted to boot from the installation media.

   a) When you are prompted, press any key to boot from the installation media.
   b) On the **Install Windows** page, for **Language to install**, select **English (United States)**.
   c) For **Time and currency format**, select **English (United States)**.
   d) For **Keyboard or input method**, select **US**.
   e) Select **Next**.
   f) In the **Windows Setup** window, select **Install now**.

3. Provide a product key, accept the license terms, and specify the installation type.
   a) If the **Enter the product key to activate Windows** page appears, type the product key provided by your instructor and select **Next**.
   b) On the **License terms** page, read the license agreement, check **I accept the license terms**, and select **Next**.
   c) On the **Which type of installation do you want?** page, select **Custom: Install Windows only (advanced)**.

4. Specify where the Windows 8.1 files should be installed.
   a) On the **Where do you want to install Windows?** page, examine the table.

Depending on what was installed on this computer before your class, you might see entries for one or more drive partitions, a drive partition that contains unallocated space, or both. To simplify the installation, you will remove all drive partitions and install Windows 8.1 in the unallocated space.

b) If necessary, select the first drive partition and then select **Delete**. If you are prompted to confirm the deletion, select **OK**.

c) Delete any remaining drive partitions, and confirm the deletions as necessary.
There should now be one drive entry, labeled **Drive 0 Unallocated Space**.

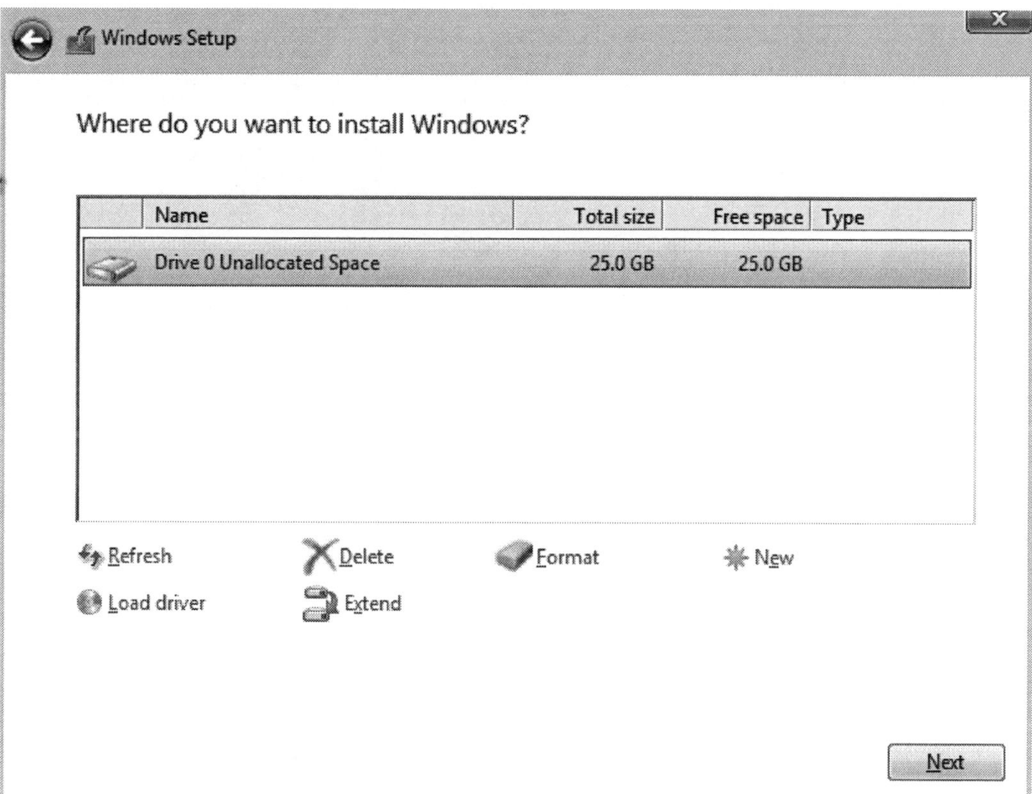

d) Verify that **Drive 0 Unallocated Space** is selected, and then select **Next**.

5. Complete the installation.

a) Wait while the Windows operating system files are installed and the computer reboots twice.

b) On the **Personalize** page, select a color.

c) In the **PC name** text box, type the first part of your assigned Microsoft account name.

For instance, if your assigned Microsoft account name were **IT_Fun_student02-10-30-14@outlook.com**, you would enter ***ITFunStudent02*** as the **PC name.**

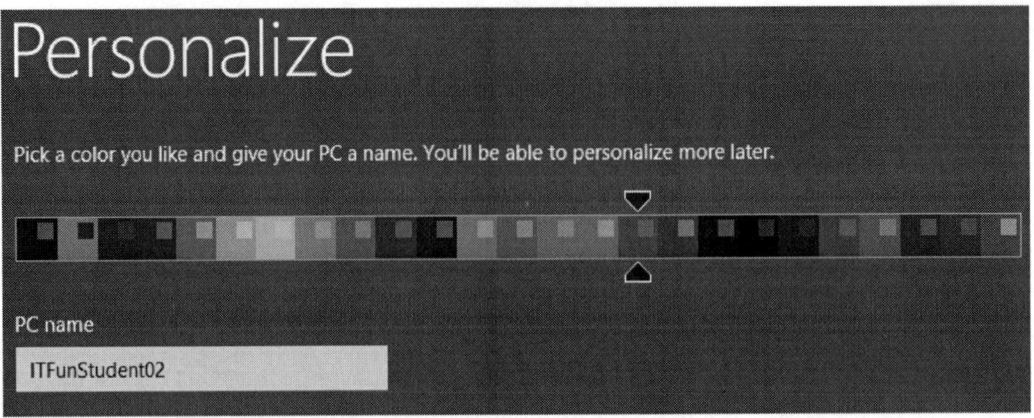

d) Select **Next**.

e) If necessary, on the **Wireless** page, follow your instructor's directions to select and connect to an available wireless network and then select **Next.**

f) On the **Settings** page, select **Use express settings**, and then select **Next**.

You will configure Windows settings in upcoming activities, so you can accept the default settings for now.

g) On the **Sign in to your Microsoft Account** page, type the email address associated with your assigned Microsoft account, and then select **Next**.

h) On the **Help us protect your info** page, select **I can't do this right now** .

i) On the **OneDrive is your cloud storage** page, select **Next**.
Windows uses your Microsoft account information to create a local computer account and applies any personalized settings to that account.

j) Observe the screen as Windows installs apps.

Several messages are displayed that are intended to help you use the Windows 8.1 interface. When the **Desktop** screen is displayed, the Windows installation process is complete.

6. If necessary, change the Time Zone setting.

a) In the taskbar, right-click the current date and time, then select **Adjust date/time.**

b) Select the **Change time zone** button.

c) From the **Time zone** drop-down listed, select the appropriate time zone for your location and then select **OK.**

d) In the **Date and Time** dialog box, select **OK**.

7. Remove the installation media from the computer.

ACTIVITY 3-3
Configuring Windows 8.1

Before You Begin

Windows 8.1 is installed on your computer.

Scenario

You just installed Windows 8.1. You are eager to begin using it and know that other users will be using it soon as well. You are sure that users are going to have questions about some of the customization features they have heard are available on this operating system, such as various sign in options, changing the desktop image, changing video settings, and creating local accounts. Before the mass rollout of Windows 8.1 to the organization, you decide you should experiment with some of these features.

---

1. Switch between showing the Desktop and the Start screen when you log in.
   a) Display the **Charms.**
   b) Select **Settings** and then **Change PC Settings.**
   c) Select **Control Panel.**
   d) Select **Appearance and Personalization.**
   e) Under **Taskbar and Navigation**, select **Navigation Properties.**
   f) In the **Taskbar and Navigation Properties** dialog box, in the **Start screen** section, uncheck **When I sign in or close all apps on screen, go to the desktop instead of Start** and then select **OK.**
   g) From the **Start** screen, select *your user name* and then select **Sign out.**

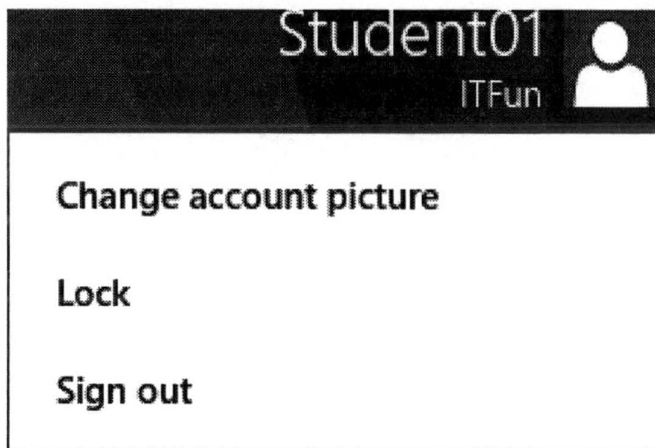

   h) Sign in again.
   You now see the **Start** screen when you log in to the computer.

2. Change sign-in options.

Note: Acknowledge any Windows 8.1 tips that are displayed.

   a) Display the **Charms**.
   b) Select **Settings→Change PC Settings.**
   c) Select **Accounts.**
   d) Select **Sign-in options.**
   e) Under **PIN**, select **Add.**

f) When prompted, type your user password and select **OK**

g) Type and confirm a four-digit number of your choice, and then select **Finish.**

Note: Consider writing down your PIN.

h) Press the **Windows** key to return to the **Start** screen.

i) Sign out.

j) Select or swipe on the Lock screen.
You are prompted for your PIN. However, don't type it yet.

k) Select **Sign-in options**.

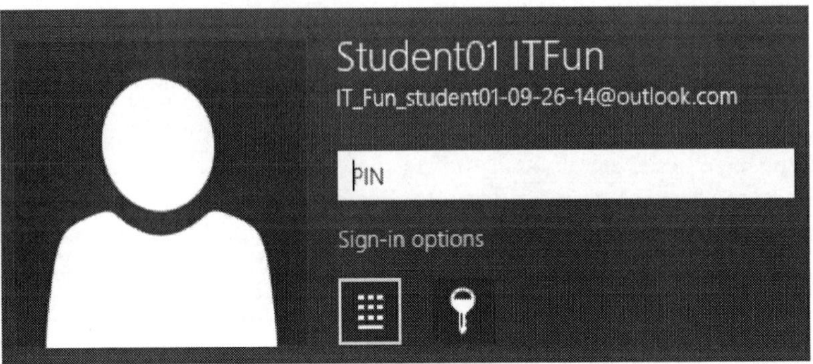

l) Select the **Microsoft account** button.
Notice that instead of being prompted for the PIN, you are now prompted to enter your password.

m) Select the **PIN** button to switch sign-in to use a PIN instead of a password.

n) Type the PIN you set. You don't need to press **Enter** after typing the numbers.

3. Change the Desktop background.

a) From the **Start** screen, select the **Desktop** tile.

b) Right-click the desktop and select **Personalize.**

c) Select the **Desktop Background** link.

d) Select the background of your choice.

e) Select **Save changes.**

4. Change video settings.

a) In the **Personalization** window, select **Display.**
b) Select **Adjust resolution.**
c) Select a lower resolution than you currently have set, and then select **OK**.
If you have a low resolution monitor, you might not be able to change the resolution.
d) Select **Revert**. If you don't make a selection, it will automatically revert to the previous resolution.
e) Close the **Screen Resolution** window.

5. Create a local user account.

a) Display the **Charms**.
b) Select **Settings→Change PC Settings.**
c) Select **Accounts.**
d) Select **Other Accounts.**
e) Select **Add an account.**
f) Select **Sign in without a Microsoft account (not recommended).**
g) Select **Local account.**
h) In the **User name** text box, type ***LocalStudentAcct***
i) In the **Password** and **Reenter password** text boxes, type ***P@ssw0rd***
j) In the **Password hint** text box, type ***cap @ zero***
k) Select **Next.**
l) Select **Finish.**
m) Press the **Windows** key, select your *username*, and, from the list, select **LocalStudentAcct.** Log in using the **LocalStudentAcct**.

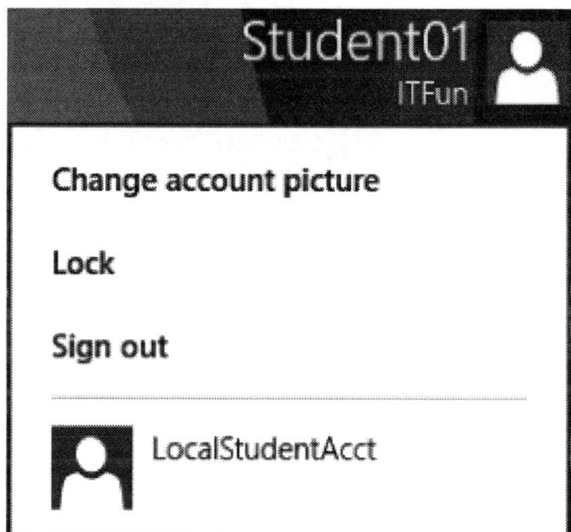

Windows will install apps for this new account. Notice that the settings you made for your regular account did not apply to this account. You still land at the Desktop when you log in with this account and are not prompted for a PIN at login.
n) Sign out.

TOPIC C

Install and Configure Applications

In the last topic, you installed and configured the operating system for a basic workstation. Although modern operating systems do offer a variety of built-in applications and utilities, the workstation will be more efficient to use once you install and configure applications on it. In this topic, you will install and configure applications.

Sometimes it seems as if there are an infinite number of software applications to choose from. And in some cases, you'll find some applications already installed on a computer by the manufacturer. The challenge is to select, install, and configure only those applications that are actually required by the user. By installing and configuring applications, you can optimize a workstation to meet the needs of its users.

Bundled Applications

Bundled applications are software programs that are sold together as a set or suite or that are sold with an operating system or with a new computer. Examples of software suites include Microsoft Office and Google Apps. Some applications commonly bundled with a new computer include security software that might combine antivirus, antispyware, and antimalware programs with firewalls and other security utilities.

Software Inventory

A software inventory is a listing of the applications that are available on a computer. You can perform a manual inventory by identifying the various applications that are installed, or you can use an inventory utility to create the inventory list. For example, you can use programs such as Belarc Advisor - Free Personal PC Audit and Microsoft Software Inventory Analyzer (MSIA) to create a detailed profile of the hardware and software installed on a computer.

Desired Applications

There are certain applications that everyone expects to be on a computer for it to be considered optimized for usability. At a minimum, these include:

- A web browser.
- An email client.
- Word processing software.
- Security software.
- Software updates, including OS updates.

Bloatware

As the cost of RAM and disk storage continues to decrease, there has been less emphasis among software developers to optimize the size of applications and the resources required to run those applications. *Bloatware* is a slang term that describes software that has lots of features and requires considerable disk space and RAM to install and run.

Application Sharing

On computers that have multiple user accounts, you have the option to configure applications so that they are available for use only to the user who installed them or to each of the user accounts on the computer. Depending on the application being installed, you might have the opportunity to specify whether the application will be available to only your account or shared with all users on the computer. Typically, desktop applications installed on the computer are available to any account on that computer, with the proper permissions.

Guidelines for Ensuring a Computer Contains Only the Necessary Applications

Note: All of the Guidelines for this lesson are also available as checklists from the **Checklist** tile on the CHOICE Course screen.

To ensure that you have the desired applications on your computer and reduce the amount of bloatware, you can use the following guidelines.

- Conduct a manual inventory or purchase an inventory utility to identify the applications currently on the computer.
- Identify one application for each of the following:
  - A web browser
  - An email client
  - Word processing software
  - Security software
  - Software updates, including OS updates
- Remove any unnecessary applications.
- Install any other necessary applications.

Access the Checklist tile on your CHOICE Course screen for reference information and job aids on How to Install and Configure Applications.

ACTIVITY 3-4

Installing and Configuring Applications

Scenario

Your manager asked you to research Windows Store apps that can be used to manage passwords. He wants to prevent users from keeping a list of passwords in their cubicles or offices. After doing some research, you have decided to install and test a free password management app that has a high rating. The Password Padlock app in the Windows Store meets these requirements. You have also been asked to help the programmers select apps that can help them be more productive. Several programmers have suggested Notepad++ because it includes line numbers by default, so you want to install it to see how it works.

---

1. Access the Windows store.
   a) Log in with your IT_Fun_student##-date@outlook.com account.
   b) From the **Start** screen, select the **Store** tile.

2. In the **Store** app, search for and select **Password Padlock.**
   a) In the **Search** text box, enter ***Password Padlock***
   b) From the search results, select **Password Padlock.**

3. Observe the information about the app. Screenshots, reviews and other details are shown.

4. Select the **Install** button. The app begins installing. A message will be displayed when the app has finished installing.
   If you are prompted to add a payment method, select **Ask me later.**

5. Close the **Store** app.

6. Open **Password Padlock.**
   a) From the **Start** screen, select **All Apps.**
   b) Under **P,** select **Password Padlock.**

7. Configure the Password Padlock app.
   a) Select **Tap here to set up your master password.**
   b) Enter and confirm the password ***P@ssw0rd!!***
   c) In the **Optional Password hint** text box, type ***cap @ zero double bang***
   d) Select the **Save** button.
   e) In the **Tip for New Users** message box, select **Close.**
   f) In the **What's New** message box, select **Close.**
   g) Close **Password Padlock.**

8. Download the most recent version of Notepad++.
   a) Open **Internet Explorer.** The MSN page is displayed with the bing web search bar near the top.

   b) In the **bing web search** text box, enter ***notepad++***

c) From the results list, select **Notepad++ - Official Site**.
d) On this page, on the navigation pane, select **download**.
e) Under the **DOWNLOAD** button, select **Notepad++ Installer.**
f) Select **Save.**

9. Install and run Notepad++.

a) Select **Run.**
b) In the **User Account Control** dialog box, select **Yes.**
c) In the **Installer Language** dialog box, with **English** selected, select **OK.**
d) Select **Next.**
e) In the **License Agreement** page, select **I Agree.**
f) In the **Choose Install Location** page, accept the default destination folder and select **Next.**
g) In the **Choose Components** page, select **Next.**
h) In the **Choose Components** page, check **Create Shortcut on Desktop** and then select **Install.**
i) With **Run Notepad++v6.6.9** checked, select **Finish.**
j) Close Internet Explorer.
k) Close the **Notepad++** window.

TOPIC D

Configure Accessibility Options

So far in this lesson, you have connected hardware, installed and configured an operating system, and installed and configured application software. To complete the basic setup of the workstation, you can configure options that help make it easier to get to and use the information on the workstation. In this topic, you will configure accessibility options.

As an IT support technician, you will discover that each user has a unique set of needs. Some users' needs are based on what they intend to accomplish with their workstations, while other needs are directly connected to the abilities of the users themselves. By configuring accessibility options, you can ensure that users who have differing access requirements can retrieve and use the data stored on their workstations.

Accessibility

Accessibility is the use of assistive technology to make computers available and easier to use. For example, users with impaired or limited vision can configure their computers to narrate the screen text and they can also increase the size of the screen components to make them easier to see. Accessibility features can be built-into the operating system or provided through specially designed applications and software.

Windows 8.1 Accessibility Options

The **Ease of Access** menu provides a way to make your computer more accessible through assistive technology. With **Ease of Access**, you can have the **Narrator** feature read aloud the text on your screen, increase the size of the page for readability, turn on an on-screen keyboard, or access other functions that offer alternative methods of making things easier to see and use.

The following table describes the features on the **Ease of Access** menu.

Ease of Access Menu Choice	*Description*
Narrator	**Narrator** will read aloud what is on the screen, including the text that you are typing, the contents of the active window, and menu options. This option is very helpful for the visually impaired. **Narrator** may not work with all applications.
Magnifier	**Magnifier** will enlarge the whole screen, or portions of the screen, to make viewing easier.
On-Screen Keyboard	Places a virtual keyboard on the screen. Useful for touchscreen PCs or when a keyboard is not available.
High Contrast	Provides a darker background to make text and images stand out for better viewing.
Sticky Keys	Sometimes two or more keys must be pressed at the same time to start an action, such as pressing **Ctrl+Alt+Del** to display **Task Manager** or to cause the computer to reboot. With the **Sticky Keys** feature turned on, you can press the keys in the combination one at a time.

Ease of Access Menu Choice	*Description*
Filter Keys	**Filter Keys** tells the PC how long to respond when a key is pressed and to ignore repeated keystrokes. This is helpful for users who shake, or who have difficulty pressing and lifting their fingers off of keys quickly enough when typing.

Note: To further explore the **Ease of Access** menu, you can access the LearnTO **Use the Magnifier** presentation from the **LearnTO** tile on the CHOICE Course screen.

Narrator

The **Narrator Settings** dialog box contains a variety of configuration options that enable you to control how Narrator starts, how it looks on screen, and how it behaves and interacts with you. Use the **Commands** category to define the specific keyboard shortcuts to start, stop, and repeat the reading; navigate to read different items on the screen; and adjust the voice volume. The **Voice** category enables you to choose between several different voices as well as control its speed, volume, and pitch.

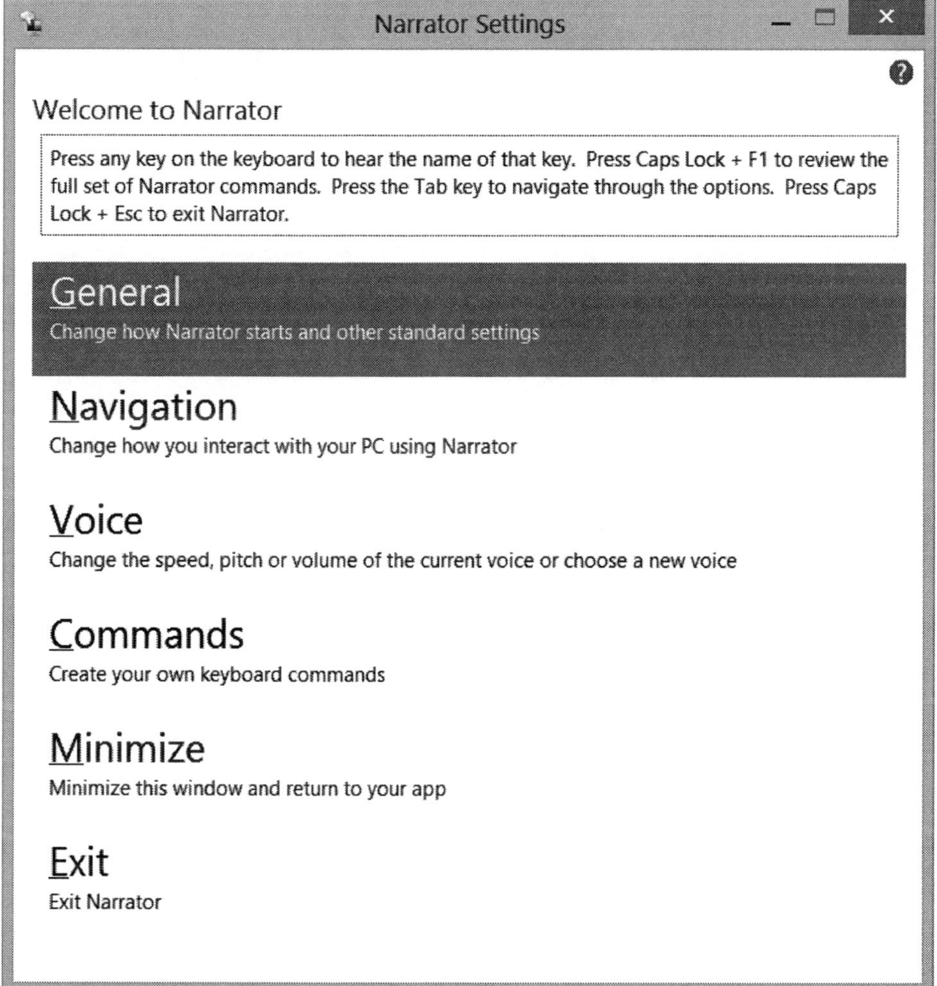

Figure 3-1: The Narrator Settings dialog box.

Magnifier

When running, the **Magnifier** toolbar is displayed and provides buttons for controlling the zoom level, what is affected, and the available options. The **Views** button contains the following choices:

- By default, the **Full Screen** is affected by the zoom level.
- **Lens** increases only the portion of the screen that's visible within the lens boundary.
- **Docked** displays the active portion of the screen in a separate window at the top of the screen.

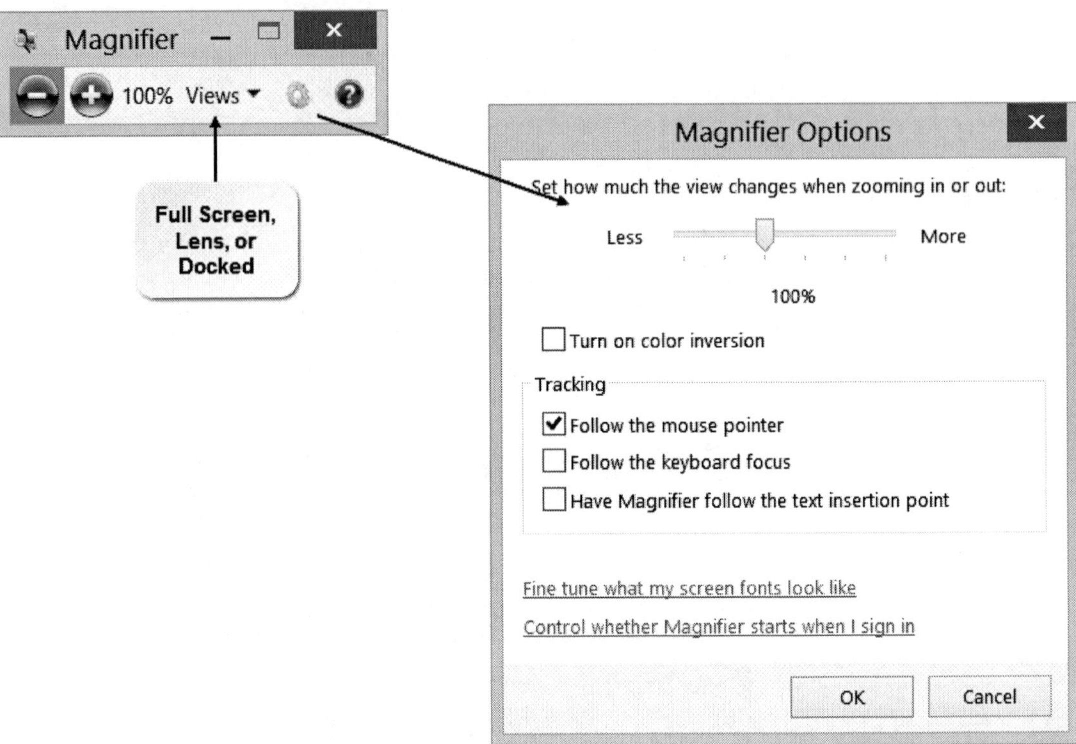

Figure 3-2: Magnifier Toolbar and Options.

Basic Accessibility Options in Other OSs

The following table lists some of the accessibility options available in various other operating systems.

Operating System	Accessibility Features
Mac OS X	• **VoiceOver** screen reader explains what is on the screen as well as reading screen text to you. • **Zoom** and **Cursor Size** enable you to magnify the full screen or a selected portion and the cursor. • **Dictation** enables you to input text by speaking instead of typing. • **Invert Colors** provides a high-contrast display to make it easier to see screen elements. • **Closed Captions** provide close captioning text when watching videos, movies, and podcasts. • **Screen Flash** flashes the screen to indicate that an app needs your attention. • **Mono Audio** plays both stereo channels in both ears. • **Switch Control** enables manipulating on-screen keyboards, menus, and the dock by using scanning. • **Slow Keys** adjusts the sensitivity of the keys. • **Sticky Keys** enables you to press keyboard shortcut combinations (such as Command+S) one at a time instead of simultaneously. • **Speakable Items** uses speech recognition to navigate within your Mac and applications, such as opening apps, switching between apps, closing windows, navigating menus, starting screen savers, and so on. • **Simple Finder** reduces the Dock to three folders. • **Text to Speech** converts highlighted text to audio.
Chrome OS	• **ChromeVOX** screen reader provides voice explanation and feedback to visually impaired users. • **Accessibility settings** enables you to configure the display (cursor size, high-contrast mode, screen magnifier) and other features (sticky keys and the on-screen keyboard).
Android OS	• **TalkBack** screen reader describes the results of actions. • **Explore by Touch** works with TalkBack to provide spoken feedback on the item that is being touched on screen. • **Accessibility settings** enables you to configure the display and sound options.

Other Adaptive Technologies

Adaptive technology includes tools that are designed to ensure that people with disabilities are able to use the software. Sometimes, the distinction is made that adaptive technology is used only by people with disabilities, whereas assistive technology tools are used by everyone. A variety of adaptive products are available on the market today. Many provide hands-free capabilities. A few examples of adaptive technologies include:

- Braille translation software converts text documents to Braille and vice versa.
- Eye-tracking devices that enable you to input by using eye movements instead of typing on a keyboard.
- Tobii EyeMobile enables you to control a Windows 8 tablet with your eyes.

For more information, you can go to the website of the non-profit organization Assistive Technology Industry Association (ATIA) and some of its partner organizations, such as the Alliance for Technology Access (ATA). Both of these sites contain information and links to a variety of companies offering products and services that help make technology accessible for all.

Access the Checklist tile on your CHOICE Course screen for reference information and job aids on How to Configure Accessibility Options.

ACTIVITY 3-5

Configuring Windows Accessibility Options

Before You Begin

To use the Narrator feature, you need speakers or headphones connected to your computer.

Scenario

As you are working through some of the help desk tickets, you see there is a category for helping users with accessibility options. You haven't used any of the accessibility options, so you decide to see how to use the magnification, high contrast, and narrator options.

---

1. Open the **Ease of Access Center**
   a) If necessary, from the **Start** screen, select the **Desktop** tile.
   b) Right-click the **Desktop** and select **Personalize.**
   c) In the left pane, select **Ease of Access Center.**

2. Use the Magnifier to enlarge the display.
   a) In the **Ease of Access Center**, select **Start Magnifier.**
   b) If necessary, select the magnifying glass to open the **Magnifier** window.

   c) In the **Magnifier** window, select the **+** to increase magnification to 300%.
   d) Select **Views** and observe the options. You can magnify the **Full screen**, a portion of the screen with **Lens** or divide the display into a normal view and a magnified view with **Docked.**
   e) From the **Views** menu, select **Lens.**
   f) Move the mouse around the screen to see the effects of magnifying through the lens option.
   g) In the **Magnifier** window, select **Views→Full screen.** Now the entire screen is magnified to 300%.

Note: If the **Magnifier** window doesn't appear, select its icon in the taskbar to bring it forward.

   h) Move the mouse to the screen edges. Notice that the display automatically scrolls to display portions that are currently off screen.
   i) Select the **Magnifying glass** to display the **Magnifier** window.

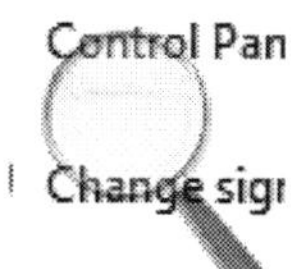

   j) Select **Views→Docked.** The top portion of the screen shows a duplicate image of the screen and is magnified.
   k) Select the **Magnifying glass** to display the **Magnifier** window.
   l) Close the **Magnifier** window.

3. Enable **High Contrast** viewing on your display.
   a) In the **Ease of Access Center**, select **Set up High Contrast.**
   b) Verify that all of the check boxes are checked under **Choose a High Contrast theme.**
   c) Observe the first option.

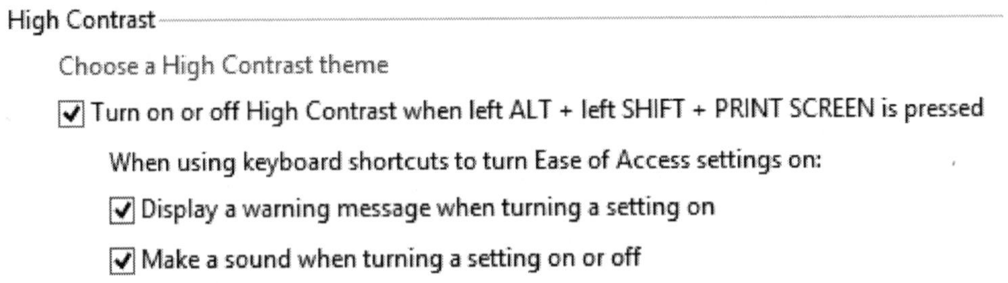

   High Contrast

   Choose a High Contrast theme

   ☑ Turn on or off High Contrast when left ALT + left SHIFT + PRINT SCREEN is pressed

   When using keyboard shortcuts to turn Ease of Access settings on:

   ☑ Display a warning message when turning a setting on

   ☑ Make a sound when turning a setting on or off

   d) Select **OK.**
   e) Press **left Alt+left Shift+Print Screen.**
   f) In the **High Contrast** dialog box, read the window content, and then select **Yes.** The display changes to a black background with white and yellow lettering.
   g) Press **left Alt+left Shift+Print Screen** to turn off **High Contrast.**

4. Enable the **Narrator** feature.
   a) In the **Ease of Access Center** select **Start Narrator.**
   b) Point to various links, icons, and text on screen to have **Narrator** read the text.
   c) Press **Caps Lock+Esc** to exit **Narrator.**
   d) Close the **Ease of Access** window.

Summary

In this lesson, you set up a basic workstation. By connecting hardware, installing and configuring various types of software, and configuring accessibility options, you can provide yourself and other users with computing devices that will meet the identified needs.

If you have experience with installing and configuring operating systems, what problems did you encounter and how did you address them?

What applications do you feel are important to include in your personal required software list?

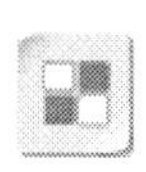

Note: Check your CHOICE Course screen for opportunities to interact with your classmates, peers, and the larger CHOICE online community about the topics covered in this course or other topics you are interested in. From the Course screen you can also access available resources for a more continuous learning experience.

4 Configuring Network Access

Lesson Time: 2 hours, 30 minutes

Lesson Objectives

In this lesson, you will configure network access. You will:

- Compare network connection types.
- Install and configure a SOHO router.
- Identify the purpose of network and alternative technologies.
- Compare methods for sharing and storing information.

Lesson Introduction

You've set up your workstation, and now you're ready to connect to and communicate with others. In this lesson, you will configure network access.

Although workstations offer some pretty powerful tools to help people be more productive, their reach and power increase dramatically when you connect them together to form a network. By configuring access to a network, you can share information and store your data in a central and easily accessible location.

TOPIC A

Network Connection Types

In this lesson, you will configure network access. To begin, you'll need some information about the various types of networks and connections that are available. In this topic, you will compare network connection types.

As an IT support technician, you will find that there are many different types of networks and ways to connect to them. By comparing network connection types, you can select the most appropriate type for each situation that you encounter.

Computer Networks

A *computer network* is a group of computers that are connected together to communicate and share network resources such as files, applications, and devices. No two computer networks are alike in size or in configuration. Each network, however, includes common components that provide the resources and communications channels necessary for the network to operate.

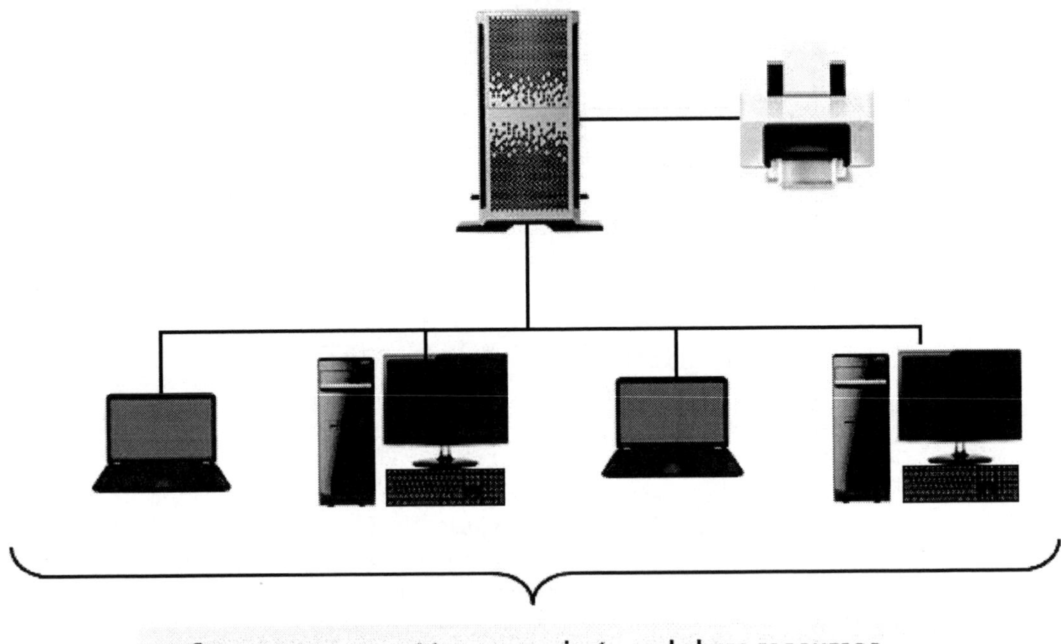

Figure 4-1: A simple computer network.

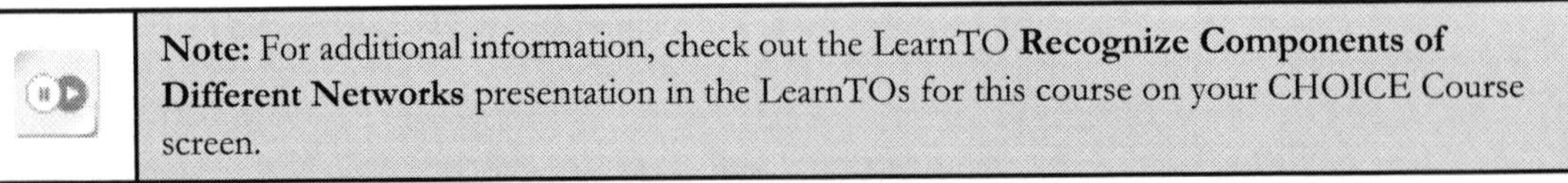

Note: For additional information, check out the LearnTO **Recognize Components of Different Networks** presentation in the LearnTOs for this course on your CHOICE Course screen.

There are several common components that make up a computer network, each of which performs a specific task.

Network Component	Description
Device	Hardware such as computers, servers, printers, fax machines, switches, and routers.
Physical media	Media that connects devices to a network and transmits data between the devices.
Network adapter	Hardware that translates data between the network and a device.
Network operating system	Software that controls network traffic and access to common network resources.

Network Types

There are several different types of networks. The two most prominent types are LANs and WANs.

A *local area network (LAN)* is a group of computers and associated devices that share the resources of a single processor or server within a small geographic area. A LAN may serve as few as two or three users or as many as thousands of users. A network set up between the computers in a home would be an example of a LAN.

A *wide area network (WAN)* is a network of computers that are spread across a large geographic area. An example of a WAN would be a company that has offices in several different cities or nations; the company's computers would be connected by a WAN.

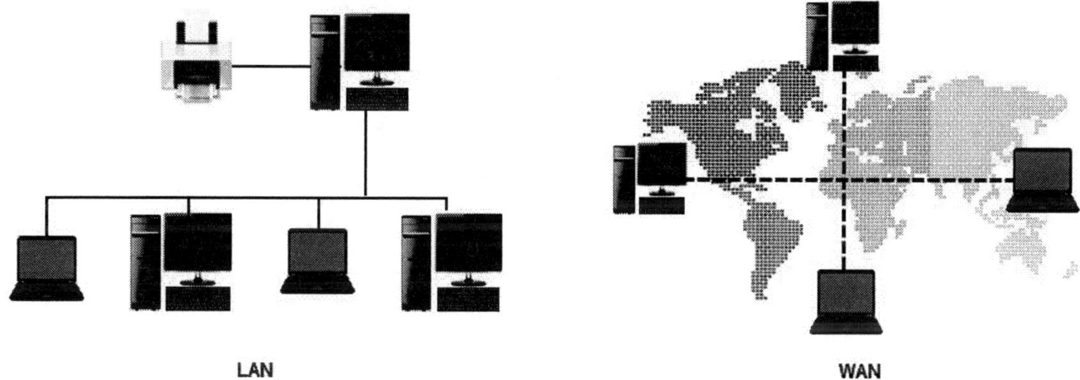

Figure 4-2: LAN and WAN wired networking.

Network Connection Methods

Connecting various devices to a network can be done in a number of ways. How devices will communicate with one another is determined by the connection method:

- Wireless
- Wired
- Cellular

Each method has its own advantages and disadvantages when it comes to certain important characteristics in networking. These characteristics describe a connection from several different perspectives.

Characteristic	Describes
Mobility	The ability to transport a device from one physical location to another without interrupting the connection.

Characteristic	Describes
Availability	A connection that stays up and operational as long as possible without interruption, as well as the ability for that connection to recover quickly should it go down.
Throughput	Throughput is the actual amount of data that is transmitted over a medium in a given time.
Bandwidth	Throughput is the maximum amount of data that is possible to transmit over a medium in a given time.
Reliability	A connection that transmits data without causing connection delays or corrupting the data.
Concurrent connections	How many users or devices can be connected to the same network at one time.
Security	How safe the network is from attack.

Note: You can think of bandwidth as theoretical, whereas throughput is a more practical description. There are many factors that could prevent a connection from reaching its maximum speeds.

Wired Network Connections

Wired computer networks use a technology called Ethernet. *Ethernet* is a set of networking technologies and media access methods specified for LANs. It allows computers to communicate over small distances using a wired medium. Networks both large and small use Ethernet to provide both backbone and end-user services.

Wireless Network Connections

A *wireless computer network* is a network in which computers use wireless connections to link with other computers. Wireless connections transmit data by using radio frequency waves. Wireless networks can connect a few devices over short distances, such as within a home or an office, or can be set up to connect computers over large distances through the Internet. Wireless networks offer affordability, ease of use, and greater mobility for the user. The most common wireless computer networking protocol is *Wi-Fi*, which is a LAN technology used by many different kinds of devices.

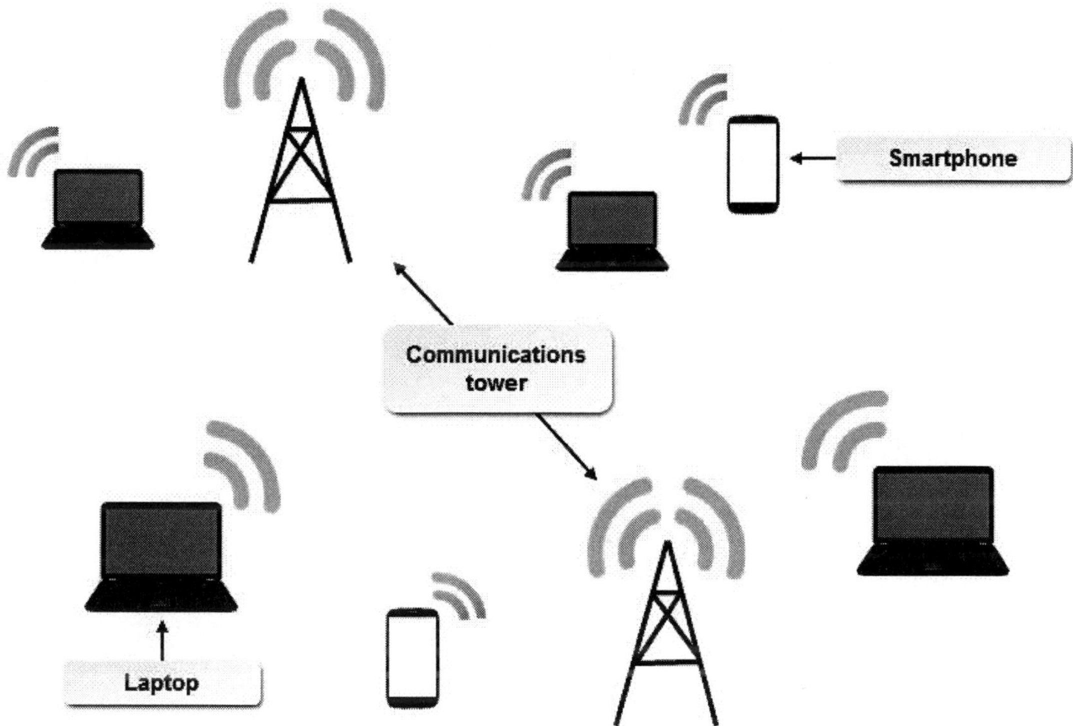

Figure 4-3: A wireless network connects devices by using radio waves.

In a wireless network, each computer has a *wireless adapter* device attached, which converts digital data into radio waves and also receives radio waves and converts them into digital data. To connect to other wireless or wired networks, wireless devices called *wireless access points (WAPs)* or wireless routers are required.

Cellular Network Connections

A *cellular network*, otherwise known as a mobile network, is a radio network. This network consists of different areas called cells, each of which has a transceiver, known as a *base station* (BS) or a cell site, and all of these cells put together allow for communication over a very large geographic area. Each cell operates on a slightly different frequency so there will be no interference between cells. The result is that mobile devices can communicate with any other mobile device on the network via the BSs in each cell.

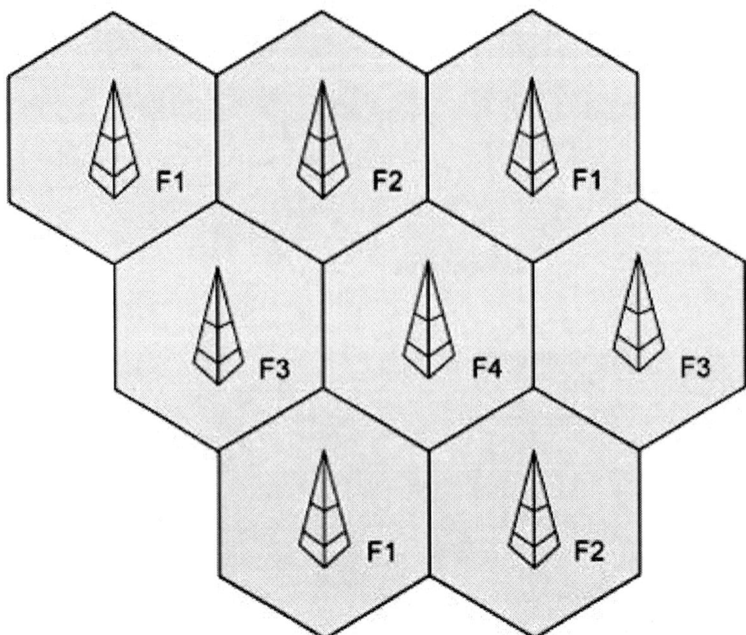

Figure 4-4: Cells in a cellular network.

Mobility

The following table compares the level of mobility available to users based on the network connection method.

Network	Mobility Level	Explanation
Wired	Little to none	By definition, a wired network requires computers and other devices to be physically attached to the network. Network devices are mobile only within the reach of the cables.
Wireless	Medium	With the use of a wireless router, network devices can travel outside of the reach of a cable but must stay within reach of the router signal. Some router signal strength requires the devices to be within the same building (such as a home router), whereas other routers are strong enough to broadcast across a university campus.
Cellular	High	The mobility of devices on a cellular network are limited only by their proximity to a cellular tower, as long as the device can receive a signal from the base station.

Availability

The following table compares the level of availability afforded to users for the different network connection methods.

Network	Availability Level	Explanation
Wired	Medium to high	A wired network's availability depends upon the health of its network devices and its cabling infrastructure.

Network	Availability Level	Explanation
Wireless	Medium to high	A wireless network's availability depends upon the health of its network devices.
Cellular	High	Large telecommunications companies have many backups in place to ensure that their networks are always up and running.

There are two primary ways to ensure high availability: resilience and redundancy. *Resilience* is the key to maintaining the availability of the network. Resilience simply means the ability of the network to survive disaster or avoid it in the first place. *Redundancy* provides an alternate way in which to keep the network operating. Think of redundancy as having a backup system in place.

Bandwidth and Throughput

The following table compares the level of bandwidth and throughput available to users for different network connection methods.

Network	Bandwidth/ Throughput Level	Explanation
Wired	High	Ethernet technology provides bandwidth up to 100 Gb/s, but is more commonly provided at 10 Gb/s and 1 Gb/s for enterprise LANs.
Wireless	Medium	Wi-Fi technology provides bandwidth up to 7 Gb/s, but is more commonly provided at 1.3 Gb/s and 600 Mb/s for enterprises LANs.
Cellular	Low	4G networks typically deliver bandwidth up to 100 Mb/s.

Reliability

The following table compares the level of reliability between the different network connection methods.

Network	Reliability Level	Explanation
Wired	High	Wired connections do not suffer from the interference issues that wireless connections do. As long as the physical cable is healthy, the connection should stay highly reliable.
Wireless	Medium	Wireless connections are susceptible to interference from other devices and phenomena that operate in the electromagnetic spectrum, which can interrupt connectivity and cause corruption of data in transit.
Cellular	Low	Cellular networks are also susceptible to interference. Additionally, despite their wide coverage, cellular networks often see a degradation in performance or a complete lack of connection in certain locations.

Concurrent Connections

The following table compares the amount of concurrent connections that each network connection method can have.

Network	*Concurrent Connection Level*	*Explanation*
Wired	Medium	The high bandwidth of Ethernet connections means that more people can connect at once without losing significant performance. However, the number of people connected simultaneously is physically limited by the cabling infrastructure of the network.
Wireless	Medium	The lower bandwidth and small coverage of wireless networks means that few users and devices can connect to a single access point. For example, a 600 Mb/s Wi-Fi signal shared among 100 people would reduce each person's bandwidth to 6 Mb/s. Some wireless routers have a built-in limit to the amount of connections they can handle.
Cellular	High	Although they offer low bandwidth, cellular networks are intended to support millions of connections at once.

Security Levels

The following table compares the level of security inherent in each network connection method.

Network	*Security Level*	*Explanation*
Wired	High	Because a wired LAN isolated from other networks requires physical access, it is much more secure from a remote breach into the network. Without this physical connection, an attacker will be unable to intercept communications.
Wireless	Medium	Attackers can intercept wireless communications without needing to be physically plugged in. The attacker just needs to be within range of the wireless network in order to monitor its transmissions. To protect against this, most modern Wi-Fi transmissions are encrypted. However, some older or poorly implemented technology may use weak encryption or none at all.
Cellular	Low	Like wireless networks, cellular transmissions are susceptible to attackers monitoring and intercepting data remotely. This is compounded by the large coverage of cellular networks and their high mobility. Many carriers implement some form of encryption, but this encryption may not be suitably strong.

Network Connection Method Comparison

The following table is an overview of the strengths and weaknesses of each network connection method.

Characteristic	*Wired*	*Wireless*	*Cellular*
Mobility	Little to none	Medium	High
Availability	Medium to high	Medium to high	High

Characteristic	Wired	Wireless	Cellular
Bandwidth/throughput	High	Medium	Low
Reliability	High	Medium	Low
Concurrent connections	Medium	Medium	High
Security	High	Medium	Low

Note: For additional information, check out the LearnTO **Select the Right Network Connection Method** presentation in the LearnTOs for this course on your CHOICE Course screen.

ACTIVITY 4-1

Comparing Network Connection Types

Scenario

Develetech uses a network to connect to printers and share information with other computers. As the company has branched into many offices across the country, your manager has asked you for help in choosing a network type to connect the computers in all the branches.

---

1. **When would a WAN be used?**
   - ○ To share files among employees within an organization
   - ○ To share files between computers in offices located in different countries
   - ○ To share a printer for printing documents
   - ○ To use resources present on a server

2. **Which tasks require the use of a network? (Choose three.)**
   - ☐ Creating a spreadsheet by using software that is installed on your computer
   - ☐ Printing a spreadsheet by using a printer that you share with the other members of your department
   - ☐ Sending an email to a group of coworkers regarding a department meeting
   - ☐ Saving a file so that others in your group can access the most updated copy of that file and make changes to it when needed

3. **Which of the following best describes Ethernet?**
   - ○ A network of computers that share a large geographic area
   - ○ A network that includes workstations and a server and supports a small geographic area
   - ○ A LAN technology used for connecting computers and servers in the same building or campus
   - ○ A LAN in which computers communicate with a server without using wires, but through a wireless device attached to a computer

4. **The accounts payable department requires a great level of security and availability. Which network connection type would you recommend for this department?**

TOPIC B

Install and Configure a SOHO Router

In the last topic, you identified basic network connection types. As an IT technician, you might be asked to implement these technologies in a small office or home office (SOHO) situation, rather than in a corporate enterprise setting. In this topic, you will install and configure a SOHO router.

Small businesses, whether located in a commercial building or in an individual's home, can benefit greatly from being able to share files and other resources. SOHO networks generally contain anywhere from two to ten computers, though there can be exceptions to this guideline. As an IT technician, you might be called upon to implement SOHO networks as part of your job duties.

SOHO Networks

A *SOHO network* is a network that provides connectivity and resource sharing for a small office or home office. Generally limited to fewer than 20 computers or nodes, a SOHO network often facilitates sharing of files and printers, as well as services such as email, faxing, and so forth. A SOHO network can contain a combination of wired and wireless computer connections, and all of the computing devices in a SOHO network usually share the same physical location.

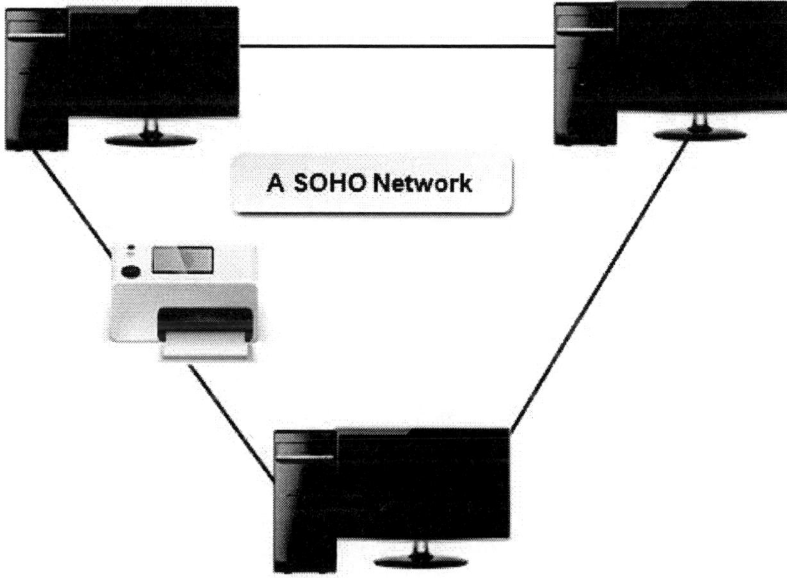

Figure 4-5: A SOHO network.

How Small Is Small?

SOHO networks can range in size, and there is no real consensus as to the maximum number of nodes that can be in a SOHO network. Some sources cite the maximum as 10 nodes, whereas others say that four or five nodes is the maximum.

SOHO Routers

A *wireless router* connects a computer to multiple networks through a wireless connection. It performs the functions of a wireless accent point (WAP) and a router. It enables wired and wireless computers to connect to the Internet. It can allow multiple users to be connected to a network at the same time. Some wireless routers have a firewall built into them.

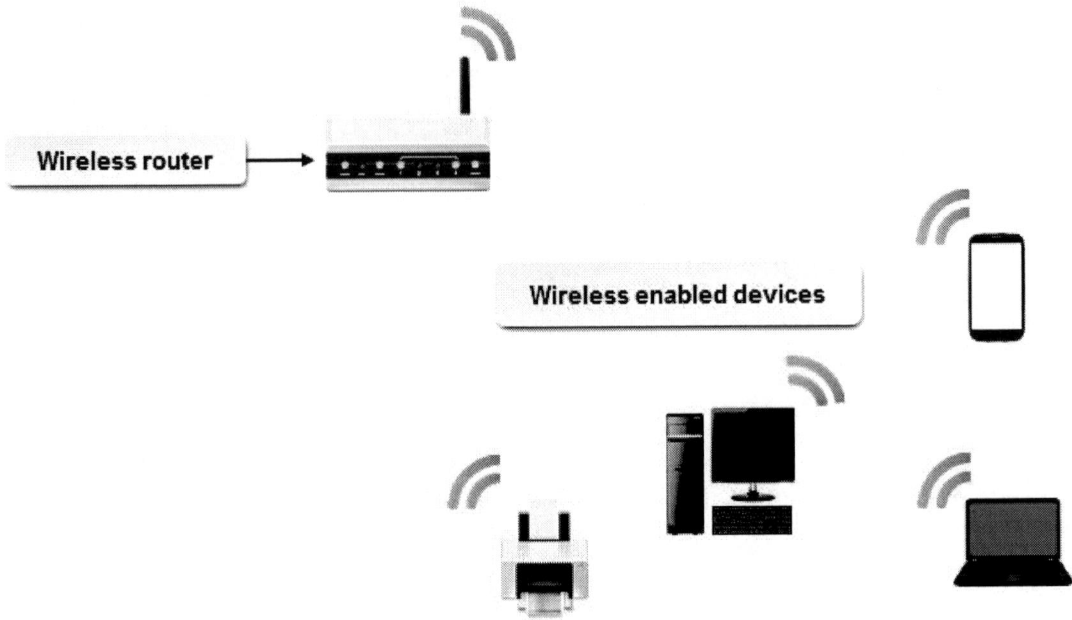

Figure 4-6: A wireless router connects a computer to multiple networks.

The following table describes the difference between the most common types of networking devices.

Network Device	Description
Hub	A *hub* is a networking device that connects multiple computers to form a LAN. The hub broadcasts data in the form of signals to all connected computers. Hubs support transmission speeds of 10 Mbps, 100 Mbps, or both.
Switch	A *switch* is a small network hardware device that joins multiple computers together within the same LAN. Like hubs, switches also have multiple ports and are responsible for forwarding data from a source to a destination. However, switches forward data packets to only the nodes or segments they are addressed to and reduce the chances of collisions among data packets.
Router	A *router* is a networking device used to send data among multiple networks that use the same protocol. A protocol is a set of rules used to establish communication between two computers on a network. Routers send data among networks by examining the network addresses contained in the packets they process. A router can be a dedicated device or can be implemented as software running on a node. Although the functions of a router are similar to that of a switch, a router has a comparatively higher data handling capacity and is mainly used in WANs.

Encryption

File encryption is a type of file protection that disguises the data within a file or message so that the specific information included within the file or message cannot be read or understood by unauthorized users. A key is used to encode the data, and neither the file nor the key contents can be read by anyone who does not have the key. File encryption can be local, where a file that is on a disk is protected, or it can be used when a file is being transmitted over a network connection.

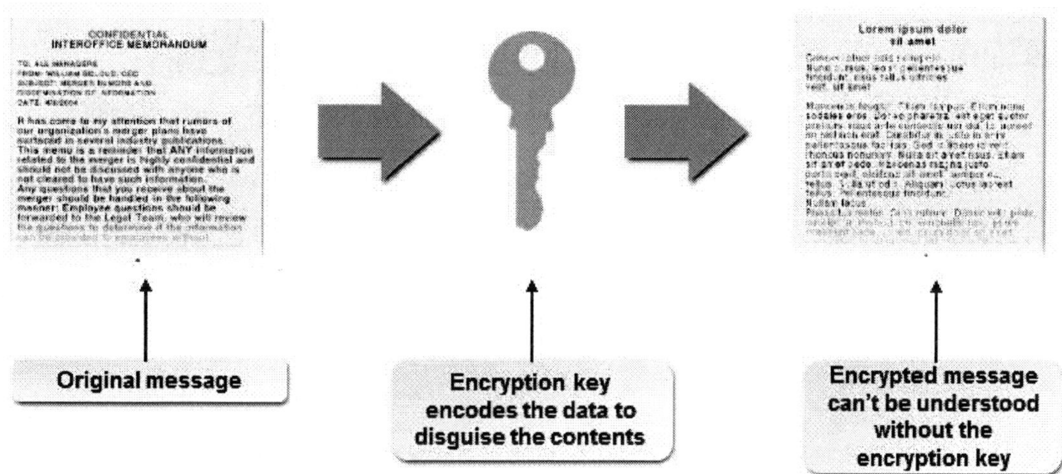

Figure 4-7: A message being encrypted.

Note: In some instances, organizational policies can restrict or require the use of file encryption.

An example of file encryption would be code that substitutes each letter of the alphabet for another letter at a specific distance in the alphabet. A rule like that was used to encode the following message: Iloh Hqfubswlrq.

The key to decoding this encrypted message would be a number that shows the distance between the original character and the encoded character. The decryption key, -3, tells you to take each letter in the encrypted message and count back three letters in the alphabet to read the message: File Encryption.

Wireless Encryption Standards

Wireless networks are not as secure as wired networks, as they operate over radio waves instead of physical cables. In an effort to strengthen the security of wireless networks, a number of *wireless encryption* protocols have been developed.

Wireless Encryption Method	*Description*
WEP	*Wired Equivalent Privacy (WEP)* is a security protocol for wireless local area networks (WLANs). WEP does not use strong encryption and is therefore considered obsolete. However, some legacy devices may only support WEP.
WPA	*Wi-Fi Protected Access (WPA)* provides a significantly stronger encryption scheme than WEP, and can use a shared private key, which are unique keys assigned to each user.
WPA2	*Wireless Protected Access 2 (WPA2)* replaced WPA encryption in 2006 and is based on the IEEE 802.11i standards. The Institute of Electrical and Electronics Engineers (IEEE) *802.11i* standard is the most recent encryption standard that provides improved encryption for wireless networking. The 802.11i standard requires strong encryption key protocols, known as *Temporal Key Integrity Protocol (TKIP)* and *Advanced Encryption Standard (AES)*. WPA2/802.11i encryption is considered to be the strongest available method of wireless security.

Service Set Identifiers (SSIDs)

A *Service Set Identifier (SSID)* is a 32-bit alphanumeric string that identifies a WAP and all the devices attached to it. A WAP typically broadcasts an SSID in plaintext. It is more appropriate to think of an SSID as a network name that is applied to the grouping of the WAP and the devices currently connected to it. Wireless connectivity devices such as a WAP or other wireless routers come with a default SSID. Instead of accepting the device's default SSID, you should manually specify an SSID to more clearly identify the device.

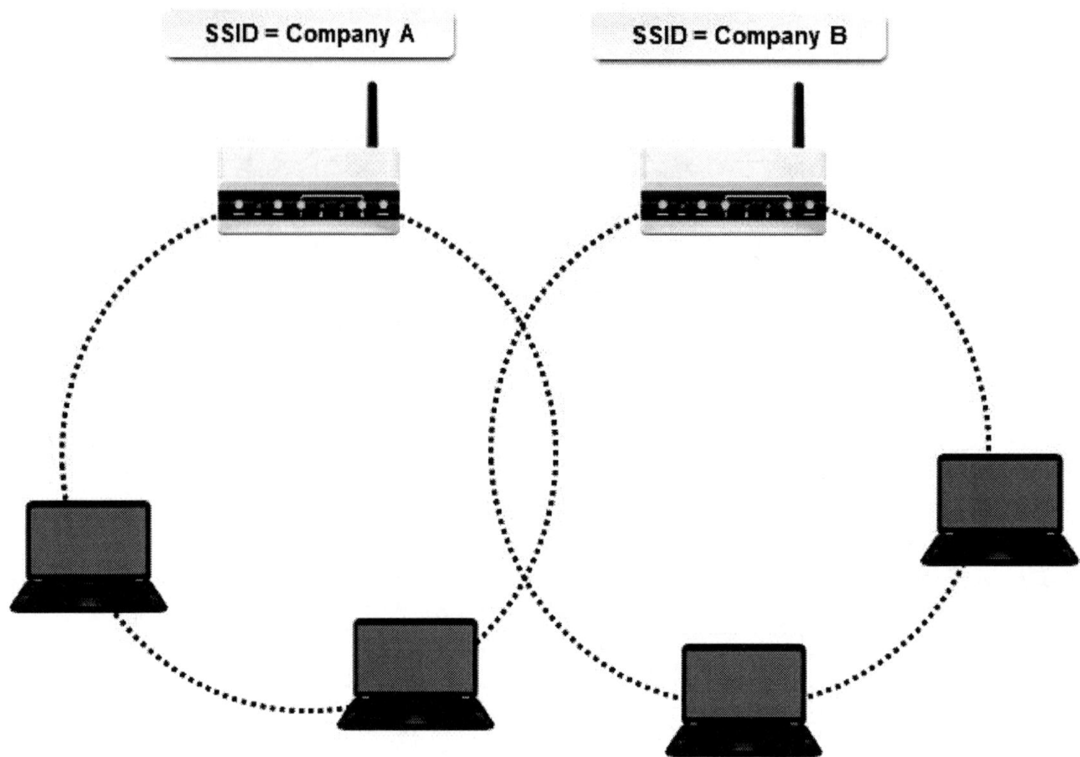

Figure 4-8: The SSIDs of two different WAPs.

SOHO Router Configuration Options

Most routers available today can be configured for wired and wireless networks. Depending on the router installation, there are several settings that you can configure to ensure connectivity, security, and access.

Setting	Description
Basics	Basic settings apply to both wired and wireless routers and can include the ability to: • Secure your router or access point administration interface. • Change default administrator passwords (and user names). • Disable remote administration. • Secure/disable the reset switch/function. • Change the default SNMP parameter. • Regularly upgrade the Wi-Fi router firmware to ensure you have the latest security patches and critical fixes.
SSID	When installing a wireless router, change the default Service Set Identifier (SSID) and verify that you are not broadcasting out to the network.

Setting	Description
Channels	Change the default channel on wireless routers. By changing the router channel, you can optimize data transmission and reduce interference with other routers in close proximity. If your router is dual channel, then you can easily change from the default channel to the other channel available. To help determine what channel is not being used, you can use one of the utilities available that can scan the local area and display used channels. This can be very helpful in choosing a different less-used channel for your router.

Firmware

Firmware is specialized software that is stored on a hardware device's read-only memory (ROM) whether or not the device is powered. It is most often written on an electronically reprogrammable chip so that it can be updated with a special program to fix any errors that might be discovered after a computer is purchased, or to support updated hardware components.

Router firmware may need an upgrade from time to time depending on manufacturer updates. These updates contain security patches, updates to performance, and updates to address any known issues. The updates can be installed in a number of ways, but most commonly can be downloaded from the manufacturer's website.

Note: Overwriting existing firmware, often through updating, is called *flashing*.

Router Setup Process

The basic setup and configuration process for a SOHO router includes:

1. Verify the wired connection, if applicable.
2. Configure encryption standard (WEP, WPA, or WPA2).
3. Change SSID from default.
4. Apply a new wireless password.
5. Change the admin password for the router.
6. Connect to the new network.
7. Verify the Internet connectivity.
8. Update firmware, if necessary.

Access the Checklist tile on your CHOICE Course screen for reference information and job aids on How to Install and Configure a SOHO Router.

ACTIVITY 4-2
Installing and Configuring a SOHO Router

Before You Begin

You will need an Internet connection to access the emulator.

Scenario

You have been assigned the task of tightening security for the sales department of Develetech Industries. Many of the employees in this department are mobile users, and they need to connect to the company network and the Internet through devices such as laptops and smartphones. Running Ethernet cables to the former is often impractical, and the latter can only connect wirelessly. However, the department manager is concerned that attackers may try to steal client information. He says that employees often run applications and transfer customer data and sales information across the network. It is your responsibility to make sure that the routers employees must connect to are configured to prevent unauthorized access.

You'll start by defining a unique SSID that employees will recognize and trust. Then, you'll use WPA2 to encrypt wireless traffic with a passphrase that only employees are told. To ensure that no one except administrators can alter these important settings, you'll change the default router administration password. In addition, you'll block any insecure connection attempts to the administration portal. With this configuration in place, your wireless users will be much less susceptible to the many dangers of Wi-Fi networking.

---

1. Connect to the wireless router's configuration interface.
   a) From the Desktop taskbar, select **Internet Explorer.**
   b) In the **Address** bar, enter ***http://ui.linksys.com***
   c) From the list of routers, select the **E1200** link.
   d) Select the **2.0.04/** link.
   e) In the **Warning** message box, check the **Do not show me this again** check box and select **OK**.

Note: This website emulates a common router configuration interface. When working with a real device, you will typically connect to http://192.168.1.1 and be prompted to enter a user name and password. For a list of default user names and passwords by router, navigate to http://www.routerpasswords.com.

2. Set an SSID for your wireless network.
   a) On the menu bar at the top of the page, select the **Wireless** tab.
   b) If necessary, select **Manual**.
   c) In the **Network Name (SSID)** text box, double-click and type ***dtech***
   d) Select **Save Settings** and, in the **Message from webpage** message box, select **OK**.
   e) Select **Save Settings** again, and then select **Continue**.

3. Set WPA2 encryption with a passphrase.
   a) Under the **Wireless** tab on the menu bar, select the **Wireless Security** link.
   b) From the **Security Mode** drop-down list, select **WPA2 Personal**.
   c) In the **Passphrase** text box, type ***!Pass1234***
   d) Select **Save Settings**, and then select **Continue**.

4. Configure the router's administration settings.
   a) On the menu bar, select the **Administration** tab.
   b) In the **Router Password** text box, double-click and type ***P@ssw0rd***
   c) In the **Re-Enter to Confirm** text box, type the same password.
   d) In the **Local Management Access** section, uncheck the **HTTP** check box and check the **HTTPS** check box.
   e) In the **Local Management Access** section, for the **Access via Wireless** option, select **Disabled.**
   f) In the **Remote Management Access** section, verify that **Remote Management** is disabled.
   g) At the bottom of the web page, select **Save Settings.**
   h) On the **Your settings have been successfully saved** page, select **Continue.**
   i) Close **Internet Explorer.**

5. **If you were configuring an actual SOHO router, how would you confirm that the configuration meets your needs?**

TOPIC C

Network and Alternative Technologies

As you configure network access, you should also be aware of some alternative technologies that you're likely to encounter in some environments. In this topic, you'll investigate these technologies to determine how they might add functionality to your network.

Virtualization

In a computing context, *virtualization* software allows for one physical device, such as a server operating system, to host multiple logical operating systems. These logical systems are called *virtual machines*. For instance, a single physical server can host several virtual servers using one hardware platform. Server, storage, and network virtualization allow for greater efficiency among fewer devices, which lowers equipment and power costs.

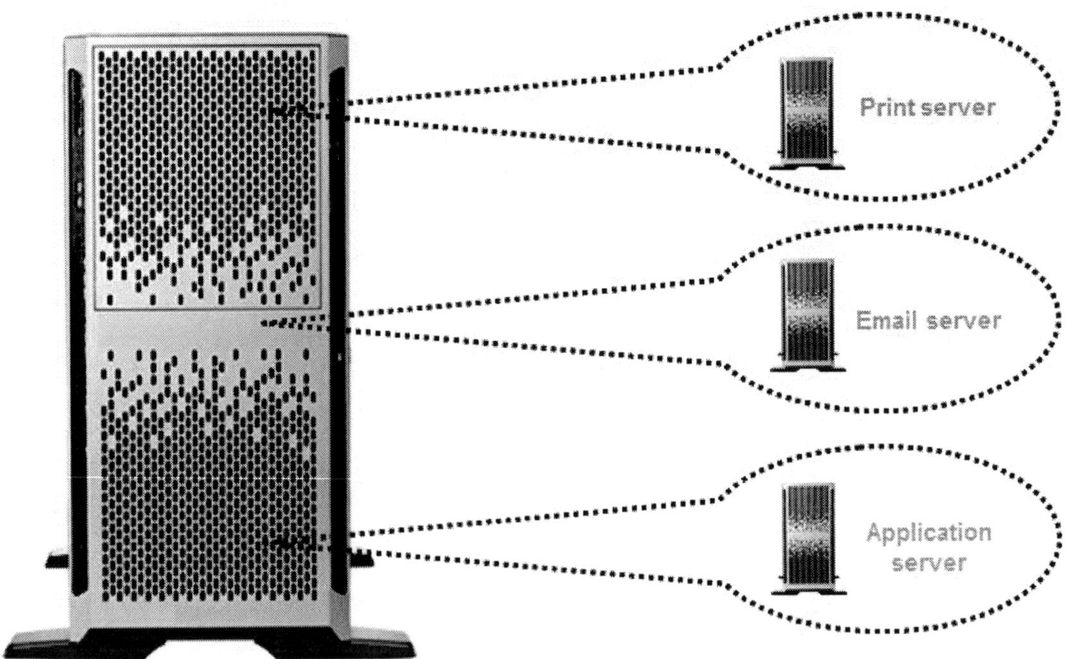

Figure 4-9: Several servers virtualized into one.

Cloud Computing

Cloud computing is a computing infrastructure in which resources, such as storage and applications, are hosted in a distributed fashion by a third party over the Internet. The "cloud" is a metaphor for the Internet and the complexity of its infrastructure. Cloud computing is an approach that allows companies to improve their efficiency by paying for only the resources used—much like paying for utilities. Since client companies no longer need to require the hardware necessary to host these services internally, less equipment and power is needed. Also, companies that provide computing resources locally typically need to provide enough to handle peak usage, which results in underutilization during non-peak workloads. Cloud computing solves this problem.

Streaming is an example of a cloud service in which media files are transmitted by a provider over the Internet and viewed by the end user in real time. Since the media is provisioned as needed, the end user transfers most of the processing responsibility onto the provider, and merely needs to maintain a strong Internet connection.

However, a major concern with cloud computing is the security of data. Since the data is hosted by a third party, there are issues involving data ownership, backup, and confidentiality.

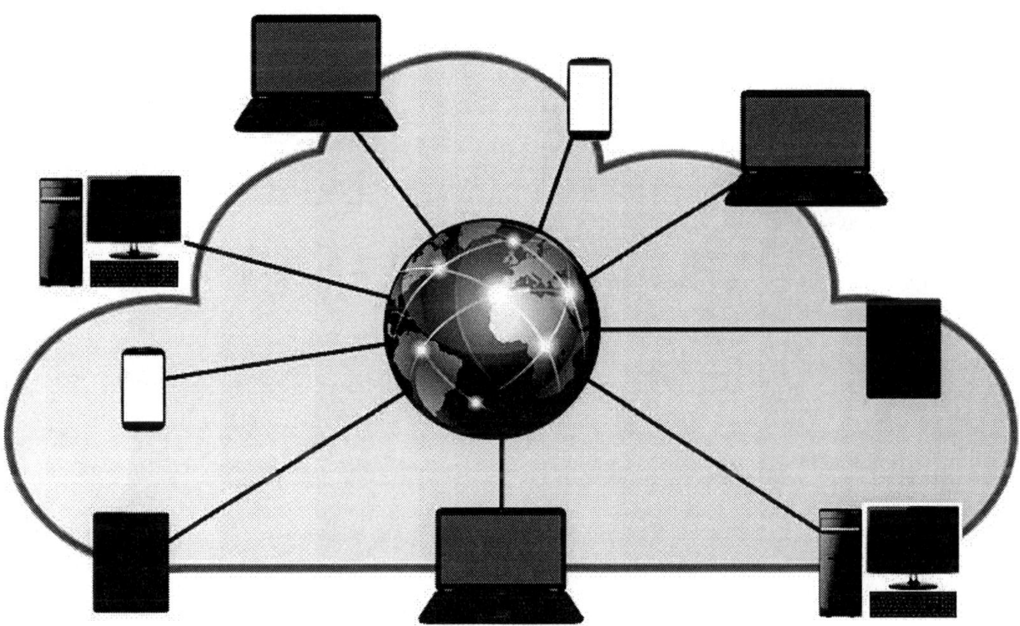

Figure 4-10: Cloud computing hosts applications over the Internet.

Web Applications

Web applications are software applications that are installed on web servers and delivered to users through the Internet. End users interact with these applications through their web browsers. This allows them to work with applications without having to install them on their systems. Such services depend on network bandwidth for efficient use as the data transfer happens in real time.

An example of a web application is Google Docs, which offers word processing, spreadsheet, and presentation programs online.

Figure 4-11: Web-delivered services deliver applications through the web.

VoIP

Voice over IP (VoIP) is the transmission of voice communications over IP networks, such as the Internet. The emergence of virtual meetings, which participants can attend remotely, is fueled by VoIP and screen-sharing technologies. Some applications even support the transmission of video and voice over the Internet. This is a significant enabler for employee telecommuting, as it often replaces traditional telephone systems.

VoIP can help a business save money as well as energy and resources for the following reasons:

- Training sessions can be done remotely; no travel is needed.
- Remote offices can collaborate without being in the same physical location.
- VoIP is very cost efficient and bypasses long-distance charges.

Voice data files are larger in size when compared to text, so upgrading to a VoIP service requires high bandwidth. You can also better support VoIP by configuring Quality of Service (QoS) on your Internet connection so that voice data will be preferred over other forms of network traffic. QoS is typically implemented on the routers or switches. By configuring QoS, you can improve the quality of voice data over the network.

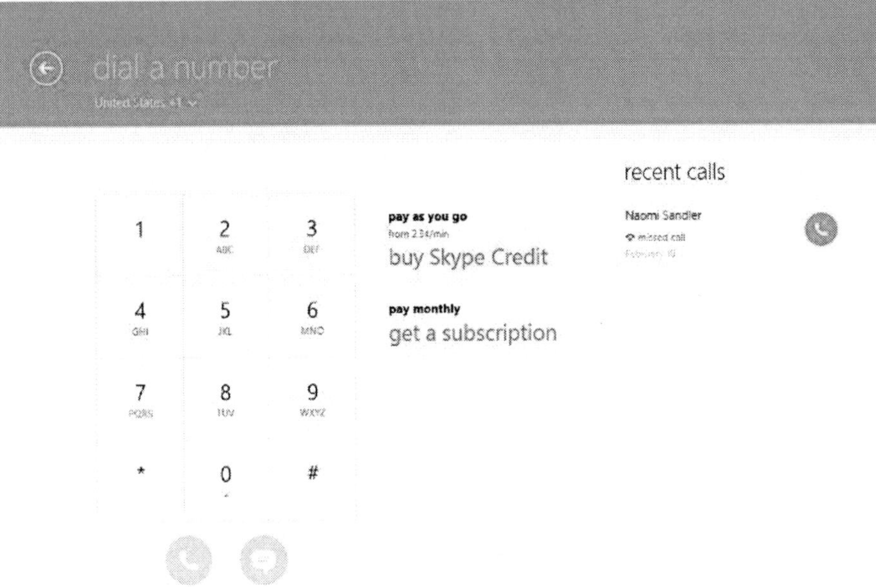

Figure 4-12: A VoIP application.

Telepresence

Telepresence is the technology that allows a person to feel as though they are present in a location different from the one they are in by including stimuli to encourage that feeling of presence. Telepresence equipment requires video, audio, and manipulation capabilities. Combining video teleconferencing equipment and mobile devices can provide some telepresence functions. Automated robots with a connected mobile computing device (tablet, laptop, or iPad) can move around freely to simulate an absent person's presence. Additionally, the ability to manipulate an object in a remote location can be accomplished by the use of robotic arms.

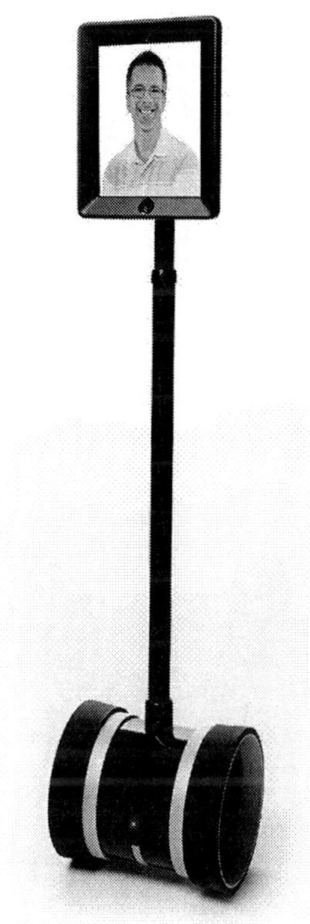

Figure 4-13: A telepresence robot.

ACTIVITY 4-3

Identifying Network and Alternative Technologies

Scenario

As an intern with the Develetech IT staff, you have been asked to identify some of the technologies than can help expand the capabilities of your network.

---

1. **What is the benefit of a cloud computing infrastructure?**
   - ○ Companies have full control over the data that is hosted.
   - ○ Companies need to pay for only the resources used.
   - ○ Companies can host all applications internally on their own servers.
   - ○ Companies do not need to worry about the security of hosted data.

2. **Why might you use virtualization?**
   - ○ To host multiple operating systems on a single computer.
   - ○ To host a single operating system over multiple computers.
   - ○ To duplicate your system for redundancy.
   - ○ To set up multiple computers from a single virtual image.

3. **Why might your organization use web applications? (Choose two.)**
   - ☐ So you don't have to install the applications on each computer
   - ☐ So you don't need networks
   - ☐ So you can use the applications on any device with an Internet connection
   - ☐ To regulate how fast the user works

4. **What is VoIP, and why has it become popular?**

TOPIC D

Sharing and Storage Methods

So far in this lesson, you have worked with connection types, hardware, and alternative technologies that are commonly encountered on computer networks. As you know, one of the primary purposes for networking computers together is to take advantage of the sharing and storage capabilities of networks. In this topic, you will compare storage devices and methods for sharing information.

Local vs. Hosted Storage

Traditionally, network services have included at least file and print sharing. One of the main requirements for file sharing is accessible storage.

Local storage refers to any storage media that is directly attached to the computer that uses it. This can include direct-attached storage such as hard drives over Serial ATA (SATA) connections, as well as external hard drives that use ports such as USB to plug in to computers. Local storage often has the advantage of speed and accessibility. These solutions are ideal for individual users who need to access, modify, and delete files quickly without relying on other machines to do the hosting for them. Because comparatively few users can access them, local storage media offer security guarantees that networked storage does not. However, local storage makes it more difficult to work collaboratively because there is not necessarily one authoritative file in one location.

Hosted storage, or networked storage, places data on specialized devices that serve files to clients in a network based on each client's need. Networked drives are available to groups of users who share access. One solution that uses networked drives is a *network-attached storage (NAS)* device. NAS devices are ideal for small-to-mid-size companies because they can combine multiple drives into one storage pool for easy access over the network. NAS devices are relatively inexpensive and typically allow administrators to easily create backups in case of failure.

Other than in-house solutions, another method of hosted storage is cloud-based storage such as Microsoft OneDrive, Amazon Cloud Services, and Google Cloud Platform. Cloud companies provide a number of services, such as storage space and collaborative applications over the Internet. This enables users and businesses to offload processing overhead onto a cloud provider. One disadvantage to using cloud storage is that you're not necessarily in complete control of your information, and you may not be able to guarantee its security.

Peer-to-Peer Networking

A *peer-to-peer network* is a network in which resource sharing, processing, and communications control are completely decentralized. All clients on the network are equal in terms of providing and using resources, and users are authenticated by each individual workstation. Peer-to-peer networks are easy and inexpensive to implement. However, they are practical only in very small organizations, due to the lack of central data storage and administration. In a peer-to-peer network, user accounts must be duplicated on every workstation from which a user accesses resources. Such distribution of user information makes maintaining peer-to-peer networks difficult, especially as the network grows. Consequently, peer-to-peer networks should not exceed 10 computers.

You can set up and use peer-to-peer networks by using several different methods:

- Direct link allows you to physically connect each PC to every other PC to form the peer-to-peer network.
- Local ad hoc networks allow peers to connect to each other and share files without needing to set up extra networking equipment such as routers or access points. Each node (a laptop, for instance) simply transmits wirelessly to other nodes without an intermediary device. This can be done by using standards such as Wi-Fi and Bluetooth.

- Online networks allow clients to connect to other peers over the Internet. BitTorrent is an example of a protocol that enables peer-to-peer file sharing over the Internet.

In Microsoft Windows operating systems, computers in a SOHO environment can join peer-to-peer networks called *workgroups* and *homegroups*. In a workgroup, typically no more than 20 peers are all connected on the same network. Homegroups are similar, but require each peer to input a password when first connecting to the group. Homegroups make it easier for peers to share files and printing services.

HTTP and HTTPS

HyperText Transfer Protocol (HTTP) is the TCP/IP service that enables clients, such as a web browser application, to connect and interact with websites. It defines how messages are formatted and transmitted and the actions web servers and a client's browser should take in response to different commands. An HTTP request includes the address of the requested web page, instructions on how and where the requested data will be stored on the client computer, protocols supported by the browser, the type of request being made, the version of HTTP supported by the browser, and so on.

HyperText Transfer Protocol Secure (HTTPS) is a secure version of HTTP that supports web commerce by providing a secure connection between web browsers and servers. HTTPS uses *Secure Sockets Layer/Transport Layer Security (SSL/TLS)* to encrypt data. Virtually all web browsers and servers today support HTTPS. An SSL/TLS-enabled web address begins with the protocol identifier https://.

Sharing data through HTTP and HTTPS comes in the form of browser-based file downloads. The user will connect to a web server and likely select a link that will enable that user to download or directly open a file from the browser. When using this form of sharing data, you need to be careful that you're downloading files from a reputable site. There are many malicious websites using HTTP that try to trick users into thinking they are legitimate, and some even convincingly spoof legitimate websites such as banks and social media sites. Always look for the HTTPS in the site's URL to verify that your browser trusts it.

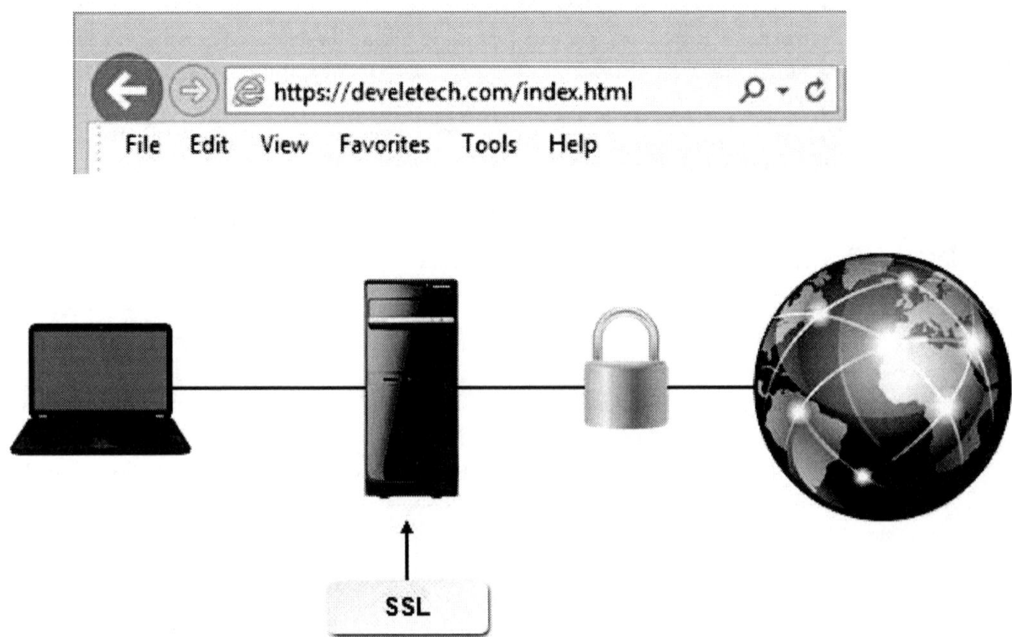

Figure 4–14: HTTPS provides a secure connection between a web browser and server.

FTP

File Transfer Protocol (FTP) is used to transfer files across a TCP/IP network, such as the Internet. FTP is intended to enable file transfers, independent of the operating system. However, computers on the network must have the FTP software installed. Operating systems that support TCP/IP almost always include some form of FTP, though you can also use an external client. FTP is the protocol that web developers use to upload web pages to a remote server. Other common uses of FTP include uploading images to photo sites, and audio and video files to media sites.

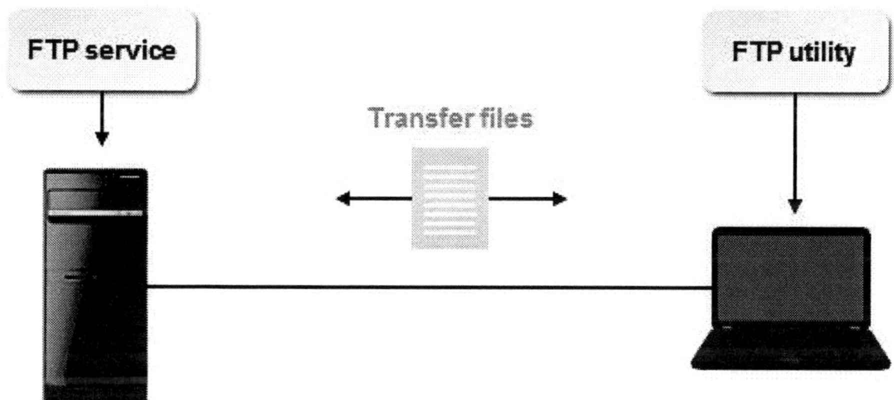

Figure 4-15: FTP is used to transfer files across a network.

In addition to standard FTP, there are other, similar file transfer protocols.

Protocol	*Description*
Simple File Transfer Protocol (SFTP)	This protocol was an early unsecured file transfer protocol that has since been declared obsolete.
FTP over SSH	Also called *Secure FTP*, FTP over SSH is a secure version of FTP that uses an SSH tunnel as an encryption method to transfer, access, and manage files. Secure FTP is used primarily on Windows systems.
File Transfer Protocol Secure (FTPS)	This protocol, also known as *FTP-SSL*, combines the use of FTP with additional support for SSL/TLS.

Printing

Printers can connect to computers by using a variety of connection types. Some printers connect locally to individual PCs over USB. A *network printer*, on the other hand, is a shared printing device that can be used simultaneously by multiple users on a network. These printers can be wired over Ethernet, but more commonly network printers offer wireless capabilities that allow users to print without being physically connected to the device. These wireless printers use standards such as Bluetooth and Wi-Fi.

Networked printers are much more useful than local printers if used in an office setting, but multiple users printing from the same device may cause delays. Wireless printers are even more convenient, but they are susceptible to interference issues associated with wireless communication in general.

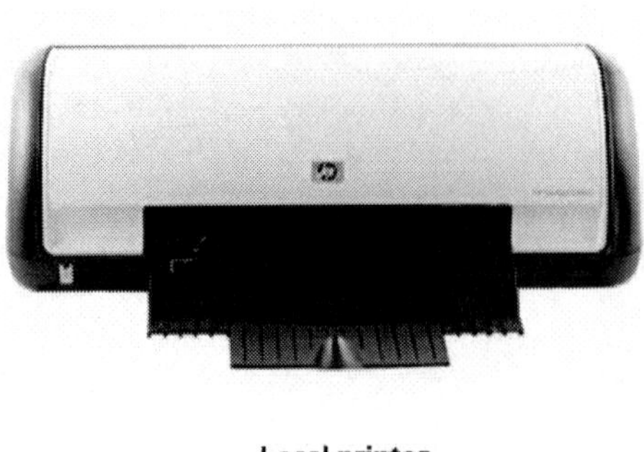

Local printer

Network printer

Figure 4-16: A local printer and a network printer.

ACTIVITY 4-4

Comparing Methods for Sharing and Storing Information

Scenario

There are many places you can save data. You want to compare the capacity of each and how secure each of the storage locations is, even without applying any additional security measures beyond those inherent in using the storage location.

---

1. **Which are examples of local storage? (Choose two.)**
   - ☐ An internal optical drive such as a DVD or Blu-ray drive
   - ☐ An external USB drive
   - ☐ A folder on OneDrive
   - ☐ A NAS device

2. **True or False? You cannot configure a wireless peer-to-peer network.**
   - ☐ True
   - ☐ False

3. **Which protocols are most commonly associated with browser-based file sharing? (Choose two.)**
   - ☐ HTTP
   - ☐ FTPS
   - ☐ FTP
   - ☐ HTTPS

4. **You can share data by using all of the devices and storage locations you examined in this topic. Which device or location is the most secure and the least secure? Why?**

Summary

In this lesson, you configured network access. Knowing how to configure your network enables your users to better communicate and share resources, as well as store their important data.

What types of network devices have you configured, and how did you secure them?

What has been your experience with wired, wireless, and cellular networks in terms of their reliability, bandwidth/throughput, and mobility?

Note: Check your CHOICE Course screen for opportunities to interact with your classmates, peers, and the larger CHOICE online community about the topics covered in this course or other topics you are interested in. From the Course screen you can also access available resources for a more continuous learning experience.

5 Working with Files, Folders, and Applications

Lesson Time: 2 hours, 30 minutes

Lesson Objectives

In this lesson, you will work with files, folders, and applications. You will:

- Create files.
- Navigate the file structure.
- Manage files and folders.
- Compress and extract files.
- Create screen captures.

Lesson Introduction

Earlier in the course, you set up a basic PC workstation. After a computer has been configured, you will need to store and access information present in the computer in the form of files and folders. In this lesson, you will work with files, folders, and applications.

Imagine that you have spent the last 20 minutes searching through the piles of papers in your office for a presentation you wrote a week ago. You need it for a meeting that will begin in the next five minutes. If only you had all your papers neatly organized in a folder within a filing cabinet, you would not be in this mess. Your computer is not much different from your desk. Keeping your files well organized on your computer can help you avoid a similar situation.

TOPIC A

Create Files

You have connected the components of your system and configured the operating system and network access according to your needs. One of the basic tasks you will do with a computer system is creating files and saving them for later use. In this topic, you will create and save files.

Years ago, creating documents with a typewriter was a cumbersome process. You needed to load paper, adjust it, and type the contents; you could not easily make a file copy or an extra copy for someone else. But with the advent of PCs and word processing software, creating and saving a document became much easier and more efficient, and as a result, this technology is now found everywhere in offices, homes, and schools. Every operating system has built-in, simple applications, such as word processors, that are very easy to learn. You can use these applications to create letters and memos without purchasing and installing any additional software, and if you can perform common tasks such as creating files in any of these applications, you'll be able to use that skill in almost any other application.

Files

A *file* is an object that stores information on a computer. It can contain user data, in the case of document files, or it can contain program code, in the case of application files. Each file has a name and usually has an extension. The nature of files may vary, depending on the applications they are associated with. Files are classified as system files and user files. The operating system and other applications run using system files; user files are created and managed by users.

Note: User files can be deleted or modified; however, do not delete or modify system files because any modification or deletion of an application's system files can affect its functionality.

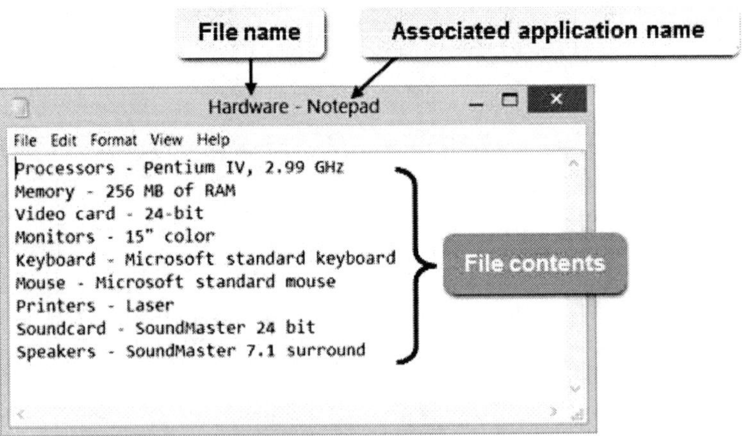

Figure 5-1: An example of a file.

File Types

During the course of a day, it is likely that you will use many different types of files. These might include documents, audio files, image files, and video files. Any time you open a program, you are using an executable file. You might also encounter or need to create a compressed file to make it small enough to send as an email attachment.

File Extensions

File extensions indicate a file's type. Operating systems such as Microsoft® Windows® use a file extension to identify the program that is associated with a file. The file extension is the last three or four characters that appear at the end of the name to the right of the period. For example, the file extension .docx identifies "qtr_report.docx" as a Word document.

When you try to open a file, it is opened in the associated application. File extensions are not always visible within applications or utilities in Windows. You can customize various settings so that you can see file extensions.

Shortcuts

A *shortcut* is a link or pointer to a program, file, or folder that is represented by a small icon. Typically, shortcuts are placed on the Desktop. Instead of needing to traverse the file structure to locate an item, if a shortcut has been created to the item, you can select the shortcut instead. Some applications create shortcuts when the application is installed. You can also create a shortcut yourself by right-clicking a file and selecting **Create Shortcut**.

Shortcut icons can be recognized by the arrow in the lower-left corner of the icon. Deleting a shortcut does not delete the item to which it is pointing.

Figure 5-2: A shortcut to an application.

Folders

A *folder* is a container object that can store your files in an organized manner. By default, a folder is represented by a folder icon. Folders can be of different types and can contain any number of other folders and files, including pictures, music, videos, documents, or any combination of these types. A folder is also referred to as a *directory*.

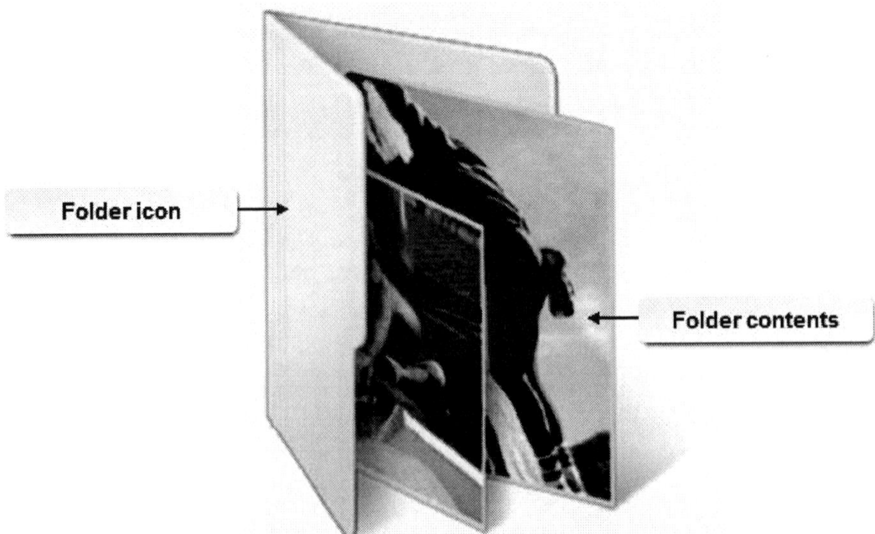

Figure 5-3: A folder.

A folder within a folder is called a subfolder. In a hierarchical folder display, folders that contain subfolders have a right-pointing arrow beside them. Selecting this arrow will either expand or collapse the directory structure inside that folder.

File and Folder Naming Conventions

When you save a document as a file, it is important to name it appropriately. Naming a folder or a file according to a logical scheme enables you to organize your data properly. When you name a folder or file, be sure to:

- Use a name that indicates the content or purpose of the document, project, or task it is related to.
- Limit the length of the name; although 260 characters can be used, file names of this length are impractical.
- Avoid special characters. The backslash (\ ), the forward slash (/), the vertical bar (|), the colon (:), the asterisk (*), the question mark (?), the quotation mark ("), the less than (<), and the greater than (>) characters are not permitted.

File and Folder Permissions

You can manage user access to file and folder objects on a computer by modifying their permissions. You can set permission levels at the folder or file level.

You can allow users to only view a file, but not modify it. You can allow users to view and modify a file. You can specify which users are allowed to access a file and what they are allowed to do with the file. You can also deny access to a file for a user or group of users.

File Explorer

File Explorer is a Windows utility application that offers a single view of all the resources and information that you can access from a computer. It displays the hierarchical structure of a computer and any network to which it is attached. These container objects are arranged hierarchically; that is, they are shown in relation to each other as the members of a family would be shown in a family tree. You can also use File Explorer to manage the information on your computer by copying and moving files.

File Explorer Components

The components of File Explorer can help you explore the Windows folder hierarchy and work with data.

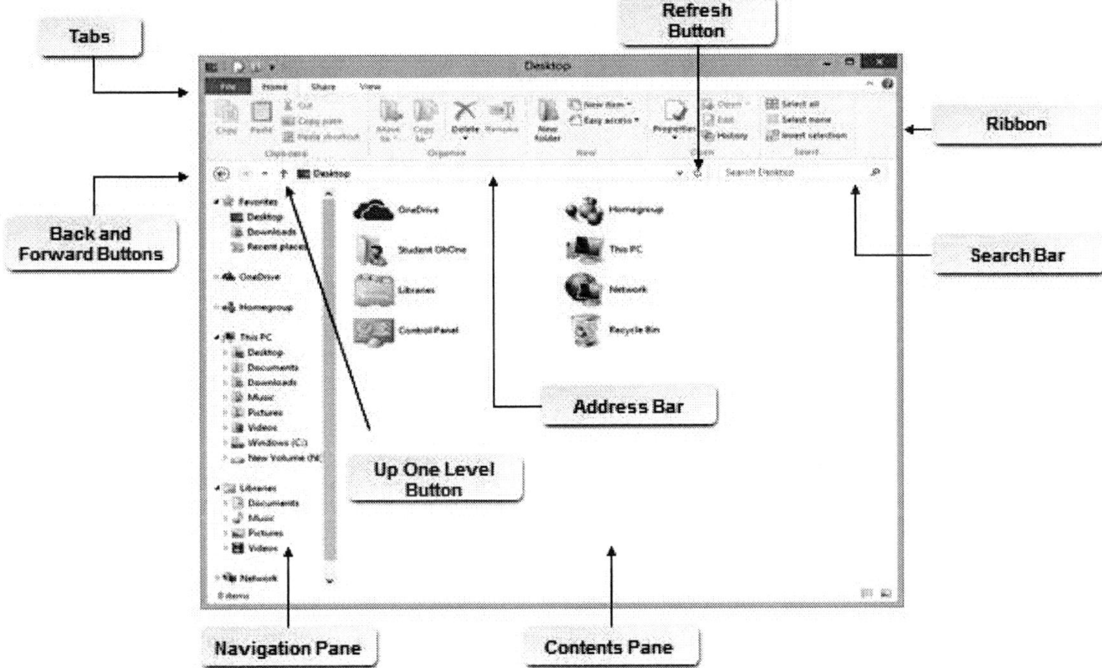

Figure 5-4: The File Explorer window.

The following table lists and defines the components of the File Explorer.

Component	Description
Address bar	The *Address bar* displays the address of an object. It is located below the Ribbon.
Navigation pane	The *Navigation pane* is located in the left pane of the window; it enables you to scroll and directly access folders on your PC, your OneDrive files and folders, drives and devices connected to your computer, or other computers on the network.
Ribbon	The *ribbon* is displayed below the title bar. It can show a list of common tasks depending upon the selected object or objects. It can be collapsed to give you more room to view files and folder, a useful feature on smaller screens.
Contents pane	The *Contents pane* displays a list of files and subfolders within a folder. It consists of column headings that help in arranging the contents in various categories such as name, size, and type of file.
Preview pane	The *Preview pane* displays a preview of files such as documents, presentation slides, and images without opening them in an application. It displays the actual file contents rather than a thumbnail or an icon. This pane is not displayed by default, but when shown it appears to the right of the Contents pane.

Component	Description
Details pane	The *Details pane* displays the file properties such as file name, file type, author, last modified, size, and other properties. Like the Preview pane, the Details pane is not displayed by default, but when displayed, it shares the Preview pane's location. You can display only the Preview pane or the Details pane, but not both at the same time.
Status bar	The Status bar displays the number of items in the selected location. If you have multiple items selected in the file list section, the number of items selected is displayed along with the total size of the selected items.
Navigation buttons	Above the Navigation pane are four buttons. The **Back** button returns you to the last location you viewed or the last search results you viewed. The **Forward** buttons returns you to the next location or search results you viewed. The **Recent locations** button shows a list of the most recent locations you visited. The **Up** button opens the location one level up from the current folder.
Search bar	The Search bar enables you to locate documents within the file structure. You can search from the current location, including any folders contained in the current folder. As you begin to type the search, any files matching what you type will be displayed in the search results list.

The Navigation and Refresh Buttons

The **Navigation** button allows you to move back and forward through the folder views in the order of their display. The **Refresh** button allows you to see the latest changes in the folder window. Any changes to the folder or file structure done outside of File Explorer will be displayed by clicking the **Refresh** button.

Types of Views in the Address Bar

In the Address bar, the path of a folder or file can be displayed in Breadcrumbs view or Address Path view. Breadcrumbs view is enabled by default and makes it easier to navigate through files and folders. You can click the small arrow next to a folder to list the subfolders within it. You can navigate to any of the subfolders by selecting them. Address Path view enables you to type an object's address to access it. You can switch from Breadcrumbs view to Address Path view by selecting the Address bar. When you select another item, it switches back to Breadcrumbs view.

Expanding and Collapsing the Windows Hierarchical Structure

In addition to adjusting the separator bar, you can also navigate by expanding and collapsing the Windows hierarchical structure. In the Navigation pane, a right-pointing arrow displayed in front of a folder indicates that the folder has other folders stored inside it. An arrow sign pointing to the lower-right indicates that the folder is already expanded and cannot be expanded any further. If neither sign is displayed, the folder has no other folders inside it, and its contents are shown in the right pane. To expand a folder, click its arrow sign. To collapse a folder, click the arrow that points to the lower-right. In the left pane, you can also click the object itself. Doing so either expands a collapsed object or collapses an expanded object. As an added bonus, clicking the object itself displays its contents in the right pane.

Access the Checklist tile on your CHOICE Course screen for reference information and job aids on How to Create Files.

ACTIVITY 5-1
Creating Files

Scenario

A group of new temporary employees has been brought in to help with the workload in the marketing department. Some of the employees are Macintosh or Linux users and are not familiar with the concept of Windows file extensions. To show the users how file extensions work, you will have them create bitmap, rich text, and plain text format files.

---

1. Set file extensions to be displayed.
   a) If necessary, from the Windows Start screen, select the **Desktop** tile.
   b) Select the **File Explorer** icon on the taskbar.
   c) Select **View→Show/hide** and check **File name extensions.**

2. Create and open a bitmap file.
   a) In the Navigation pane, select **This PC.**
   b) In the Details pane, select the **C** drive.

   Note: The C drive label will be preceded with the text **New Volume** or **Local Disk** and **C:** will be enclosed in parentheses.

   c) In the Details pane, navigate to **Users→*your_student_account*→Documents**.
   d) Right-click a blank area in the **Documents** pane of File Explorer and select **New→Bitmap image**. An empty file named **New Bitmap Image.bmp** is created with **New Bitmap Image** selected, ready for you to rename it.
   e) With **New Bitmap Image** selected in the file name, press **Enter** to accept the default name.
   f) Right-click **New Bitmap Image.bmp** and select **Open With→Paint**.
   g) Draw any shape in the open file and select the **Save** icon.
   h) Select the **Close** button to close Paint. You are returned to File Explorer.

3. Create and open a text file.
   a) In File Explorer, right-click a blank area and select **New→Text Document.**
   b) Replace the selected text *New Text Document* with the text ***My new txt file*** and then press **Enter.**
   c) Double-click **My new txt file.txt** to open it in the default application associated with TXT files, Notepad.

   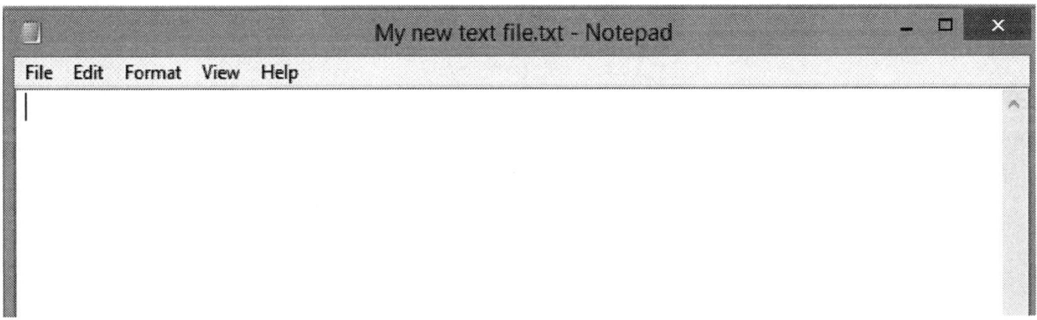

   d) Type any text in the document and then select **File→Save.**
   e) Select **File→Exit** to close Notepad. You could have also used the **Close** button to close Notepad.

4. Create and open a rich text file.
   a) In File Explorer, by using the same technique as you used to create the previous files, create a new rich text document and name it ***My new rtf file***
   b) Double-click the RTF file. It will open in the default application associated with RTF files on your computer. This might be WordPad or, if it is installed, Microsoft Word.
   c) Enter some text in the file, save the file, and close the application.

5. Create a new file from within Notepad.
   a) Press the **Windows key** to return to the Windows Start screen.
   b) Type ***notepad*** and from the Search results, select the Notepad application.

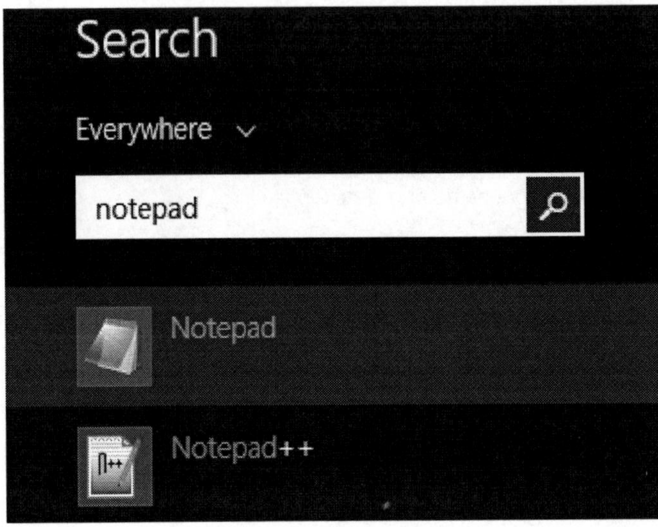

   c) Type some text in Notepad.
   d) Select **File→Save As**.
   e) Verify that the file will be saved to the local drive in the **Documents** folder.
   f) In the Save As dialog box, type ***my new file*** and select **Save.**
   g) Select **File→Exit** to close Notepad.
   h) Locate the **my new file.txt** file in File Explorer.

Name	Date modified	Type	Size
New Bitmap Image.bmp	9/30/2014 6:00 AM	Bitmap image	829 KB
My new text file.txt	9/30/2014 6:01 AM	Text Document	1 KB
My new rtf file.rtf	9/30/2014 6:01 AM	Rich Text Docume...	1 KB
my new file.txt	9/30/2014 6:06 AM	Text Document	1 KB

TOPIC B

Navigate a File Structure

You have created and saved a file. In your normal work routine, you will create many files and save them in different folders. To access and store data more efficiently, you will need a tool that enables you to view and manage files and folders. In this topic, you will navigate a file structure.

All the information present in a computer is stored in files or folders. In a normal work routine, you will need to work on files in different folders. By navigating through the hierarchical structure, you can easily maintain and organize the information stored on your computer.

Shortcut Keys

It can slow users down if they are using the keyboard and then they need to use the mouse to perform an action. Shortcut key combinations enable users to perform the same actions that are normally performed by using the mouse, but instead by using the keyboard. Many of the commands on the File Explorer ribbon have shortcut key equivalents. If you point to the button or command on the ribbon, you will see the shortcut key combination listed. You can use many of these shortcut key combinations within files in other applications.

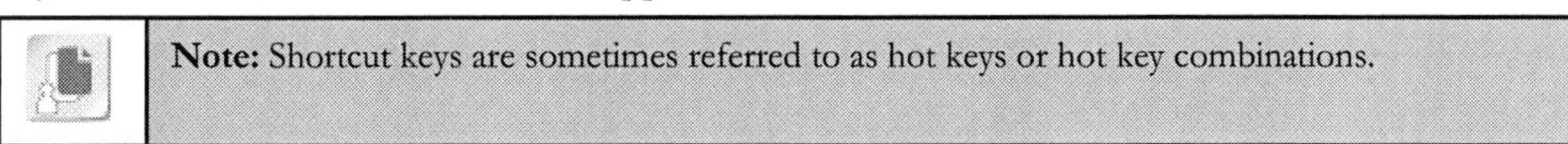

Note: Shortcut keys are sometimes referred to as hot keys or hot key combinations.

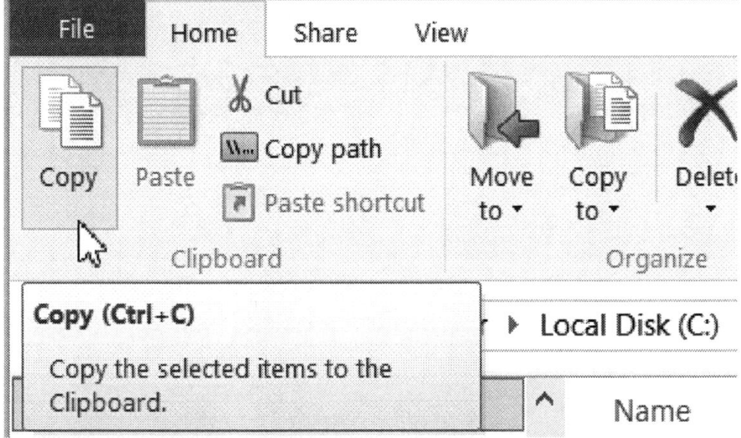

Figure 5-5: Shortcut keys.

Common Windows Shortcut Keys

The following table lists some of the most common Windows shortcut key combinations.

Key Combination	Used to Perform
Ctrl+C	Copy the selected file or folder.
Ctrl+X	Cut the selected file or folder.
Ctrl+V	Paste the selected file or folder.
Ctrl+D	Delete and send object to the Recycle Bin.
Ctrl+S	Save the file from within a Windows application.

Key Combination	Used to Perform
F1	Display the application's Help window.
F2	Rename the selected file or folder.
Alt+Enter	Display properties for the selected file or folder.
Ctrl+A	Select all of the contents of the current folder or all of the text within a document.

Note: You can use many of these shortcut key combinations within applications for selected file content.

File Structure Navigation on Non-Windows Devices

On non-Windows devices such as Mac, Linux, and Android™ devices, the file structure is still hierarchical. However, these other operating systems do not use letters to identify different drives on which content is stored.

These operating systems do not use File Explorer either. They each have their own file management system. Mac computers use an application called Finder. Most Android devices do not have a default file management application, but there are many free file management apps available to download.

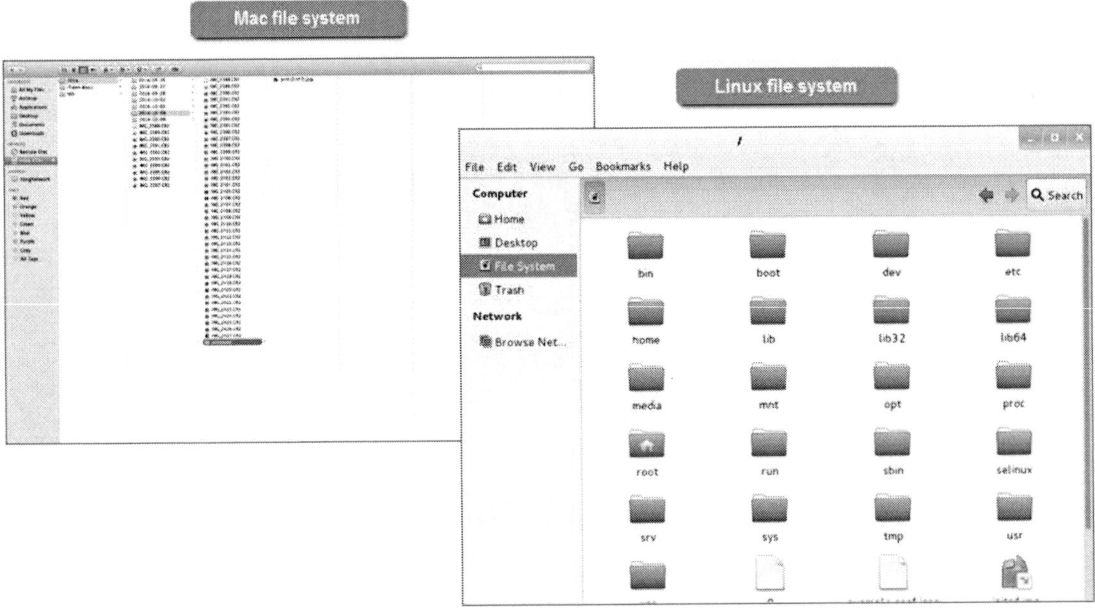

Figure 5-6: Examples of the Mac and Linux file systems.

Access the Checklist tile on your CHOICE Course screen for reference information and job aids on How to Navigate a File Structure.

ACTIVITY 5-2

Navigating a File Structure with File Explorer

Before You Begin

You previously created several documents that begin with "my" in the file name.

File Explorer is open.

Scenario

One of the employees seems to be having trouble navigating through the file system. He also seems to have trouble figuring out where he saved files, so when he needs to access the file later, he can't find it. You set aside some time to help him with file system navigation and searching with File Explorer.

---

1. Navigate File Explorer by using the left navigation pane.
   a) In the **Navigation** pane, select the triangle to the left of **This PC**. If This PC is not shown, collapse all of the objects in the left pane, and expand them until you see This PC.
   Several objects should be displayed below **This PC**, including the C: drive.
   b) Select the triangle to the left of **This PC** again to collapse the list of objects under it.

2. Display Libraries.
   a) Select the **View** tab.
   b) Display the **Navigation pane** drop-down menu.
   Only the items with a checkmark next to them are currently displayed.
   c) Select **Show libraries.**

   Note: Show libraries is not available in Windows 8.1 without Update 1 applied.

   Libraries is now shown as a separate listing in the **Navigation** pane in File Explorer.

3. Navigate Libraries by using breadcrumbs and paths.
   a) Expand **Libraries** if it is not already expanded.
   Under **Libraries,** you should see **Documents**, **Music**, **Pictures**, and **Videos**.
   b) Select **Documents** to view the contents of the Documents library in the **Files** pane.
   You should see some files you created in the previous activity.
   c) Select in the **Address bar** to change from Breadcrumb view to Path view.
   d) Expand **This PC** and select the **C:** drive.
   Notice that the Address bar went back to Breadcrumb view instead of Path view when you selected another object.

4. Search for files containing **my** in the file name.
   a) Place the insertion point in the **Search** text box located to the right of the Address bar.
   b) Type ***my***
   c) From the **Search Tools→Search** contextual tab, select **This PC**
   d) Observe the results in the File list area of File Explorer.
   All of the files that contain My (or my) in the file name are listed.
   e) Select **Search Tools→Search→Location→Search again in→Libraries.**
   Now only the My files in the folders in the Libraries are listed.
   f) Select the **Close search** button to close the search results screen. 

TOPIC C

Manage Files and Folders

Now that you've created a few files and navigated the file system, there are a few tips and tricks you can use to become even more efficient. In this topic, you will manage files and folders.

As you begin to add more and more files to your computer, it can become difficult to locate the file you want to work with. Organizing the content into hierarchical folders helps you maintain organization in your file structure. Items can be stored in more than one location or can be moved to a different location. The default folders are a good starting point for organizing your data, but you will likely need to create additional folders to store your data.

Basic File and Folder Management Techniques

You can perform basic folder and file management actions in any File Explorer window and in many other applications.

Action	*Description*
Create objects	When you create a folder or a file, you need to decide where to store it in the overall Windows hierarchy. You can create folders and files on the desktop or on any drive, though it is recommended that you confine your data to the **Documents** folder. You can also create new files and folders within existing folders. This is called nesting folders. If you create a new folder or a file object in File Explorer, it is given a default name that depends on the nature of the object. For example, a new folder object would be named "New Folder" until you explicitly rename it. Each object within a container must have a unique name, so additional new folders in the same location will be named "New Folder (2)," "New Folder (3)," and so on. This applies to default file names as well.
Select multiple objects	In File Explorer, you can select several objects at the same time as long as they are in the same location. Being able to select multiple files, for instance, is handy if you want to rename, copy, or move many of them in one single action. These objects may be listed next to each other (contiguous) or they may be separated by other objects that you do not want to select (non-contiguous). • To select contiguous objects, select the first one and then press **Shift** when you select the last one. • To select non-contiguous objects, press and hold **Ctrl** while you select each one. • To select everything in a container, select **Edit→Select All** or press **Ctrl +A.**
Open files	If you double-click a file in File Explorer, it will open in the default application associated with the file type assigned to the file. If no application is associated with the file type, you will be prompted to select an application to use to open the file. If you want to use a different application than the default application to open the file, you can right-click the file and select **Open With**. From the submenu, you can then select the desired application to use to open the file.
Edit files	When you have a file open, you can change the contents of the file.

Action	Description
Save files	When you have edited a file, you need to save it to be sure that your changes are preserved.
Rename objects	As you create and manage folders and files, you may at some point want to rename them. You can rename a file or folder by selecting **File→Rename.** You can also rename several objects at the same time. You can mix file types (you can rename word processing files and picture files at the same time), you can rename files and folders at the same time, and you can also rename multiple folders at the same time.
Copy objects	Sometimes, you may want to duplicate a file or a folder and all of its contents, leaving the original intact. Perhaps you want to make a copy of an important document in case you make a mistake while editing the original. You can make a copy of a folder or file and store it in a different location or in the same location as the original folder or file. If you make a copy in the same location, the name of the copy ends with "- Copy."
Move objects	If you accidentally create an object in the wrong location or if you just want to reorganize your folders, you can easily move the object or folders to any desired location. In most cases, you will have the option of cutting the object from its original location and pasting it to a new location, or moving the object in one single action.
Delete objects	When you do not require a file, folder, or any such object any longer, you can either delete these items permanently or move them to the **Recycle Bin** temporarily. This will help you reduce clutter and retain only the files that you require and use. When deleting, ensure that you delete only the files that you have created, and not the system or program files.
Undo last action	In Windows 8 and most Windows-based programs, if you ever make a mistake while moving, deleting, cutting, copying, pasting, or formatting folders, files, or text, you have an opportunity to undo the last action. For instance, if you move a file to the wrong location, and realize it immediately, you can select **Edit→Undo Move.** The **Undo** action adjusts itself to reflect the last action performed. So, if the last thing you did was to delete a folder, the menu choice would be **Edit→Undo Delete.**

Note: For additional information, check out the LearnTO **Manage Files and Folders on Macintosh Devices** presentation in the LearnTOs for this course on your CHOICE Course screen.

Note: For additional information, check out the LearnTO **Manage Files and Folders on Linux Devices** presentation in the LearnTOs for this course on your CHOICE Course screen.

The Recycle Bin

The *Recycle Bin* is a container object located on the desktop that temporarily stores deleted files. It is called the **Recycle Bin** because you can restore deleted files and folders from it, unless you either purposely empty the **Recycle Bin** or it reaches its capacity, at which point Windows begins permanently deleting the oldest files in the **Recycle Bin** to accommodate the newest ones.

The **Recycle Bin** does not store files that are deleted from removable media such as USB drives or network drives—they are always deleted permanently. It stores only those folders and files that were deleted directly from your hard drive. When files are in the **Recycle Bin**, its appearance changes from an empty bin to one with sheets of paper in it.

Figure 5-7: The Recycle Bin is a repository for deleted items such as files and folders.

Note: Even if the **Recycle Bin** contains only one file, it is generically referred to as full because the icon looks full.

You should delete files only from folders that you create or from the Documents folder. You should not delete files or folders from any other location. Two folders that you should strictly avoid deleting are the Program Files and Windows folders.

- The Program Files folder is where Windows installs your software.
- The Windows folder is where the Windows operating system resides.

M odifying or deleting files from either of these folders can damage programs or your PC. Therefore, follow this rule of thumb: Never access these two folders unless there is a need for it.

File Attributes

File attributes are characteristics that can be associated with a file or folder that provide the operating system with important information about the file or folder and how it is intended to be used by system users.

There are several standard attributes that you can enable for files or folders on Windows systems.

File Attribute	*Description*
Archive (A)	Indicates that a file has not been backed up. Windows automatically sets the Archive attribute on any file you create or modify. When you back up data, you can choose to back up only the files on which the Archive attribute is set.
Hidden (H)	Hides a file from view in file management tools such as File Explorer, Computer in Windows 8, or My Computer in Windows XP.
Read-Only (R)	Enables users to read the contents of a file or execute it (if a program file), but prevents users from changing the contents of a file.
System (S)	Indicates that a file is used by the operating system. Some applications use this attribute to restrict user access to these files. The System attribute in Windows automatically hides the file or folder.
Index (I)	This Windows-specific attribute enables the Windows Indexing Service to create an index of the file to speed up the Search function.

By default, files you create are able to be modified. Operating system and application files are usually marked as read-only to prevent you from accidentally deleting them. If you want to change any of your data files to read-only, you can change the attributes on the file so that it can no longer be modified. If at a later date you need to change the file, you can remove the read-only attribute from the file.

You can view or change most attributes of a file or folder object by opening the properties of the object in File Explorer. You can view and manage the System attribute at the command line by using the `attrib` command. For information on the functions and syntax of the `attrib` command, see the Windows Help system.

Display Options

You can change how you view the files and folders in File Explorer. You can view the items as lists with or without details, or as various-sized icons. You can change the way they are sorted and whether the sort is in ascending or descending order. You can also specify which folders to include in each Library.

By default, the changes you make to the display options apply only to the current folder. However, you can apply the change to all folders of the same type. There are five folder types:

- General items
- Documents
- Pictures
- Music
- Videos

Common modifications to the File Explorer layout include:

- **Changing the layout for the display of folder contents.** You can display the list of files and folders within a location either as a list or as a series of icons. If you decide to use icons, there are four sizes to choose from. There are also several options for displaying folder content as a list. The **List** view shows only the file or folder name. If you want to view details such as the date the file was modified, the item type, its size, or whether or not it is available offline, then you need to select the **Details** view. In **Details** view, there are six columns displayed by default. You can add columns to the view. You can also remove columns from the view, except for the **Name** column. You can also rearrange the order in which the columns are displayed.
- **Changing the order in which items are displayed.** By default, items in a folder are sorted with folders first, followed by all files, in ascending order by name. You can change the sort order to sort by another column or category, and change between ascending and descending order. A common need is to sort by **Date modified** in descending order so that the most recently modified files are shown at the top of the list. From the **View** tab, you can also specify whether to group the items by a category. By default, there are no groupings.
- **Changing how libraries are displayed.** Libraries are not listed in the **Navigation** pane by default. You can add or remove folders from the various libraries. You can add folders from internal drives on your PC, USB drives or other flash memory cards, indexed network locations, and other PCs in your homegroup. The same display options apply to libraries as apply to other folders. If you apply your display options to all folders of a specific type, the options will also be applied to the folder in the library. Each of the locations included in your library are grouped together separately in the **Navigation** pane.
- **Displaying file sizes.** File sizes are displayed by default in the **Details** view. For other views, you can point to the item to display a pop-up window with file size information. Folders do not display the file size in the **Details** view. Another way to view the file size is to display the

Details pane. This is not displayed by default. The **Details** pane displays the **Date modified**, **Size**, **Date created**, and **Availability** information for the selected file.

Access the Checklist tile on your CHOICE Course screen for reference information and job aids on How to Manage Files and Folders.

ACTIVITY 5-3
Managing Files and Folders

Data Files

All of the files in the **093004Data** folder on the removable media provided by your instructor.

Before You Begin

Your instructor will provide you with removable media containing the course data files. Insert the removable media into your computer.

Scenario

You are helping a new project manager start a project by basing it on the skeleton of an existing project. After discussing the file structure, you both decide it would be good to keep the original project files in its own folder and to make it so that those files cannot be accidentally modified. Right now there are only a few files in the structure, but as the project progresses, there will be many files. You and the project manager decide to try several different views to see which one will work best.

---

1. Rename, copy, and move files to better organize the project.
   a) Navigate into the **093004Data** folder. This folder is located on the removable media you inserted into your computer.
   b) Drag the **File Management** folder to **C:**. This will copy the files from the removable media onto your hard drive.
   c) Right-click the **C:\File Management** folder and select **Rename.** Rename the **File Management** folder to ***My Current Project***

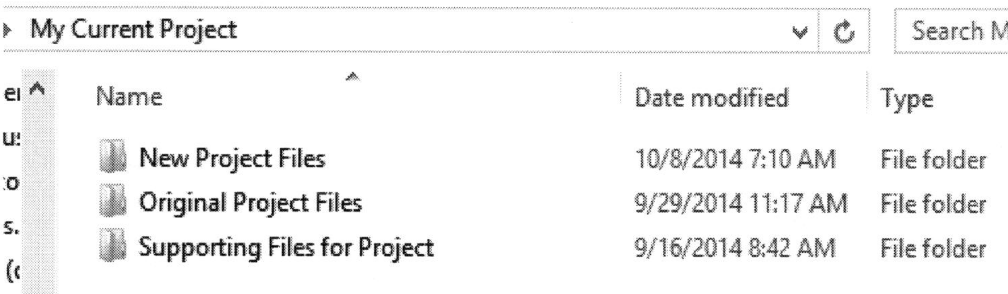

   d) Open the **My Current Project** folder, and then open the **Original Project Files** folder.
   e) Press **Ctrl+A** to select all of the contents of the folder.
   f) Press **Ctrl+C** to copy the selected items to the Clipboard.

g) Paste the contents of the Clipboard into the folder **New Project Files**.

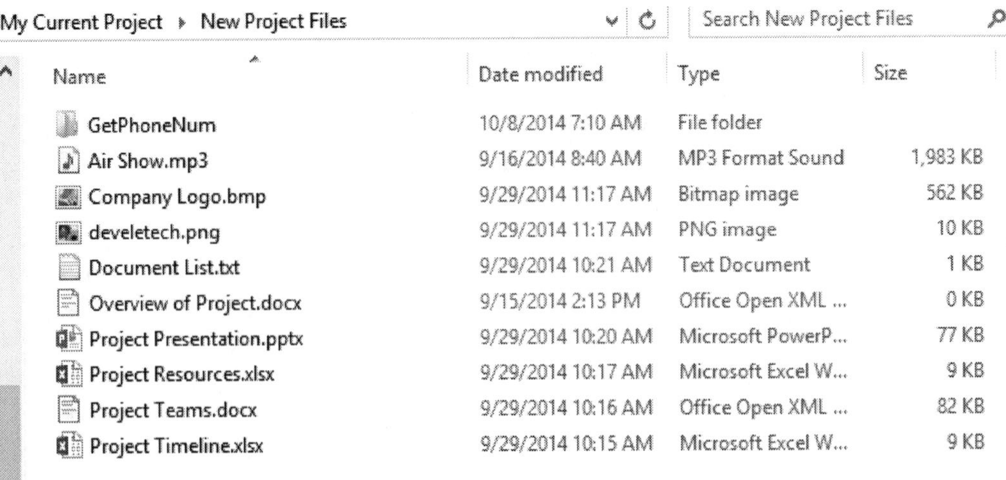

2. Change the file attributes on the content under **Original Project Files** to **Read-only.**
   a) Open the folder **Original Project Files.**
   b) Select all of the files in the folder, and then select **Home→Open→Properties.**
   c) In the **GetPhoneNum, ... Properties** dialog box, on the **General** tab, in the **Attributes** section, select **Read-only**, and then select **OK.**

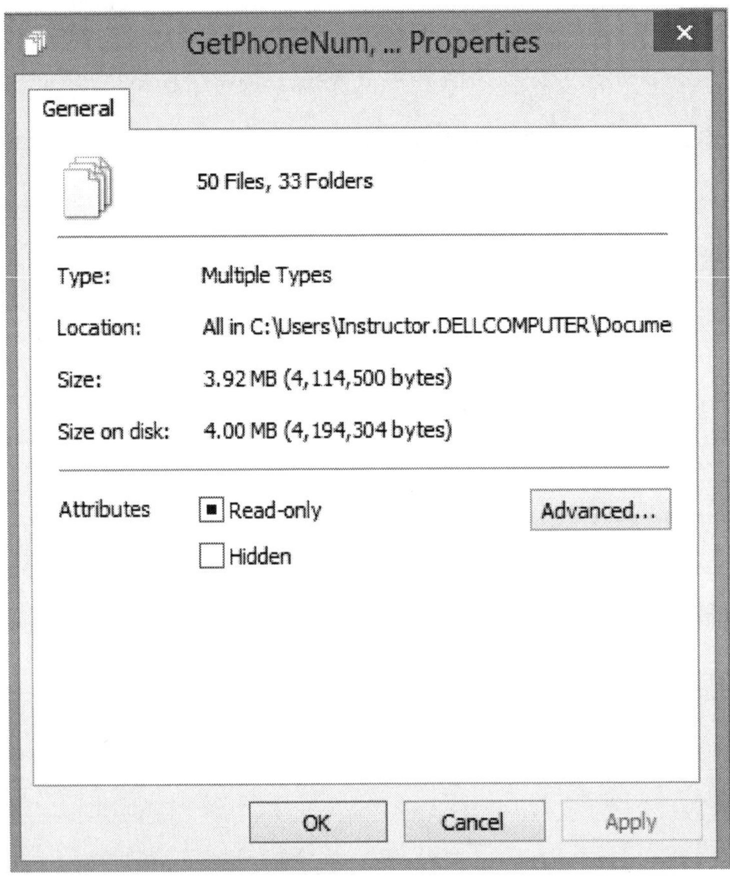

d) In the **Confirm Attribute Change** dialog box, with **Apply changes to the selected items, subfolders and files** selected, select **OK.**

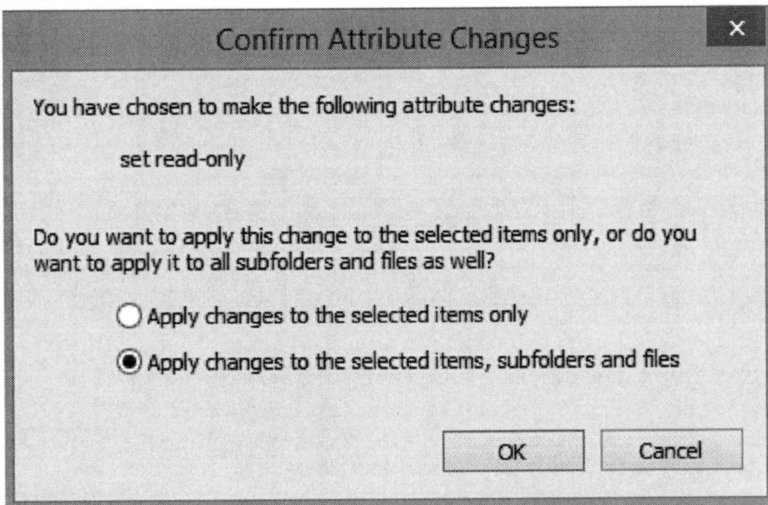

e) Right-click any one of the files in the folder and select **Properties.**
f) Verify that **Read-only** is selected, and then select **Cancel.**
g) Verify that files in the **New Project Files** folder are **not** marked as read-only.

3. Change the display options and then apply them to all folders of the same type.

a) With the **Original Project Files** folder open, select the **View** tab on the ribbon.
b) Select **View→Layout.**

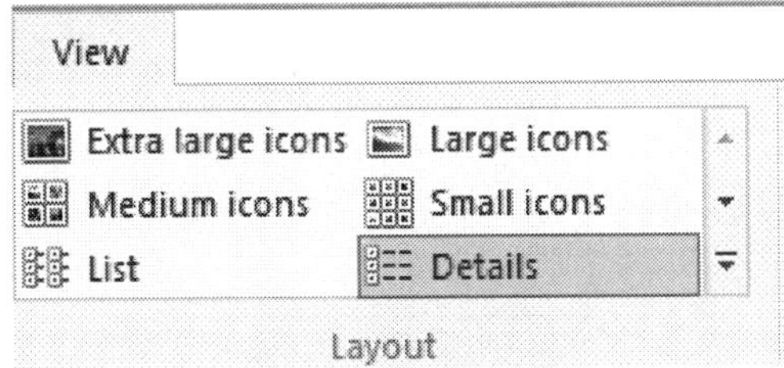

c) Point to each of the layout view options to get a preview of how each layout view displays the contents of the folder.
d) Select **List.**
e) Select and open the **New Project Files** folder.
The files are still shown in **Details** view.
f) With the **Details** view selected in the current window, select **View→Options→Change folder and search options.**
g) Select the **View** tab.

h) Select **Apply to Folders** and then select **OK.**

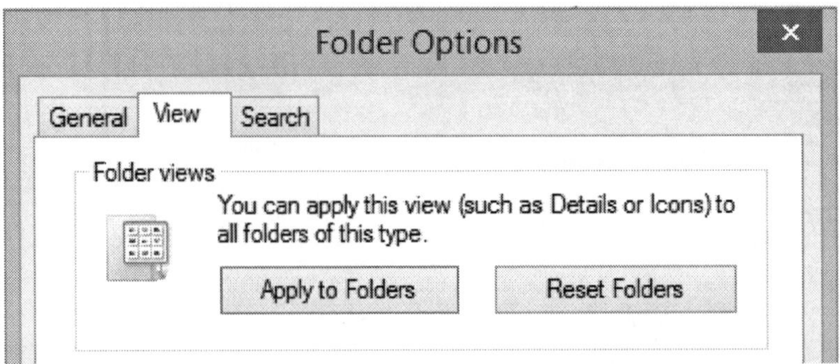

i) In the **Folder Views** dialog box, select **Yes.** Select **OK** again.
j) Open the **Original Project Files** folder and verify that it now shows the files in **Details** view.
k) Select the files **Company Logo.bmp** and **Project Presentation.pptx**. From the **Home** tab on the ribbon, select **Move to→Choose location.** In the **Move Items** dialog box, select **This PC→C→My Current Project→Supporting Files for Project** and then select **Move.**

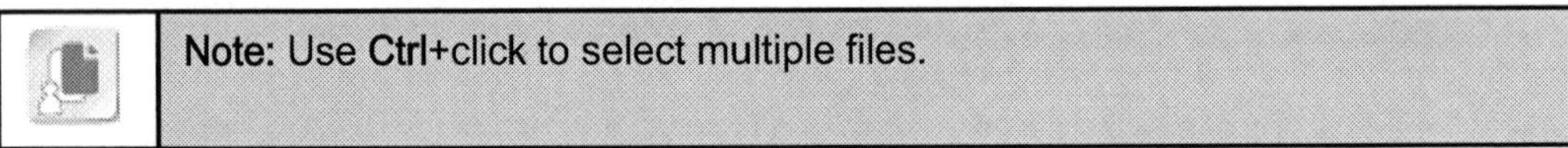

Note: Use **Ctrl+click** to select multiple files.

l) Open the **Supporting Files for Project** folder and change the display type to **Medium icons.**

4. View the file sizes.
   a) In the **Supporting Files for Project** folder, point to a file. A pop-up window shows the file size.
   b) Open the **New Project Files** folder. The file sizes are listed under the **Size** column.

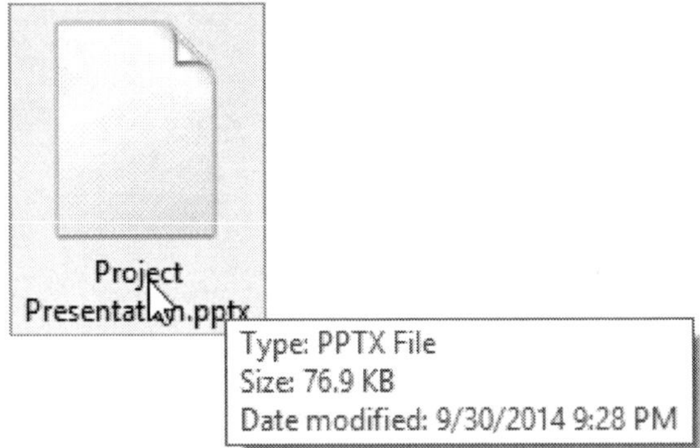

   c) Select **Size** to change the sort order of the files.

5. Rearrange and change which properties are displayed in the **Details** view of File Explorer.
   a) Select the **Size** column heading and drag it so it is between the **Name** and **Date modified** column headings.
   b) Right-click any of the column headings, and then select **Date created** to add another column to the display.
   c) Move the **Date created** column to the left of the **Date modified** column.

d) On the ribbon, select **View→Current view→Group by→Type.** Notice that each type of file is listed in ascending order in separate sections.

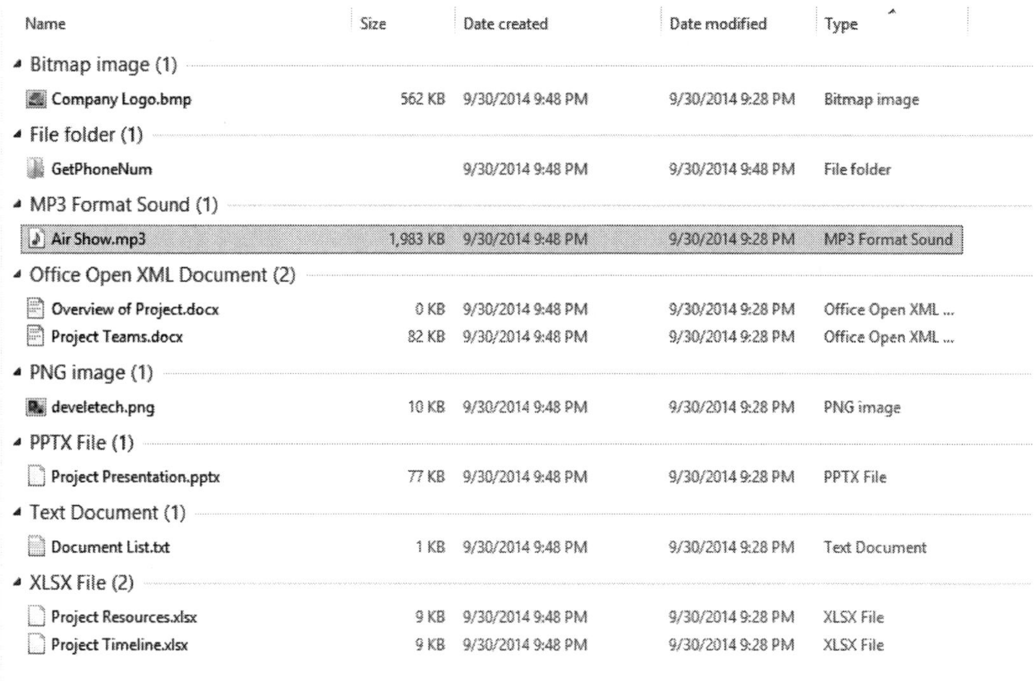

Name	Size	Date created	Date modified	Type
Bitmap image (1)				
Company Logo.bmp	562 KB	9/30/2014 9:48 PM	9/30/2014 9:28 PM	Bitmap image
File folder (1)				
GetPhoneNum		9/30/2014 9:48 PM	9/30/2014 9:48 PM	File folder
MP3 Format Sound (1)				
Air Show.mp3	1,983 KB	9/30/2014 9:48 PM	9/30/2014 9:28 PM	MP3 Format Sound
Office Open XML Document (2)				
Overview of Project.docx	0 KB	9/30/2014 9:48 PM	9/30/2014 9:28 PM	Office Open XML ...
Project Teams.docx	82 KB	9/30/2014 9:48 PM	9/30/2014 9:28 PM	Office Open XML ...
PNG image (1)				
develetech.png	10 KB	9/30/2014 9:48 PM	9/30/2014 9:28 PM	PNG image
PPTX File (1)				
Project Presentation.pptx	77 KB	9/30/2014 9:48 PM	9/30/2014 9:28 PM	PPTX File
Text Document (1)				
Document List.txt	1 KB	9/30/2014 9:48 PM	9/30/2014 9:28 PM	Text Document
XLSX File (2)				
Project Resources.xlsx	9 KB	9/30/2014 9:48 PM	9/30/2014 9:28 PM	XLSX File
Project Timeline.xlsx	9 KB	9/30/2014 9:48 PM	9/30/2014 9:28 PM	XLSX File

ACTIVITY 5-4
Using the Recycle Bin

Scenario

You want to clean up some of the files you created when you were experimenting with the file system. You also want to make sure you understand how the Recycle Bin works so if any of the users you support accidentally delete files, you can help them recover the files.

---

1. Delete and then undo a deletion.
   a) In the **New Project Files** folder, select any file and press **Delete.** The file is sent to the Recycle Bin.

   Note: By default, you are not prompted to confirm deletion of files from the hard drive. You can change it so that you are prompted to confirm file deletions.

   b) On the Desktop, select the **Recycle Bin** to open it. Notice that the file you deleted is listed in the files pane of the Recycle Bin window.
   c) Position the **New Project Files** and **Recycle Bin** windows so that you can see them both.
   d) Switch to the **New Project Files** window and press **Ctrl+ Z**. This is the keyboard shortcut for the Undo command.
   Notice that in the **Recycle Bin** window the file is no longer listed, and it has been returned to the **New Project Files** file list.

2. Delete the files from the **Documents** folder that begin with **My**.
   a) Navigate to the **Documents** folder.
   b) Select all of the files that begin with **My**.
   c) On the ribbon, select **Home→Organize→Delete→Recycle** to move the files to the Recycle Bin.

3. Examine Recycle Bin properties and restore a file.
   a) In the **Recycle Bin** window, select **Recycle Bin Tools→Manage→Manage→Recycle Bin properties.** Observe the **Space Available**, the **Custom Size**, and the **Display delete confirmation dialog** settings.
   b) Select **Cancel.**
   c) Select one of the deleted files in the **Recycle Bin** window.
   d) Select **Recycle Bin Tools→Manage→Restore→Restore the selected items.**

4. Empty the Recycle Bin.
   a) In the **Recycle Bin** window, select **Recycle Bin Tools→Manage→Manage→Empty Recycle Bin.**
   b) Select **Yes** to confirm that you want to permanently delete the contents of the Recycle Bin.

5. Permanently delete a file without it going to the Recycle Bin.
   a) In the **Documents** window, select the file that begins with **My**.
   b) Select **Home→Organize→Delete→Permanently delete.**
   c) Select **Yes.**
   d) Verify that the file did not go into the Recycle Bin.
   e) Close the **Recycle Bin** window.

TOPIC D

Compress and Extract Files

You have created and managed folders and files and navigated the file structure of your desktop computer. As you complete your computing tasks, you might need to reduce the size of files to transfer them more easily. In this topic, you will compress and extract files.

The size of some types of files, such as image files and presentation files, is large. If you could reduce the size of file without distorting the file, you could use less storage space and transfer the file in less time. Also, transferring many files can be made easier by compressing them into a single file.

File Compression and Extraction

Compressing a file is the process of reducing the size of a file. The major advantage of a compressed file is that it makes it easier to transfer files from one location to another. One example of a program that compresses files is WinZip®. Files that are compressed with this utility will have a .zip extension.

You can compress a single file to make it smaller. You can also compress multiple files and folders into a single compressed file, making it easier to move the group of files to another location. Restoring a compressed file to its original size is called *extracting*.

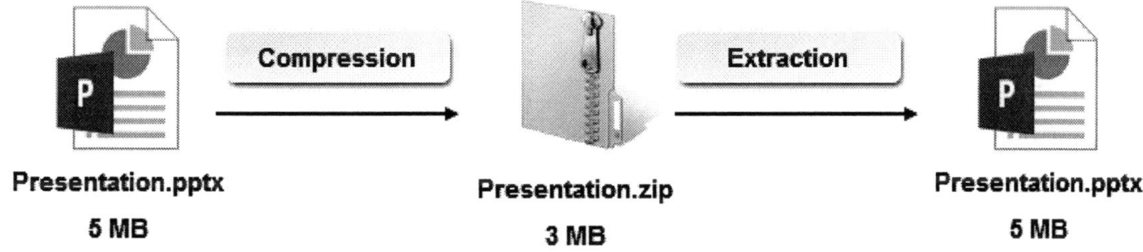

Figure 5-8: The compression and extraction process.

Access the Checklist tile on your CHOICE Course screen for reference information and job aids on How to Compress and Extract Files.

ACTIVITY 5-5

Compressing and Extracting Files

Before You Begin

You have moved the File Management folder to your C drive and changed the name to **My Current Project**.

Scenario

The project manager wants to share all of the files she has been working on with the team before their first meeting. Because there are several files, and some of them are large, she would like to find a way to optimize the files before sharing them. You suggest that she might want to compress the files and folders into a single compressed file. She is unsure of how this works, so you walk her through compressing and then extracting the files.

---

1. Compress all of the files under the **My Current Project** folder into a single compressed file.
   a) Navigate to the **My Current Project** folder on the C drive.
   b) Right-click the **My Current Project** folder and select **Send to→Compressed (zipped) folder.**

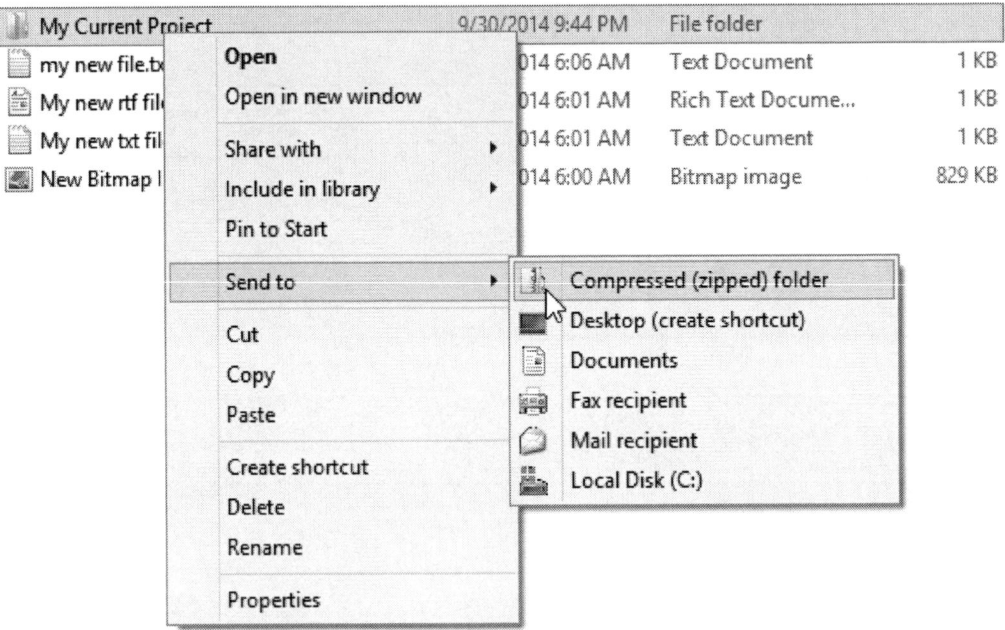

   c) In the message box stating that the compressed file cannot be created in the current location, select **Yes** to create the compressed file on the Desktop.
   d) Navigate to the **Desktop** folder to locate the **My Current Project.zip** file.

2. Extract the files from the My Current Project.zip file.
   a) Right-click **My Current Project.zip** and select **Extract All**.
   b) Observe the **Extract Compressed (Zipped) Folders** dialog box.
   The folder where the files will be extracted to is listed. If you wanted to extract the files to a different location, you would select the **Browse** button and navigate to the desired folder.
   c) Select **Browse**.

d) In the **Select a destination** dialog box, navigate to **This PC→C:→Users→*your_student_folder*→Documents** and then select **OK.**
e) Select **Extract.** By default, **Show extracted files when complete** is selected. This will open the folder in a new window and show you the extracted files.
f) Navigate through the file structure under the **My Current Project** folder to verify that all of the files were extracted and placed in this new location.
g) Close all open File Explorer windows.

TOPIC E

Create Screen Captures

So far in this lesson, you have created and managed files and folders. When you are working with files, folders, and applications, it is sometimes easier to show someone what you see on your screen, instead of trying to describe what is there. In this topic, you will create screen captures.

It is often said that a picture is worth a thousand words. This can be especially true when trying to provide documentation or when trying to describe a computer-related problem a user is having. Windows comes fully equipped with the ability to capture what is shown on your screen and save the results to a file.

Screen Captures

A screen capture is a picture, or image, of what is displayed on your computer monitor. It is also known as a screenshot, screen grab, or screen dump.

You can take screen captures of Windows 8 Store apps and Desktop apps. You can capture the whole screen or the active window. You can also grab a portion of a window. Full screen captures taken with the key combination **Windows+Print Screen** are automatically saved to a **Screenshots** folder in your **Pictures** folder. The files are saved as PNG files.

Note: On Windows tablets on which there might not be a **Print Screen** button, you can use the key combination of the **Windows** key and the volume down button.

You can also create active window screen captures with the key combination **Alt+Print Screen**. These captures are not automatically saved as files, but they are copied to the Clipboard and can be pasted into any location where you can paste images. If you want to save one of these screencaps as an image, you can paste it into Paint and then save the file.

You can also purchase third-party screen capture applications. Some of these applications give you more flexibility in the types of files you can save your captures to, the resolution of the images, and the ability to include or exclude the mouse pointer.

The Snipping Tool

The **Snipping Tool** desktop application was introduced in Windows 7 and is still available in Windows 8/8.1/RT. You can use it to capture anything on the Desktop. To capture Windows 8 apps, it's recommended to use **Windows+Print Screen**.

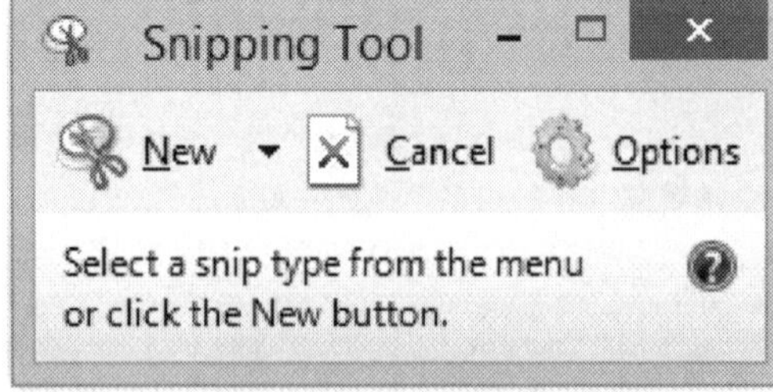

Figure 5-9: The Snipping Tool.

The Snipping Tool enables you to capture rectangular areas, freeform areas, a specific window, or the full screen. The captured image is then displayed in the **Snipping Tool** application window. Once an image is captured, you can save, copy, or send the image. You can also use the **Pen** tool or the **Highlighter** tool to annotate the image before saving, copying, or sending it. If you snap a

Windows 8 store app next to the Desktop, you can use the Snipping Tool in both windows. However, the Snipping Tool border is not displayed when used in a Windows 8 store app window.

If you decide to save a screen capture obtained with the Snipping Tool, by default it is saved to your **Pictures** folder as a .png file. You can navigate through the file system to save it in a different location if desired. You can also save it as PNG, GIF, JPG, or MHT file types.

Access the Checklist tile on your CHOICE Course screen for reference information and job aids on How to Create Screen Captures.

ACTIVITY 5-6
Creating Screen Captures

Before You Begin

The Desktop is open.

Scenario

The project manager you have been working with will be creating documentation for her current project. One of the things she would like to include are screen captures showing specific project-related details. Because her project is confidential, she cannot have you show her how to create screen captures within the project. You decide to show her how to use the Windows key combinations to capture Windows 8 Store apps and to use the Snipping Tool in Desktop style apps.

---

1. From the Windows Start screen, open the **Maps** app.
   a) Switch to the Windows **Start** screen.
   b) Select the **Maps** tile.
   c) Select **Allow** to allow Maps to use your location.
   d) Zoom out and reposition the map as needed to display all of the borders of the state of Iowa.

2. Take a full screen capture by using the Windows key combination.
   a) With the **Maps** app open, press **Windows+Print Screen.** The print screen button might have a different abbreviation printed on it, such as Print Scr, PrtScn, or PrtSc.
   b) Switch to the **Desktop.**
   c) Open **File Explorer** and navigate to your Users **Pictures** folder.
   d) Open the **Screenshots** folder. A **Screenshot(1).png** file should be listed in the folder.

   Libraries ▸ Pictures ▸ Screenshots

   Screenshot (1).png

   e) Snap the **Maps** app and the **Desktop** so both are visible on screen next to each other.
   f) Press **Windows+Print Screen.**

g) Notice that another file is added to the **Screenshots** folder. This screenshot shows both the map and the Desktop in the screenshot.

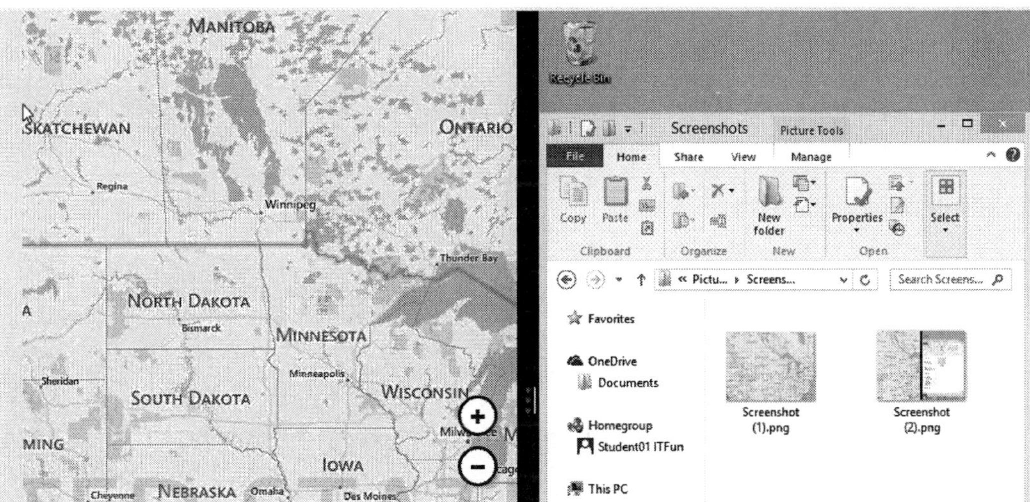

3. Take a screen capture of the active window by using the Windows key combination.
   a) Select the **Maps** app to make it the active window. Make sure both windows stay snapped.
   b) Press **Alt+Print Screen** to take a screen capture.
   c) Observe the **Screenshots** folder. The screen capture is on the Windows Clipboard, but it is not saved into a file.
   d) Use the **Search** charm to open **Paint.**
   e) In the **Paint** app, press **Ctrl+V** to paste the contents of the Clipboard into the blank Paint file.

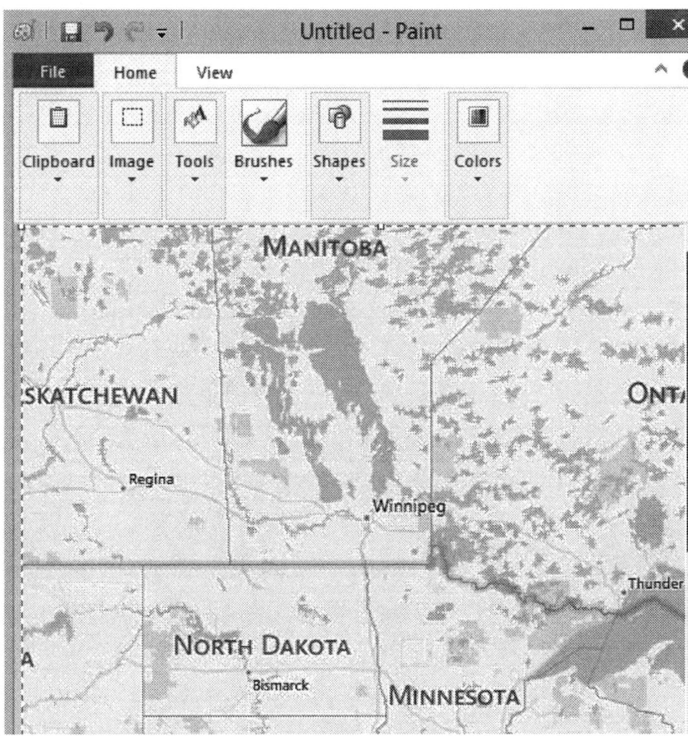

   f) On the **Quick Access Toolbar**, select **Save.**
   g) Observe the path and file type. The file will be saved as a PNG file in the **Pictures** folder.
   h) Save the file as ***My Screen Capture.png***

i) Close **Paint.**
j) Navigate up to the **Pictures** folder. This is the default location for **Paint** to save files.

4. Take a rectangular screen capture by using the Snipping Tool.
   a) Use the **Search** charm to open **Snipping Tool.**
      The Snipping Tool app is a Desktop app and opens on the Desktop.

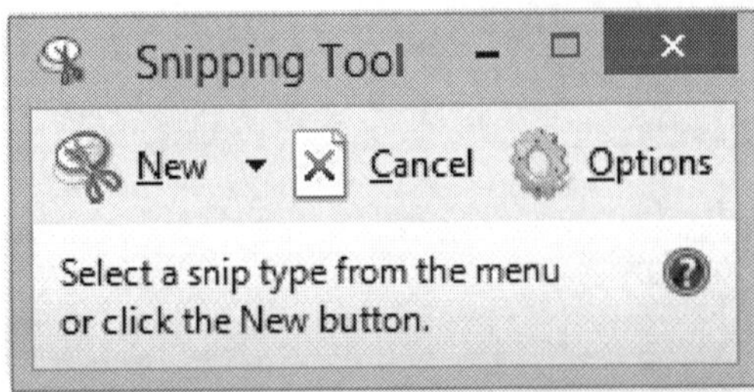

Note: It is likely that you won't see the outline of the area being selected when you are using the Snipping Tool.

   b) In **Snipping Tool,** on the **New** button, select the drop-down arrow.
   c) Select **Rectangular Snip.** A gray mask covers the screen and the cursor changes to a crosshair.
   d) In the **Maps** app, with the map of the United States displayed, place the crosshair at the upper left corner of the state of Iowa and drag to the lower right, making sure to capture the entire state borders.
   e) Observe the screen capture in the **Snipping Tool** window. You also got part of Illinois and Nebraska if you got all of the borders of the state of Iowa. You won't save this image.

5. Take a free-form screen capture by using the Snipping Tool.
   a) In the **Snipping Tool,** select **New.**
   b) Select the **New** drop-down arrow, and then select **Free-form Snip.** The cursor changes to a pair of scissors when moved out of the **Snipping Tool** window.
   c) In the **Maps** app, while holding down the mouse button, drag around the borders of the state of Iowa. Get as close as you can to the borders, but don't worry about being exactly on the borders for this activity.
   d) Observe the screen capture in the **Snipping Tool** window. Only the shape you traced is included in your screen capture.

6. Save your Snipping Tool screen capture to a file.
   a) In the **Snipping Tool** window, select the **Save** button.
   b) Save the file as *Iowa.png*

7. Close all open windows.

Summary

In this lesson, you worked with files, folders, and applications. The skills you practiced in this lesson should assist you in more easily creating and managing files and folders at work, at school, and at home.

How might you use file compression utilities to manage files and folders on your computer?

What is the advantage of capturing screens on your computer?

Note: Check your CHOICE Course screen for opportunities to interact with your classmates, peers, and the larger CHOICE online community about the topics covered in this course or other topics you are interested in. From the Course screen you can also access available resources for a more continuous learning experience.

6 Configuring and Using Wireless Devices

Lesson Time: 2 hours

Lesson Objectives

In this lesson, you will configure and use wireless devices. You will:

- Configure wireless devices.
- Use wireless devices.

Lesson Introduction

So far in this course, you've set up a basic desktop computer, connected it to a network, and managed files, folders, and applications. As an IT support technician, you might also be asked to assist users with setting up and using their tablets and smartphones. In this lesson, you will configure and use wireless devices.

Mobile wireless devices today can do just about anything a desktop computer can do when it comes to end-user productivity such as making and receiving phone calls, emailing, capturing and editing photos and videos, accessing the Internet, and in some cases, remotely accessing data and resources on a private or public network.

TOPIC A

Configure Wireless Devices

In previous lessons, you learned about the characteristics of wireless and cellular networks. In this topic, you'll configure wireless devices so they can communicate and exchange data with other devices.

Certain basic functions and features are common to all wireless computing devices. What differs is how you set up those functions and features to optimize your use of the device. Configuring your wireless device enables you to take advantage of its features and functions.

Wireless Device Configuration Options

There are virtually thousands of options that you can configure on a typical wireless device. Most of these, however, fall into the following general categories:

- Security
- Sharing
- Communication
- Data management

Basic Security Configuration Settings

Securing a mobile device is a necessary task that should be required and enforced by any employer or user. You can implement several security methods to provide the right level of security while still providing access to desired resources and applications.

Security Control	*Description*
Enable screen lock and passcode settings	Consider enabling the screen lock option on all mobile devices, and make sure that you require a passcode. In addition, consider specifying strict requirements on when the device will be locked. You can specify how long the device is active before it locks, which typically ranges from 1 minute to 5 minutes. Once the device is locked, you can access it only by entering the passcode that has been set up by the user. This security control prevents access to the device if it is misplaced or stolen. On some devices, you can configure the passcode settings to erase all data stored on the device after a certain number of failed logon attempts. Often, enabling screen lock is a requirement in an organizational security policy, no matter if the mobile device is provided by the employer or the individual. Pattern passcodes require a user to complete a specific action on the touchscreen to activate the device. Most of the time, the smudge pattern is visible on the surface and can be re-created to gain access to the device. Using a numeric PIN or a password is considered more secure.

Security Control	Description
Configure device encryption	When available, configure all mobile devices to use data encryption to protect company-specific and personal data that may be stored and accessed on the device. This method is effective as long as the hardware cannot be accessed to steal the data. Along with device encryption, use data encryption so when data is accessed by physically taking the device apart, the data remains secured. Device encryption can also be a requirement in an organizational security policy.
Require remote wipes	*Data wiping* is a method used to remove any sensitive data from a mobile device and permanently delete it. Remote wiping is also available for some devices, so you can perform these functions remotely if the device is lost or stolen. Wipe and sanitization guidelines and requirements might be included in an organization's security policy if mobile devices are issued to employees for professional use. In some cases, administrators will have rights to remotely connect to any device that is supported by the organization.
Enable location services and applications	GPS tracking service functionality is available on most mobile devices and can usually be added when required for business reasons. This feature is used as a security measure to protect and track mobile devices that may be lost or stolen. If a mobile device does not have the locating functionality built in, then you can download a locator application that can track and locate a lost or stolen device.
Enable remote backup	Depending on the type of mobile device, there are remote backup services available through the operating system (OS). For example, Apple offers remote backup services to its iCloud® through the **General Settings** of the device. From there, you can specify what application data to back up. Android™ offers remote backup using Google Drive. Both of these services offer the first 5 GB of data for free; then you can purchase more backup space as needed. These features enable you to recover your data when a device is lost or stolen.
Install antivirus software	There are many options when it comes to mobile antivirus solutions. Organizations that allow mobile devices to connect to the network and transfer data should require that antivirus get installed to prevent unauthorized access to data, systems, and resources. Available solutions include: • BullGuard Mobile Security • Kaspersky Mobile Security • ESET Mobile Security • Lookout Premium • Trend Micro Mobile Security • Webroot SecureAnywhere Mobile
Install updates and patches	Mobile device updates are similar to other computing device updates and patches. Verify that devices are set up to automatically install updates from the manufacturer. Updates and patches can resolve security issues and systems flaws that present a security risk.

Bluetooth

Bluetooth® is a wireless technology that facilitates short-range wireless communication between devices. Both voice and data information are exchanged among these devices at 2.4 GHz within a range of approximately 30 feet. You can connect up to eight Bluetooth devices to each other at a time; this connection of two to eight Bluetooth-enabled devices is known as a *piconet.* Bluetooth devices operate at very low power levels of approximately 1 milliwatt (mW).

Bluetooth is predominantly used in wireless personal area networks to transfer information between two computers or other devices. Other common uses include:

- In mobile headsets for hands-free communication with mobile phones.
- For computer peripherals such as the mouse, keyboard, and printer.
- For Bluetooth-enabled devices such as gaming consoles and global positioning system (GPS) receivers.

Bluetooth Pairing

Bluetooth enables mobile devices to connect wirelessly to devices such as headsets, "carputers," laptops, MP3 players, and gaming consoles. Newer computers come with a Bluetooth radio built right into the system, while older computers require an adapter, such as a USB-enabled Bluetooth adapter. Devices in *discovery mode* will transmit their Bluetooth-friendly name, which is usually the manufacturer's name. Once the name has been transmitted, the device can be paired with any other device that is also transmitting a signal. By using Bluetooth technology, mobile devices can establish a connection through a process called *pairing.* When two devices pair, they share a secret key to establish a wireless connection and then begin data transfer.

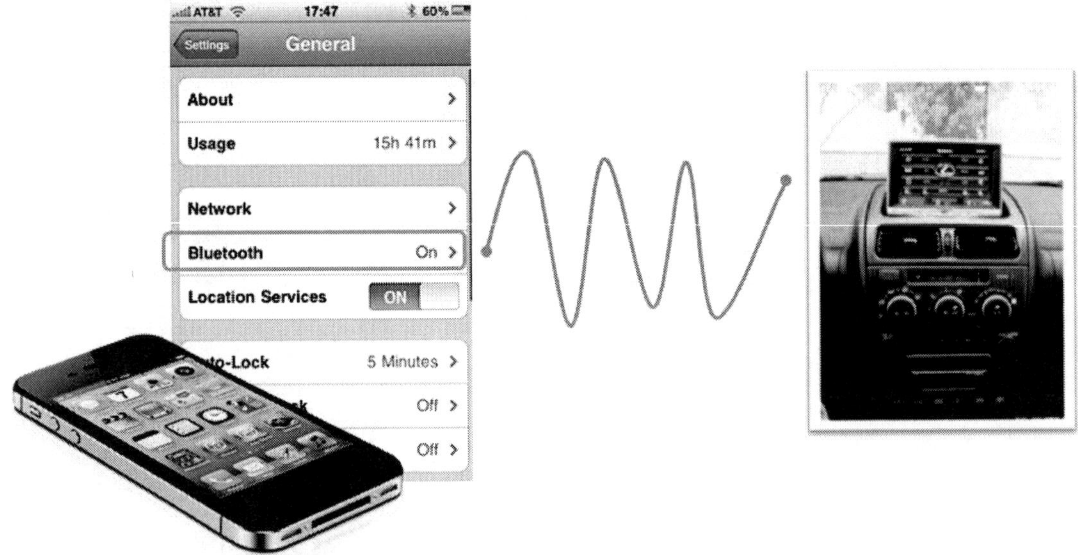

Figure 6-1: Bluetooth pairing.

The basic steps in this process include:

1. Enable Bluetooth on the mobile device through system settings.
2. Enable pairing on the device.
3. On your mobile device, find a device for pairing.
4. Once the device is found, it will ask for a PIN code.
5. Depending on the type of device, the PIN code will be sent via a text, or it will be a standard code such as "0000" used for wireless headsets.
6. Verify that a connection message has been displayed.

7. Test the connection by using the two devices together to either make a phone call, transfer data, or play music.

Near Field Communication

Near Field Communication (NFC) is a standard of communication for mobile devices, such as smartphones and tablets, that are in very close proximity, usually when touching or being only a few inches apart from each other. NFC is most often used for in-person transactions or data exchange. Aside from having a shorter range of operation, NFC cannot transfer as much data as Bluetooth. On the other hand, it is faster and easier to establish NFC communication compared to Bluetooth.

Figure 6-2: NFC allows for data exchange between two devices that are within inches of each other.

The Google Nexus smartphone running a version of the Android operating system is an example of an NFC-enabled device.

The Wireless Connection Setup Process

You can use the following general process to set up wireless connections:

1. Verify that wireless capabilities are available.
2. If necessary, turn on Wi-Fi on the wireless device.
3. Locate and select the SSID for the WAP.
4. If necessary, enter the password for the wireless network.
5. Verify that your wireless device can connect to the Internet.

Email Configuration

Once you've established a network connection with your mobile device, you can set up and configure email. You can configure mobile devices to automatically update your email account information and manage mail. Mobile devices support many different email providers, such as Yahoo! Mail, Microsoft Exchange, Windows Live, Gmail, and Hotmail/Outlook.

On a mobile device, you can access email in one of two ways: web-based or client-based.

- To use web-based access, install the email provider's app, which is available in the mobile device's app store. You will need to enter your user name and password to access the web-based email application.
- Client-based email access is a bit more complicated and requires more information to access email services. Microsoft Exchange is a client-based email system that allows mobile devices to sync with the server.

Before you can set up your mobile device's email, you need to determine the type of email account you will be configuring.

Email Protocols

Depending on your email provider, you may need to configure additional settings based on which protocol it uses.

Protocol	Description
POP3	*Post Office Protocol version 3 (POP3)* is a protocol that enables an email client application to retrieve email messages from a mailbox on a mail server. With POP3, the email messages wait in the mailbox on the server until the client retrieves them, either on a schedule or manually. Once the messages are retrieved and downloaded to the client, they are generally deleted from the server. The client then stores and works with the email messages locally.
IMAP	*Internet Mail Access Protocol version 4 (IMAP4)* is a protocol that enables a client to retrieve messages from a mail server. With IMAP4, messages generally remain on the server while the client works with them as if they were local. IMAP4 enables users to search through messages by keywords and to choose which messages to download locally. Messages in the user's mailbox can be marked with different status flags that denote states such as "deleted" or "replied to." The messages and their status flags stay in the mailbox until explicitly removed by the user. Unlike POP3, IMAP4 enables users to access folders other than their mailbox.
SMTP	*Simple Mail Transfer Protocol (SMTP)* is used to send email from a client to a server or between servers. It uses a store-and-forward process, in which the sender starts the transfer. An SMTP server can store a message until the receiving device comes online. At that point, it contacts the device and forwards the message. If all devices are online, the message is sent quickly.

Note: For additional information, check out the LearnTO **Configure Email on a Mobile Device** in the LearnTOs for this course on your CHOICE Course screen.

Synchronization of Wireless and Other Devices

Data synchronization is the process of automatically merging and updating common data that is stored on multiple devices. For example, users can access their email contact lists from both their mobile devices and laptop computers. Synchronization can begin when the devices are connected via a cable, wirelessly, or over a network connection. In some cases, you may need to install synchronization software on the devices you choose to synchronize. You can control the synchronization rate, and you can limit the synchronization process to allow and restrict push and pull notifications from the cloud over the Internet. The types of data that you can synchronize include:

- Contacts
- Programs
- Email
- Pictures
- Music
- Videos

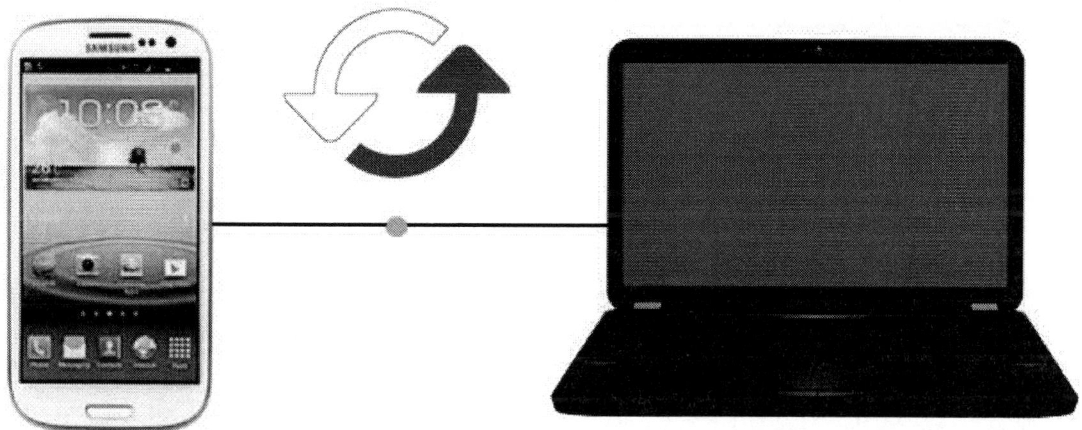

Figure 6-3: Data synchronization.

Exchange ActiveSync

Microsoft has its own synchronization protocol called *Exchange ActiveSync (EAS)* that enables mobile devices to connect to an Exchange Server to access mail, calendars, and contacts. Exchange administrators can limit what devices can connect and synchronize with the server and can control which ones are blocked.

Synchronization Requirements

Synchronization requirements will vary and will be specific to each mobile device. Factors to consider when enabling data synchronization on a mobile device include:

- You might need to use a specific system account to enable synchronization.
- You might require an email account.
- If you are using Microsoft Exchange, then control may be given to the admin.
- Organizations may have specific requirements to synchronize data.
- Certain devices might require additional software to enable synchronization.

Access the Checklist tile on your CHOICE Course screen for reference information and job aids on How to Configure Wireless Devices.

ACTIVITY 6-1

Configuring Wireless Devices

Before You Begin

You will need an iPhone or iPad, or Android device, along with a Bluetooth device for this activity.

Scenario

You are assisting with the rollout of new smartphones and tablets for the sales force. Some employees are getting iOS devices, and some are getting Android devices. Smartphones come with a Bluetooth earpiece, and tablets include a Bluetooth keyboard. You will be helping the employees pair their Bluetooth devices with their wireless devices. You will also be helping them set up email on their devices.

---

1. Determine which operating system your device uses.
   a) Turn on the device.
   b) Access the settings on the device.
   The settings will indicate which operating system is installed and the version of the operating system.

2. If you have an iOS smartphone or tablet, perform these steps to pair the mobile device with a Bluetooth-enabled device.
   a) Place the iOS smartphone or tablet and the Bluetooth device near each other.
   b) Referring to the device documentation, place the Bluetooth device in discoverable mode.
   c) From the home screen of your iOS device, tap **Settings** app, and then tap to open **General settings.**
   d) Verify that the **Bluetooth** setting is **On.** If it is not on, then tap **Bluetooth** and tap the **OFF** setting to switch it to **ON.**
   The device will search for the Bluetooth device.
   e) When the Bluetooth device is found, tap to select it from the list.
   f) If a passcode is required, enter the correct passcode provided by the manufacturer or sent from the device to which you are connecting.
   g) Test the pairing by using the devices.

3. If you have an Android smartphone or tablet, perform these steps to pair the mobile device with a Bluetooth-enabled device.
   a) Place the Android smartphone or tablet and the Bluetooth device near each other.
   b) Referring to the device documentation, place the Bluetooth device in discoverable mode.
   c) Open the **Settings** menu on your Android device.
   d) Tap to open **Wireless→Networks→Bluetooth** settings.
   e) Tap to turn on the **Bluetooth** setting if it isn't already turned on.
   f) When the Bluetooth device is found, tap to select it from the list.
   g) If a passcode is required, enter the correct passcode provided by the manufacturer or sent from the device to which you are connecting.
   h) Test the pairing by using the devices.

4. If you are using an iOS device, configure email on the phone or tablet.
   a) From the home screen, open the **Settings** app.
   b) Tap the **Mail, Contacts, Calendars** option.
   c) Tap **Add Account.**
   d) Tap to select the email account type you are configuring.

e) Enter your email account authentication information and tap **Next.**
f) After the phone or tablet loads your account, tap to choose the options you want synchronized, and then tap **Save.**
g) Open the inbox and read the message to confirm that the email account was successfully set up.

5. If you are using an Android device, configure email on the phone or tablet.

a) From the **Home** screen, open the **Email** application.
b) On the **Your Accounts** page, tap **Next.**
c) Enter your email account address and password information.
d) Select the appropriate email protocol setting.
e) Enter the incoming mail settings, and then tap **Next.**
f) Enter the outgoing mail settings, and then tap **Next.**
g) Verify that **SSL** is selected and then tap **Next.**
h) Customize the settings as needed and close the application.
i) Open the inbox and read the message to confirm that the email account was set up correctly.

TOPIC B

Use Wireless Devices

In the last topic, you configured wireless devices. The next logical step is to make use of them. In this topic, you will use wireless devices.

Wireless communication is prevalent in almost every aspect of today's world, so being comfortable with common ways to use mobile devices should help you be more productive and accessible to others.

Gesture-Based Interactions

Many modern computing devices have touchscreens. Users convey instructions by touching designated areas on the screen.

The following table describes gestures that are universally recognized on devices that have touchscreens.

Gesture	*Description*
Tap	Tap an item, such as a button or link, to select it or tap an app to launch it. Starting with your finger off the screen, touch the screen on the item you wish to activate. Then immediately pull your finger away from the screen. This is comparable to clicking an item with a mouse.
Tap & Hold	Tap an item and continue to hold your finger steady until a shortcut menu appears or the app icons jiggle.
Double-Tap	Tap an item twice in rapid succession. Double-tap the **Home** button to display the multitasking bar.
Pinch	Pinch an item to zoom out or make it smaller. Starting with your index finger and thumb apart from each other, touch both to the screen on the item you want to pinch. Without releasing the screen, move your fingers together, and then release the screen.
5-Point Pinch	With all five fingers making contact with the screen, pinch to quickly return to the **Home** screen.
Spread	Stretch an item to zoom in or make it larger. Starting with your index finger and thumb together, touch both to the screen on the item you want to stretch. Without releasing the screen, move your fingers apart, and then release the screen.
Swipe	Swipe an item to reveal a setting or change the screen display. Starting with your finger off the screen, touch the screen on the item you wish to swipe. Without releasing the screen, drag your finger across the screen. You can slide a control by swiping the button to the left or right.
Drag	Tap and hold an item and then move the item to drag it to a new location.
Flick	Flick your finger up or down on the screen to scroll through the items displayed on the screen. This gesture uses the concept of *kinetics* to emulate the feeling of sliding sheets of paper. A flick is quicker than a swipe.
Slide	Slide controls by swiping left or right to change the setting.

Screen Orientation

On most mobile devices, the screen orientation changes automatically with the position of the device. This function is possible due to advanced mobile OS technology that includes an *accelerometer* and a *gyroscope*. The accelerometer reads and measures the orientation of the device by using a sensor that can measure the acceleration of the direction the device is moving in order to reposition the screen. This technology works when the device is in motion and upright. When the device is flat on a surface, the gyroscope changes the orientation of the device by reading the x and y coordinates as the device is moved to quickly update the orientation of the screen. These technologies work together to provide an instant update to the screen in all environments.

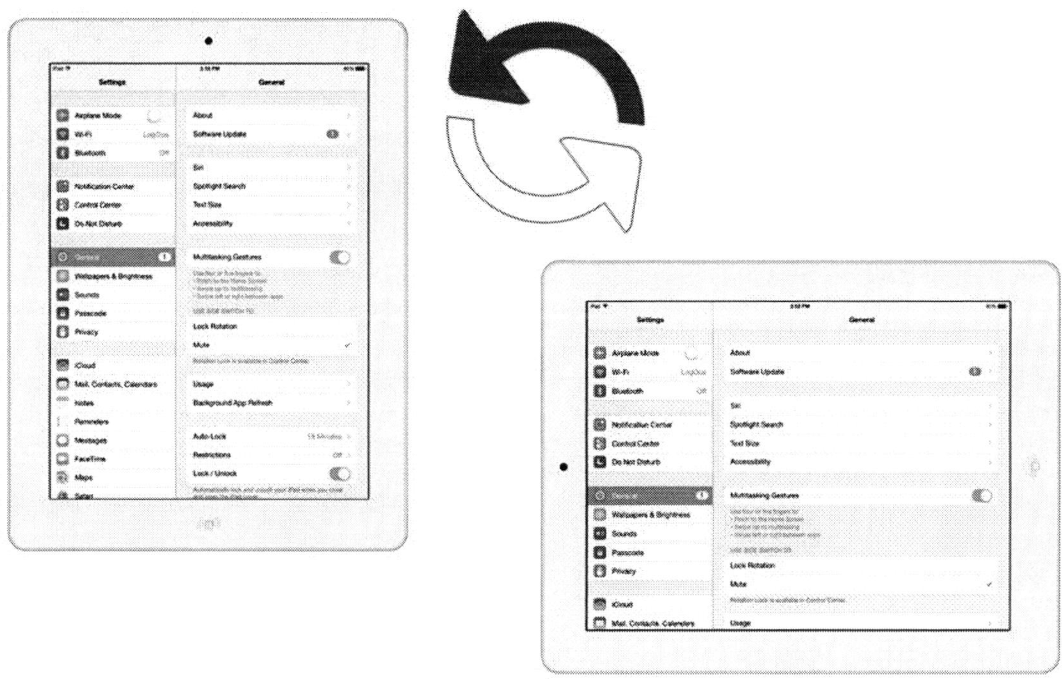

Figure 6-4: Tablet screen orientation adjusting to rotation.

Airplane Mode

You can use the *airplane mode* setting to quickly disconnect a mobile device from Wi-Fi and cellular connections, disabling the ability to send and receive calls, email, and text messages. By using airplane mode, you are complying with safety regulations while in flight, but you still have access to other built-in features and apps that don't require sending or receiving data. You might also decide to use airplane mode to conserve battery life or avoid roaming charges when traveling abroad.

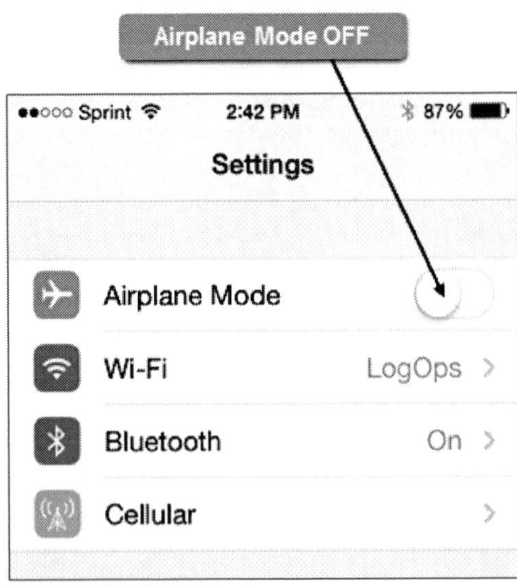

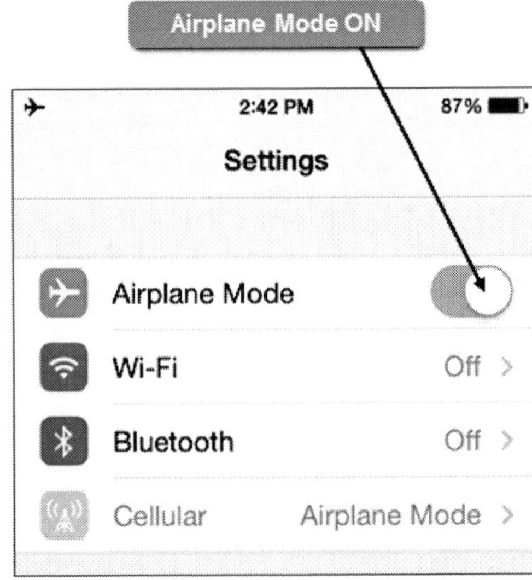

Figure 6-5: Airplane mode.

Mobile App Stores

Mobile apps are compact software programs that are developed to perform a predefined function. They are designed to work on a smartphone or a handheld mobile device such as a mobile phone, tablet, or feature phone. You can download and use mobile apps for many different purposes.

Note: Look at your mobile phone for a moment, and set a reminder to review your *CompTIA® IT™ Fundamentals* material. You have just used a mobile app developed to perform a predefined function (setting a reminder and alerting you at the set time). Keep in mind that all mobile apps are not the same.

There are mobile apps for just about everything, including games, calorie counters, virtual sticky notes, recipes, and many more. These apps are developed for personal and professional use and are intended to make life easier, to entertain, or to connect businesses with consumers. Some apps come preloaded on smartphones; others can be downloaded for free or for a small fee from the following stores:

- The App Store contains apps for Apple iOS devices.
- Google Play™ store and Amazon Appstore contain apps for Android devices.
- The Windows® Store contains apps for Windows devices.
- Company app stores contain proprietary apps created by in-house developers.

Access the Checklist tile on your CHOICE Course screen for reference information and job aids on How to Use Wireless Devices.

ACTIVITY 6-2

Using Wireless Devices

Before You Begin

You have access to a wireless mobile device.

Scenario

As the mobile device rollout to the sales reps continues, you will next show them how to install and use an app on their device. Because the sales force often travels by air, you decide that a flight tracker app would be an appropriate app to install.

---

1. On your wireless device, open the app store.
   If the app store icon is not displayed on the Home screen, navigate to the app listing and select the appropriate icon.

   Note: If a wireless network is available, you might want to connect to it so you don't use data from your data plan while downloading and working with the app.

2. If necessary, create an account for the app store.

3. Search for and install a free flight tracking app.
   a) Use the app store's **Search** feature to find a free flight tracking app.
   b) Select a free flight tracking app from the search results list.
   c) Tap **Install**.
   d) Follow any prompts displayed to download and install the app. Depending on your device, you might be prompted for your user name and password, account information, payment methods (which you can skip because it is a free app), or other required information.
   e) When the app is finished installing, tap **Open**.

4. Rotate the device and verify that the screen orientation changes.

5. Activate Airplane mode.
   a) Access the **Settings** menu on your device.
   b) Set **Airplane mode** to **On.**

c) Observe the connection icons.

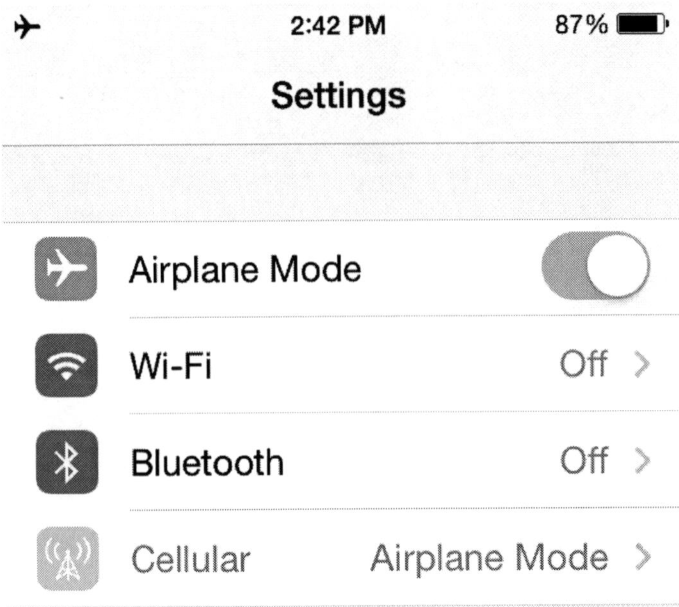

If you were connected to a Wi-Fi network, your connection was disabled. If Bluetooth was turned on, it is now off. If a 3G or 4G indicator was displayed, it is no longer displayed.

d) Try to make a phone call to verify that the phone is disconnected from the cellular network.

e) Set **Airplane mode** to **Off.**

f) Verify that Wi-Fi, Bluetooth, and cellular connections have been restored.

Summary

In this lesson, you configured and used wireless devices. By configuring communication methods such as Bluetooth sharing, NFC, and email, and establishing data synchronization, as well as installing mobile apps, you can maximize the functionality of any mobile device.

What are some examples of using Bluetooth pairing in real life?

What other sorts of wireless device uses would you expect to encounter in a business environment?

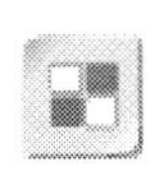

Note: Check your CHOICE Course screen for opportunities to interact with your classmates, peers, and the larger CHOICE online community about the topics covered in this course or other topics you are interested in. From the Course screen you can also access available resources for a more continuous learning experience.

7 Securing Computing Devices

Lesson Time: 2 hours, 30 minutes

Lesson Objectives

In this lesson, you will secure computing devices. You will:

- Identify common security threats.
- Apply security best practices.
- Perform secure web browsing.

Lesson Introduction

In this course, you have set up and worked with a variety of computing devices. One of the major issues surrounding the use of computing devices is how to keep information safe from harm. In this lesson, you will secure computing devices.

You might feel comfortable browsing the Internet and using it to send and receive messages, download music, and shop online, but you need to be aware of the threats associated with downloading information from the Internet. Whether the threat comes in the form of an attacker trying to gain access to your logon credentials or in the form of a malicious piece of code such as a virus, you must be able to protect sensitive data that resides on your computer.

TOPIC A

Identify Security Threats

Security threats come from many sources. A threat could be instigated by another person who is fraudulently representing himself or an institution, or the threat could be a software-based event caused by unknowingly downloading malicious code from the Internet. Online attacks at best can affect one computer, or at worst they can bring an entire organization to a grinding halt. By identifying and responding appropriately to potential social engineering attacks, and understanding the risks associated with working online, you can protect not only your system, but also the entire infrastructure of your organizational network.

Hackers and Attackers

Hackers and *attackers* are related terms for individuals who have the skills to gain access to computer systems through unauthorized or unapproved means. Originally, a hacker was a neutral term for a user who excelled at computer programming and computer system administration. Hacking into a system was a sign of technical skill and creativity that also became associated with illegal or malicious system intrusions. Attacker is a term that always represents a malicious system intruder.

Note: The term *cracker* refers to an individual who breaks encryption codes, defeats software copy protections, or specializes in breaking into systems. The term "cracker" is sometimes used to refer to as a hacker or an attacker.

A *white hat* is a hacker who discovers and exposes security flaws in applications and operating systems so that manufacturers can fix them before they become widespread problems. The white hat often does this professionally, working for a security organization or a system manufacturer. This is sometimes called an ethical hack.

A *black hat* is a hacker who discovers and exposes security vulnerabilities for financial gain or for some malicious purpose. Although the black hats might not break directly into systems the way attackers do, widely publicizing security flaws can potentially cause financial or other damage to an organization.

People who consider themselves white hats also discover and publicize security problems, but without the organization's knowledge or permission. They consider themselves to be acting for the common good. In this case, the only distinction between a white hat and a black hat is one of intent. There is some debate over whether this kind of unauthorized revelation of security issues really serves the public good or simply provides an avenue of attack.

White hats and black hats get their names from characters in old Western movies: The good guys always wore white hats and the bad guys wore black hats.

Malware

Malware is any unwanted software that has the potential to damage a system, impede performance, or create a nuisance condition. The software might be introduced deliberately or inadvertently and might or might not be able to propagate itself to other systems.

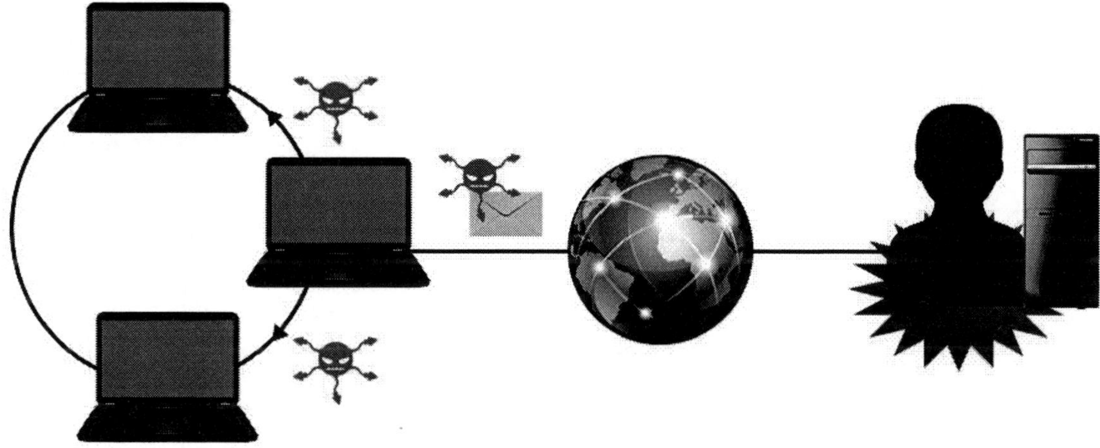

Figure 7-1: Malware.

Types of Malware

Many malicious code attacks fall into the general malware category. Having a good antivirus program installed and running prevents most of these types of attacks from affecting you, your files, and your computer.

Malware Type	Description
Virus	A piece of code that spreads from one computer to another by attaching itself to other files. The code in a virus executes when the file it is attached to is opened. Frequently, viruses are intended to enable further attacks, send data back to the attacker, or even corrupt or destroy data.
Worm	A piece of code that spreads from one computer to another on its own, not by attaching itself to another file. Like a virus, a worm can enable further attacks, transmit data, or corrupt or erase files.
Trojan horse	An insidious type of malware that is itself a software attack and can pave the way for a number of other types of attacks. There is a social engineering component to a Trojan horse attack since the user has to be fooled into executing it.
Logic bomb	A piece of code that sits dormant on a target computer until it is triggered by a specific event, such as a specific date. Once the code is triggered, the logic bomb detonates, and performs whatever actions it was programed to do. Often, this includes erasing and corrupting data on the target system.
Spyware	Surreptitiously installed malicious software that is intended to track and report the usage of a target system, or to collect other data the author wishes to obtain. Data collected can include web browsing history, personal information, banking and other financial information, and user names and passwords.
Adware	Software that automatically displays or downloads advertisements when it is used. Although not all adware is malicious, many adware programs have been associated with spyware and other types of malicious software. Also, it can reduce user productivity by slowing down systems and simply by creating annoyances.

Malware Type	Description
Rootkit	Code that is intended to take full or partial control of a system at the lowest levels. Rootkits often attempt to hide themselves from monitoring or detection, and modify low-level system files when integrating themselves into a system. Rootkits can be used for non-malicious purposes such as virtualization; however, most rootkit infections install backdoors, spyware, or other malicious code once they have control of the target system.
Spam	Spam is an email-based threat that presents various advertising materials, promotional content, or get-rich-quick schemes to users. The messages can quickly fill a user's inbox and cause storage issues. Spam can also carry malicious code and other types of malware.
Ransomware	Ransomware is malicious software that prevents you from using your computer. It usually displays a message stating that you must pay a fee or face some other penalty before you can access your files and computer again. Paying the ransom doesn't necessarily mean that you will regain access to your files or computer.

Social Engineering Attacks

A *social engineering attack* is a type of attack that uses deception and trickery to convince unsuspecting users to provide sensitive data or to violate security guidelines. Social engineering is often a precursor to another type of attack. Because these attacks depend on human factors rather than on technology, their symptoms can be vague and hard to identify. Social engineering attacks can come in a variety of methods: in person, through email, or over the phone. Social engineering typically takes advantage of users who are not technically knowledgeable, but it can also be directed against technical support staff if the attacker pretends to be a user who needs help. Social engineering attacks can be prevented with effective user education.

Types of Social Engineering Attacks

There are various types of social engineering attacks.

Social Engineering Type	Description
Shoulder surfing	This is a human-based attack where the goal is to look over the shoulder of an individual as he or she enters password information or a PIN. Shoulder surfing can happen in an office environment, a retail environment, at an ATM or at the entryway of a secure physical facility. When you are setting up workstations, the monitors should be placed so that they are not facing hallways or windows and giving passersby an opportunity to view information on the screen. This also applies to employees who work from home. Their equipment should not be accessible by other family members or visible to people walking past their homes.
Spoofing	This is a human-based or software-based attack where the goal is to pretend to be someone else for the purpose of identity concealment. Spoofing can occur in Internet Protocol (IP) addresses, network adapter's hardware (Media Access Control [MAC]) addresses, and email. If employed in email, various email message headers are changed to conceal the originator's identity.

Social Engineering Type	Description
Impersonation	This is a human-based attack where an attacker pretends to be someone he is not. A common scenario is when the attacker calls an employee and pretends to be calling from the help desk. The attacker tells the employee he is reprogramming the order-entry database, and he needs the employee's user name and password to make sure it gets entered into the new system.
Hoax	This is an email-based or web-based attack that is intended to trick the user into performing undesired actions, such as deleting important system files in an attempt to remove a virus. It could also be a scam to convince users to give up important information or money for an interesting offer.
Phishing	This is a common type of email-based social engineering attack. In a phishing attack, the attacker sends an email that seems to come from a respected bank or other financial institution. The email claims that the recipient needs to provide an account number, Social Security number, or other private information to the sender in order to verify an account. Ironically, the phishing attack often claims that the account verification is necessary for security reasons. Individuals should never provide personal financial information to someone who requests it, whether through email or over the phone. Legitimate financial institutions never solicit this information from their clients. A similar form of phishing called *pharming* can be done by redirecting a request for a website, typically an e-commerce site, to a similar-looking, but fake, website.
Vishing	This is a human-based attack where the goal is to extract personal, financial, or confidential information from the victim by using services such as the telephone system and IP-based voice messaging services (Voice over Internet Protocol [VoIP]) as the communication medium. This is also called *voice phishing*.
Whaling	This is a form of phishing that targets individuals who are known to possess a good deal of wealth. It is also known as *spear phishing*. Whaling targets individuals that work in Fortune 500 companies or financial institutions whose salaries are expected to be high.
Spam and *spim*	Spam is an email-based threat that presents various advertising materials, promotional content, or get-rich-quick schemes to users. The messages can quickly fill a user's inbox and cause storage issues. Spam can also carry malicious code and other types of malware. Spam can also be categorized as a type of social engineering because it can be used within social networking sites such as Facebook and Twitter. Spim is an Internet messaging (IM)-based attack similar to spam that is propagated through IM instead of through email.

Social Engineering Type	Description
Dumpster diving	Most people and companies are environmentally aware and recycle papers that they are done using. If that piece of paper contains company confidential information, be sure that it is shredded and placed in a secure recycle bin. Attackers are not above jumping into a Dumpster or large recycling location in an attempt to obtain information they can use or sell. Outdated hardware should never be thrown in the trash. The hardware contains heavy metals that could contaminate the soil. Also, hard drives and other storage devices might contain sensitive information. It is not uncommon to find thieves searching for such hardware in the hopes of finding valuable information on the devices. By properly disposing of paper and hardware, you can protect your organization from Dumpster divers.

Password Cracking

A *password attack* is any type of attack in which the attacker attempts to obtain and make use of passwords illegitimately. The attacker can guess or steal passwords or crack encrypted password files. A password attack can show up in audit logs as repeatedly failed logons and then a successful logon, or it can show as several successful logon attempts at unusual times or locations.

Figure 7-2: Attacker guesses the password to gain network access.

Types of Password Attacks

Hackers use several common categories of password attacks. Creating complex passwords can increase the amount of time it takes for an attack to succeed.

Password Attack Type	Description
Guessing	A *guessing attack* is the simplest type of password attack and involves an individual making repeated attempts to guess a password by entering different common password values, such as the user's name, a spouse's name, or a significant date. Most systems have a feature that will lock out an account after a specified number of incorrect password attempts.
Stealing	Passwords can be stolen by various means, including sniffing network communications, reading handwritten password notes, or observing a user in the act of entering the password.

Password Attack Type	Description
Dictionary attack	A *dictionary attack* automates password guessing by comparing encrypted passwords against a predetermined list of possible password values. Dictionary attacks are successful against only fairly simple and obvious passwords, because they rely on a dictionary of common words and predictable variations, such as adding a single digit to the end of a word.
Brute force attack	In a *brute force attack*, the attacker uses password-cracking software to attempt every possible alphanumeric password combination.
Hybrid password attack	A *hybrid password attack* utilizes multiple attack vectors including dictionary, brute-force, and other attack methodologies when trying to crack a password.

Physical Security Issues

Physical security threats and vulnerabilities can come from many different areas.

Threat/Vulnerability	Description
Internal	It is important to always consider what is happening inside an organization, especially when physical security is concerned. For example, disgruntled employees may be a source of physical sabotage of important network security-related resources.
External	It is impossible for any organization to fully control external security threats. For example, an external power failure is usually beyond a network technician's control because most organizations use a local power company as their source of electrical power. However, risks posed by external power failures may be mitigated by implementing devices such as an uninterruptible power supply (UPS) or a generator.
Natural	Although natural threats are easy to overlook, they can pose a significant risk to the physical security of a facility. Buildings and rooms that contain important computing assets should be protected against likely weather-related problems including tornadoes, hurricanes, snow storms, and floods.
Man-made	Whether intentional or accidental, people can cause a number of physical threats. Man-made threats can be internal or external. For example, a backhoe operator may accidentally dig up fiber optic cables and disable external network access. Alternatively, a disgruntled employee may choose to exact revenge by deliberately cutting fiber optic cables.

Environmental Threats and Vulnerabilities

Natural, environmental threats pose system security risks and can be addressed with specific mitigation techniques.

Environmental Threat	Effects and Mitigations
Fire	Fire, whether natural or deliberately set, is a serious network environment security threat because it can destroy hardware and therefore the data contained in it. In addition, it is hazardous to people and systems. You need to ensure that key systems are installed in a fire-resistant facility, and that there are high-quality fire detection and suppression systems on-site so that the damage due to fire is reduced.

Environmental Threat	Effects and Mitigations
Hurricanes and tornadoes	Catastrophic weather events such as hurricanes and tornadoes are major network security threats due to the magnitude of the damage they can cause to hardware and data. You need to ensure that your information systems are well-contained and that your physical plant is built to appropriate codes and standards so that damage due to severe weather is reduced.
Flood	A flood is another major network security threat that can cause as much damage as fire can. Your organization should check the history of an area to see if you are in a flood plain before constructing your physical plant, and follow appropriate building codes as well as purchase flood insurance. When possible, construct the building so that the lowest floor is above flood level; this saves the systems when flooding does occur. Spatial planning together with protective planning in concurrence with building regulations and functional regulations are precautionary measures that should be looked into as well.
Extreme temperature	Extreme temperatures, especially heat, can cause some sensitive hardware components to melt and degrade, resulting in data loss. You can avoid this threat by implementing controls that keep the temperature in your data center within acceptable ranges.
Extreme humidity	Extreme humidity can cause computer components, data storage media, and other devices to rust, deteriorate, and degrade, resulting in data loss. You can avoid this threat by ensuring that there is enough ventilation in your data centers and storage locations, and by using temperature and humidity controls and monitors.

Theft

You must find a way to prevent theft of both data and hardware. The items most often stolen are portable devices such as laptops, tablets, and smartphones. These pieces of hardware often have highly valuable data on them. You can physically secure laptops and tablets by using a cable, but determined thieves will cut through a cable. You can install software and encrypt the information on all of these portable devices to make it more difficult for the thieves to access the information contained on the devices.

Another type of theft is theft of software and licensing. Most software has a software license agreement that allows the user to install and use the software on a single computer. Unless the license explicitly states that the software can be used on more than one computer, installing it on additional computers is illegal. Also, be sure that you are buying legitimate copies of the software and not bootlegged copies.

ACTIVITY 7-1
Identifying Security Threats

Scenario

As part of your internship, you are working with the security team to create a security policy for the company. There currently isn't anything in writing about how to protect systems from hackers or protecting hardware and data from being stolen. Recently, there have been several viruses discovered on computers. One of the employees had his laptop stolen from his hotel room while he was traveling. Also, some of the old equipment was recently set out on the shipping dock awaiting disposal and some of it seems to have gone missing.

---

1. **What should be included in the policy manual regarding virus protection?**

2. **How can computing devices be secured while an employee is traveling to help prevent theft of the devices?**

3. **Why should the organization be concerned about someone taking old equipment that was going to be recycled anyway?**

TOPIC B

Apply Security Best Practices

You've just learned about the different types of security threats to computers and networks. Some of the threats are introduced to the network by the actions of a single user; other threats and attacks can be more widespread in nature. This topic addresses some of the ways you can protect your computers and network.

Types of User Accounts

Windows includes several built-in user accounts to provide you with initial access to a computer.

User Account	*Provides*
Administrator	Complete administrative access to a computer. This is the most powerful account on a computer and should be protected with a strong password. In some situations, you might also consider renaming this account.
Standard User	Access to use most of the computing software on the computer. However, higher permission is required to uninstall or install software and hardware. This account also limits the configuration of security settings, operational settings, and deletion of necessary system files. This account is sometimes referred to as a non-privileged user account.
Guest	Limited computer access to individuals without a user account. By default, the **Guest** account is disabled when you install the operating system. You enable this account only if you want to permit users to log on as a guest.

Note: Other operating systems have similar types of accounts.

Authentication

User authentication is a network security measure in which a computer user or some other network component proves its identity in order to gain access to network resources. There are many possible authentication methods; one of the most common is a combination of a user name and a password.

There are three phases in the user access process that a person or system must perform in order to gain access to resources:

- Identification: The claim of identity made by the user when entering a user name and password.
- Authentication: The verification of that claim.
- Authorization: The action taken as a result of verifying the claim.

Authentication Factors

Most authentication schemes are based on the use of one or more authentication factors. You can combine these authentication factors for multi-factor authentication. The factors include:

- Something you know, such as a password.
- Something you have, such as a key or an ID card.
- Something you are, including physical characteristics, such as fingerprints.

Multifactor authentication is any authentication scheme that requires validation of two or more authentication factors. It can be any combination of who you are, what you have, what you know, where you are or are not, and what you do. Requiring a physical ID card along with a secret password is an example of multi-factor authentication. A bank ATM card is a common example of this. Keep in mind that multi-factor authentication requires the factors to be different, not just the specific objects or methods.

Single Sign-On

Single sign-on (SSO) is an access control property that you can use to provide users with one-time authentication to multiple resources, servers, or sites. Users log in once with a single user name and password to gain access to a number of different systems, without being asked to log in at each access point. Different systems may use different mechanisms for user authentication, so SSO has to use different credentials to perform authentication. With the widespread use of SSO, it is important to ensure that user authentication is strong for the login; with one potential user name and password providing access to a host of systems, it is critical that this single access point is being properly secured.

Password Management Best Practices

You should ***always*** change any default passwords to strong passwords to protect your computer and data. A strong password is one that cannot be easily guessed by others and is often referred to as a complex password.

To create a strong password:

- Use at least seven characters.
- Use a combination of uppercase letters, lowercase letters, numbers, and symbols.
- If you are replacing a previously created password, make sure that your new password is significantly different from the last one.
- Do not use common words, your name, your user name, or other words that people might associate with you, such as a pet's name.

A password is your access to your computer, and it should be protected so that the information on your computer is safe and inaccessible to others.

To protect your password, make sure that you:

- Do not write it down or share it with others.
- Do not use your network password for other purposes.
- If you are a computer administrator, create a new administrator account other than the normal login for security purposes.
- Do not re-use passwords.
- Change your password at least every 60 to 90 days, especially if your account is not configured so that the password expires automatically.
- Always use password protection whenever you're given the option.
- Change your password if you suspect that it has been compromised.
- Do not save your password on the computer.

Password-Protected Screen Savers

Setting a password to your screen saver is a security measure that prevents unauthorized access to confidential information and passwords associated with your user account. This can be enabled by checking the **On resume, display logon screen** check box in the **Screen Saver Settings** dialog box.

Device Hardening Best Practices

One important risk mitigation technique is device hardening. *Device hardening* is a collection of security tasks used to reduce the scope of the device's vulnerability and attack surface. There are many technologies included with today's devices, some of which you use often, some that you need to use only occasionally, or some that you never use. You might not always be in front of your device and attackers might take advantage of an unattended device to illicitly access information on the device or the network to which it is connected.

Disabling features you don't regularly use is one way you can harden your device against attack. Making sure you lock the screen on unattended devices is another prudent method of hardening devices against unwanted intruders.

The following table summarizes some device hardening techniques.

Device Hardening Technique	*Description*
Timeouts and lockouts	User accounts should be configured so that after a specified number of incorrect login attempts, the account is locked. The account can be configured to remain locked until an administrator unlocks it for the user, or it can be configured to remain locked for a specified amount of time. The lockouts and timeouts are a common method used to prevent attackers from breaching a user account by trying to guess the user's password.
Software firewall	Although most desktop and server operating systems ship with a pre-configured software firewall, today's mobile devices still do not have any such protection. *Firewalls* use administrator-defined rules to inspect traffic flowing in and out of a device. They look for and block malicious packets. A firewall can inspect each packet individually (stateless packet filtering) or watch whole conversations between the device and some other node on the network (stateful packet filtering). Firewall rules can be based around any of the following criteria: • IP addresses • Domain names • Protocols • Ports • Keywords/phrases • Types of files (such as executables or images) A good firewall should offer the following services: • Packet filtering: Stateless inspection of each packet against a pre-defined rule set. • Stateful inspection: Monitoring of an entire session of Transmission Control Protocol (TCP), from handshake to teardown, or User Datagram Protocol (UDP), through requested and opened ports. • Content filtering: Permit or block specified attachment and payload types, keywords, and file formats. • Proxying: Placing the client session on hold while retrieving content on behalf of the client and caching the content for later use.
Antimalware	As we have mentioned previously, make sure that a good antivirus program is installed on your system. Make sure the virus definitions are kept up-to-date. In addition, you might install ad blocking software. Be sure to use antivirus software on desktop, laptop, tablet, and smartphone devices.

Device Hardening Technique	Description
Disable Bluetooth	Bluetooth technology connects headsets and audio headphones, keyboards, and even printers to computing devices, especially mobile devices. It is rarely secured. For this reason, these devices are also potentially subject to bluejacking and bluesnarfing as their communications and data can be accessed easily. If you don't use Bluetooth devices, or only use them occasionally, you should consider disabling the service so it isn't used to compromise your system. *Bluejacking* is a method used by attackers to send out unwanted Bluetooth signals from mobile phones and laptops to other Bluetooth-enabled devices. Because Bluetooth has a 30-foot transmission limit, this is a very close-range attack. With the advanced technology available today, attackers can send out unsolicited messages along with images and video. These types of signals can lead to many different types of threats. They can lead to device malfunctions or even propagate viruses, including Trojan horses. Users should reject anonymous contacts and configure their mobile devices to the non-discoverable mode. *Bluesnarfing* is a method in which attackers gain access to unauthorized information on a wireless device by using a Bluetooth connection within the 30-foot Bluetooth transmission limit. Unlike bluejacking, access to wireless devices such as mobile phones and laptops by bluesnarfing can lead to the exploitation of private information including email messages, contact information, calendar entries, images, videos, and any data stored on the device.
Disable NFC	*Near Field Communications (NFC)* is used on smartphones and other mobile devices to enable radio communication when the devices touch each other or are a few centimeters apart. Any time you don't need to use this feature, turn it off to prevent intruders from accessing your phone or mobile device.
Encryption options	*Encryption* is the process of converting data into a form that is not easily recognized or understood by anyone who is not authorized to access the data. Only authorized parties with the necessary decryption information can decode and read the data. Encryption can be one-way, which means the encryption is designed to hide only the cleartext and is never decrypted, or it can be two-way, in which the encryption can be decrypted back to cleartext and read.

Wireless Networking and Security

Whenever possible, use a secured wireless network rather than an open wireless network. Open wireless networks are a major security risk when accessed directly. Because they are insecure, attackers can perform any number of attacks on the network, as well as compromise every user's communications. The protocols used on a secure wireless network help protect your data from attack.

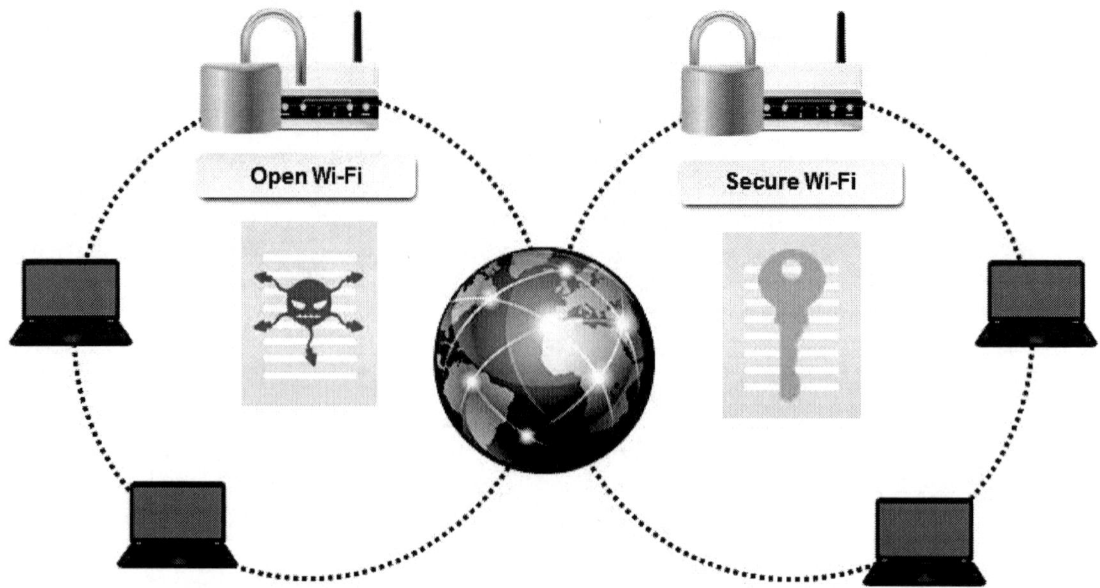

Figure 7-3: Open Wi-Fi vs. secure Wi-Fi.

Email Best Practices

If there are noticeable changes to an email account, such as an excess amount of spam or you find that there have been emails sent from the account that the email account owner was unaware of, then the computer's security has been jeopardized. Suspicious email issues to be aware of include:

- **Spam** is an email-based threat where the user's inbox is flooded with emails that act as vehicles carrying advertising material for products or promotions for get-rich-quick schemes and can sometimes deliver viruses or malware. Spam can harbor malicious code in addition to filling up your inbox. Spam can also be utilized within social networking sites such as Facebook and Twitter.
- **Hijacked email** is an account that has been accessed by an attacker and is being used by the attacker to send and receive emails. This means that an attacker can read, edit, and send email messages from an account. In a corporate environment, a hijacked email account can result in unauthorized data access.

Avoid selecting links in emails whenever possible. Sometimes an email message looks like it came from a legitimate source with the correct logos, but look for misspellings and bad grammar. This is a good indication that the message is not actually from specified source. Look at the address of the sender as well. If the email address doesn't seem to match the content, then delete the message.

If you don't know the sender, do not open any attachments to the email message. Even if you do know the sender, be careful of opening attachments that you weren't expecting to receive. Someone may have hacked the sender's account and the message could easily contain malware.

If you discover that your email account has been compromised, the first thing to do is change your password and alert the network administrator. You should also perform a complete scan of your system with antivirus software to locate and remove any malware that might have been introduced onto your system.

Cloud Storage Best Practices

Cloud storage has become a very popular method for backing up data and for sharing data. Many providers offer cloud storage. Some of the most popular include Microsoft's OneDrive, Google's GoogleDrive, Apple's iCloud, and Dropbox. There are other providers as well. You will need to research to see which one provides the amount of storage and access you are seeking and how much it will cost.

Some things to consider when deciding to use cloud storage include:

- Which data do you feel comfortable storing in the cloud?
- How much encryption will you place on content stored in the cloud?
- Will the cloud be your primary backup location?
- What other backup locations will you need?

As with any other service that has user names and passwords, make sure not to share your credentials.

Security Software Alerts

As fast as software companies update and patch vulnerabilities in their software, attackers come up with new ways to breach the software. This includes operating system software as well as application software and mobile apps. You might see alert boxes pop up on your display letting you know that new patches and updates are available for your software. Be sure to apply them in a timely manner. In some organizations, users are not allowed to install the updates themselves. This is usually because the IT department needs to test the patch before deploying it throughout the organization. The patch might cause issues with features that you use in the software or with how the application interacts with other applications on your system.

You might see pop-up messages saying that you need to install updates to your software, but it is for software that you don't actually have installed on your device. This is often the case for alerts from antivirus software that you don't have installed. If you see such an alert for an application that you don't have installed, but sure ***not*** to select the link for the update. Having conflicting antivirus software applications on your system can prevent either of them from trapping attacks on your system.

Guidelines for Applying Security Best Practices

Note: All of the Guidelines for this lesson are also available as checklists from the **Checklist** tile on the CHOICE Course screen.

An effective security policy clearly states the organization's policies on how best to protect hardware and software from unauthorized access.

To apply security best practices and prevent unauthorized access to your systems and data, use these guidelines:

- Disable or rename default user accounts.
- Use the Administrator account only when necessary, and use a regular user account the rest of the time.
- Safeguard your authentication credentials by not sharing them with anyone or posting them where they are visible. Consider using multi-factor authentication methods.
- Consider using SSO so that signing in to the device also signs you in to the applications or services you use on the device.
- Make sure passwords are not dictionary words, are easily remembered but not easily cracked, and are never shared.
- Harden devices by:
    - Implementing lockouts and timeouts when the wrong password is entered after a specified number of times.
    - Configuring a software firewall to protect mobile device data.
    - Disabling Bluetooth and NFC when not in use.
    - Installing antivirus software and keeping it up to date.

    - Encrypting data.
- Avoid connecting to unsecured wireless networks.
- Be aware of suspicious email messages that aren't from who they say that they are from. Be sure that you change your password if your account has been compromised.
- When using cloud storage, be sure the data is encrypted.
- Install patches and updates to applications as soon as possible to address security alerts. Most patches are designed to protect you from security holes in the application.

ACTIVITY 7-2
Applying Security Best Practices

Scenario

You are assisting in the creation of a security policies document at Develetech. The section of the document you are currently working on deals with making sure all employees have a secure user experience. This includes having the appropriate type of user account, secure authentication methods, that their devices are secure, and that they practice safe use of apps, email, and cloud storage.

---

1. **In this organization, some employees travel between sites. This group of users does not use laptop computers, but does use desktop computers at each of the sites they visit. Which type of user account should be created for these users and how can they be sure not to leave traces of their presence on the computers they use?**

2. **Users who travel between sites have been using thumb drives to take their documents with them to other sites. You suggest that they use Microsoft OneDrive instead. What are pros and cons of using OneDrive versus a thumb drive?**

3. **Sales team members have smartphones, tablets, and laptops they take with them when they travel. What policies should be put in place to keep these items secure?**

TOPIC C

Perform Secure Web Browsing

Web browsers can store information that you enter, such as the URLs of sites you visit, items you add to an online shopping cart, user names and passwords, and other information. This can make it easier and faster for you to access sites, but if the information falls into the wrong hands, your user name, password, credit card information, and even your identity can be compromised.

So much of our personal and professional time is spent browsing the Internet and using it for email communications, industry research, business transactions, online shopping, and entertainment. The openness of the Internet and web browsing also opens the door to security threats that can range from annoying to destructive. It's important to know about and apply the web browsing best practices introduced here.

Cookies

A *cookie* is a text file that is created by a website and placed on a computer's hard drive to store information that is used to identify users and, possibly, to prepare customized web pages for them. A cookie can store technical information about the user's actions at a website, such as the links the user clicked. It also stores personal information, but not before the user completes a form or clicks buttons that indicate interests.

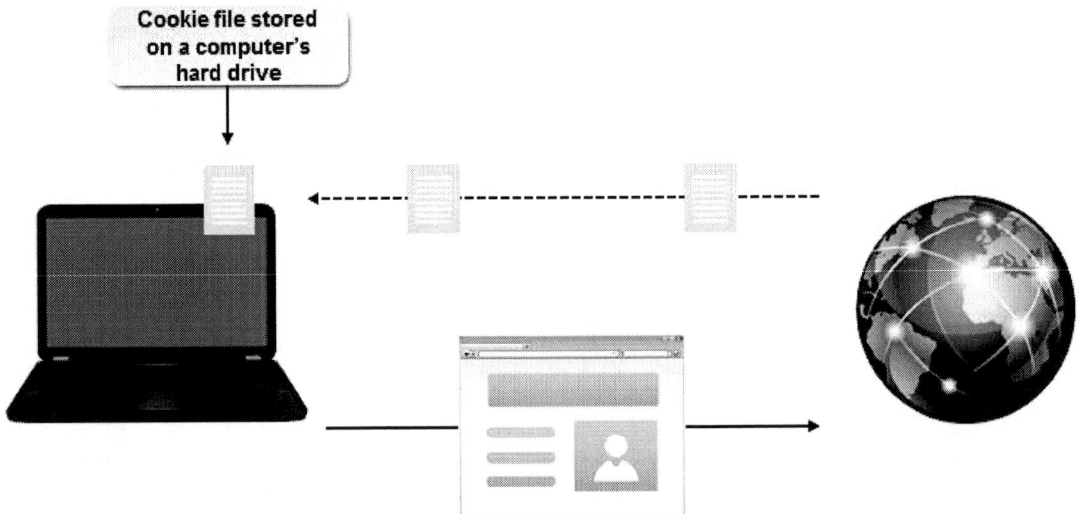

Figure 7-4: A cookie file with user information.

Cookies can be temporary or persistent. Temporary cookies, which are also referred to as session cookies, are stored on a computer only for the duration of the web session. They are deleted once the browsing session ends. Persistent cookies are saved on the hard drive and remain there even after the browsing session ends. Once a website's persistent cookie is stored on a computer, the browser sends the cookie back to the originating website to be reread or updated on any subsequent visit or request from that website.

Note: Cookies can also be first-party or third-party cookies. First-party cookies originate on, or are sent to, the website that is currently being viewed. Third-party cookies originate on, or are sent to, a website other than the one currently being viewed, such as an advertising or a marketing site.

Internet Cache

An *Internet cache* is a local storage area that holds the files saved by a web browser to decrease the time it takes to reload a web page. The browser cache includes all the text, image, and script files necessary to create and display a given web page when you first access it. When a web page that has been cached is changed, you might not see the most current information unless you clear the cache or manually reload the page. Also, some secure websites, such as those associated with banks, might cache personal information that you supply.

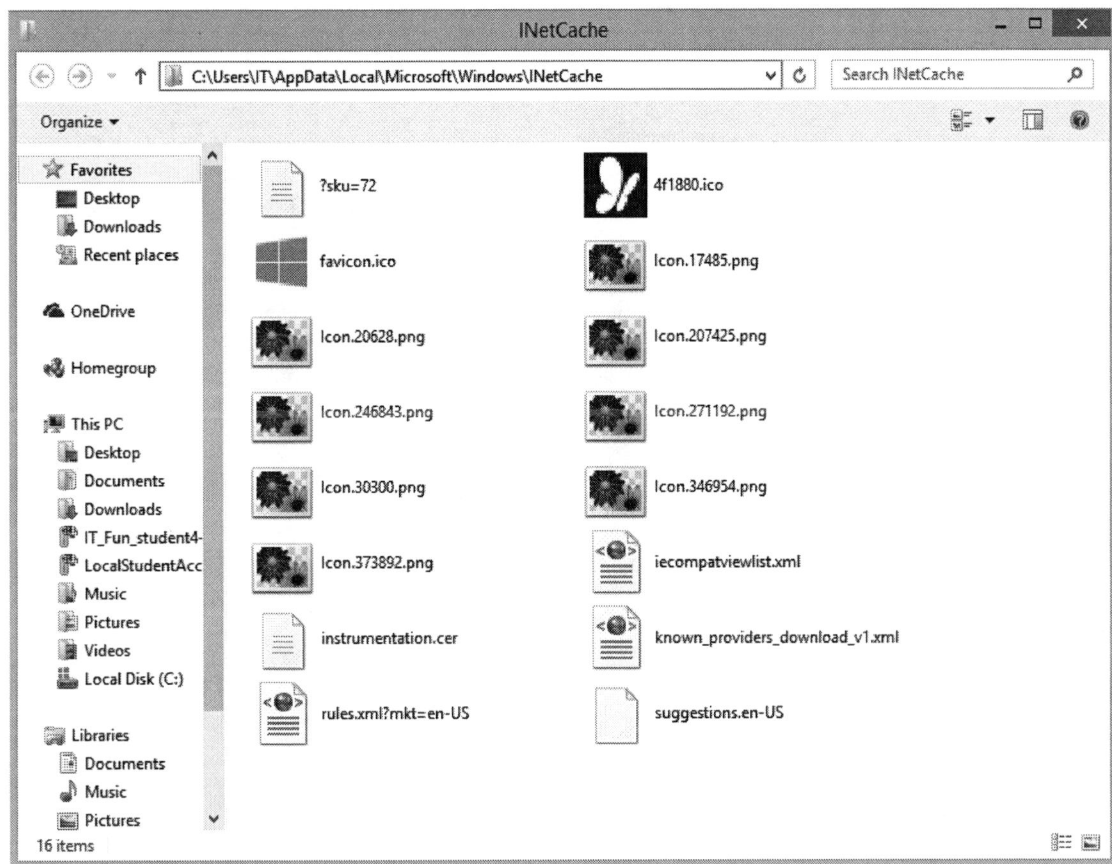

Figure 7-5: Web pages stored in a local folder.

If you visit secure websites on a shared computer, clearing the browser cache can help keep your personal information safe. In Internet Explorer, the browser cache is referred to as **Temporary Internet Files.**

Browser Enhancements

By default, web browsers can process and display HTML code, but many websites include additional content that the browser isn't initially designed to display. You can install additional software that enables you to view and interact with this additional content.

Browser enhancements include:

- Plug-ins: A *plug-in* enables the browser to process specific types of content. For example, the Adobe® Flash® player plug-in enables you to view Flash files. Other commonly installed plug-ins include the Java plug-in to allow Java applets on the page to run in a Java virtual machine on your computer and video player plug-ins.

  If you browse to a site that uses a plug-in that you don't currently have installed, a message will appear at the top of the browser page prompting you to install the plug-in. Typically, you will download an installation file, and then run the executable file to install the plug-in.

- Extensions: An extension adds additional features to the browser and becomes part of the browser application. Some of the extensions users install might enhance the browser by adding toolbars, shortcut menu options, or helper objects that are loaded each time the browser is launched.

As with other software, developers often need to update plug-ins and extensions. This might be to address security concerns or to increase or enhance functionality. You should update the plug-ins and extensions whenever you are prompted to do so.

If you find that you are not using a plug-in, or that a plug-in has been installed without your knowledge, you should disable it. If you find that a plug-in is a security risk, you should block it. Some browsers will automatically block any plug-in that is outdated or hasn't been used for some time. Plug-ins can be disabled by using the Settings feature of your browser.

Digital Certificates

A *digital certificate* is an electronic document that provides for the secure exchange of information over a network. A certificate can verify the validity of a website, the identity of a person, or the integrity of a file. Certificates are digitally signed by the issuing authority and can be issued to users, computers, services, or files. In many cases, digital certificates work in the background, but sometimes you have to decide whether or not to accept one when you are downloading programs or files. If you do not accept the certificate, you probably won't get access to the file or service.

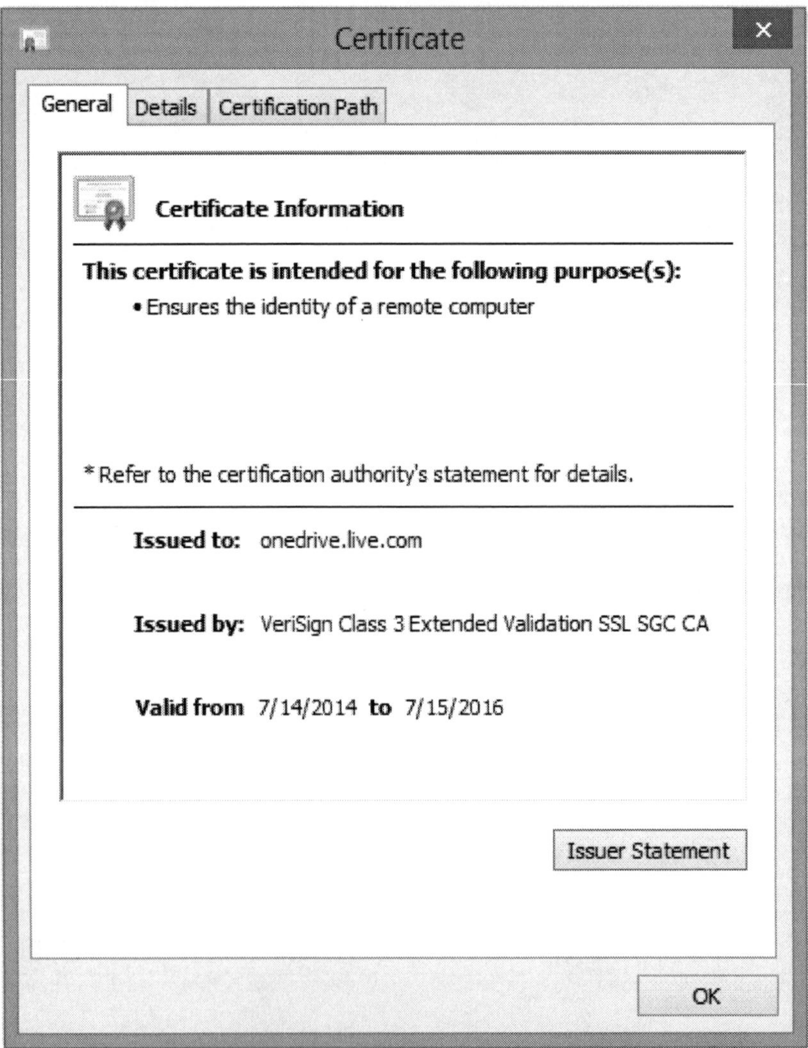

Figure 7-6: Certificates ensure the security of information exchanged.

Invalid Certificates

When you attempt to access a site, you might receive a warning that the digital certificate is invalid. If this is happening on all of the sites you visit, you should check to see if there is a browser update available or try a different web browser. You should also check that your date and time are correct on your computer. Certificates are issued to be valid for a set period of time. If you access the site before or after the certificate is valid, then you will receive a message that the certificate is invalid.

If the certificate has been tampered with, then you will also receive an invalid certificate warning message. If the site content has been tampered with, it can also invalidate the certificate.

Unless you are very sure that the site is safe, do not access a site that displays an invalid certificate warning. In fact, most browsers will not allow you to access a site if the warning is displayed.

Secure Web Connections

Attackers often use seemingly valid web page components such as links and banner ads to mask their activities. Before you select a link to access an ad or a website, hover over the link or ad and look closely at the URL of the site to which you will be taken. Attackers often copy the content of legitimate sites onto their own server, but modify the content so that your information is directed to their server instead of the server of the site you thought you were accessing.

One of the first things to look at is whether they are using HTTP or HTTPS. Banks, PayPal, and other secure sites will always use a secure HTTPS URL. Attackers usually just use HTTP addresses. Look for additional information in the URL that shouldn't be there. In most cases, the address should be **https://www.*sitename*.com**. Attackers usually alter that address to include additional words or letters so that they could register the domain name, but still keep the *site*.com portion of the address. For example **https://www.paypal.com** would be the actual PayPal address, but **http://www.mypaypal.com** would not actually take you to the official PayPal website.

Look for the secure lock icon in the address bar or in the status bar, depending on which browser you are using. If you are going to a secure HTTPS site, the lock icon should be closed, indicating that you are actually on a secured HTTPS site.

Adware Symptoms

Symptoms of adware include:

- Your home page in your browser has been changed to something other than what you configured it to be.
- Your browser is loading pages noticeably more slowly than it previously did.
- Additional toolbars have been added to your browser.
- When you select a link in a web page, you are directed to a different page than where you expected to be taken.
- There are a lot of pop-up advertisements being displayed. In fact, sometimes there are so many ads appearing that you can't close them all, and they just keep on appearing.
- Additional programs have been installed and you did not install them.

Untrusted Sources

Different content has various ways of letting you know that the content is from an untrusted source. You might get a dialog box with a warning, or you might see a message displayed under the menu or toolbar. Java displays one type of icon for trusted content and a different icon for untrusted content.

You will be given the option to continue to load the content or to close the page. Unless you are positive that the content can be trusted, close the page.

Personal Identifying Information

Personal identifying information (PII) is any information that can be used to determine who a person is. This information includes a person's Social Security number, financial account information, or driver's license number. Preventing another person from using this identifying data is essential in protecting you from identity theft. You should never allow a browser to store this information.

Automated Forms

Avoid using the autofill feature of web browsers. Although it might make it easier for you the next time you need to enter the same information, if your computer or portable computing device falls into someone else's hands, the information is also available to them as well. Use the Settings feature of your browser to disable autofill of forms.

Browsing on Public Workstations

You now know many of the dangers that lurk in web browsers and online. When you are using your own computer, you can be sure that you have turned off all of the features that would make your online experience insecure. Public computers are available in libraries, Internet cafes, airports, some hotel conference centers, and other places. When you are using a public computer, or someone else's computer, there are certain precautions you can take to make sure your PII is safe.

Steps to take include:

- Log out of sites rather than just closing the web page.
- Log out of the computer as well as any sites to which you are logged in whenever you step away from the computer.
- Be aware of your surroundings and of other people who might be attempting to shoulder surf.
- Avoid entering sensitive information such as credit card numbers, financial institution logins, or any other private data.
- Be sure that the browser is not set up to remember your user name or password.
- Delete the temporary Internet files.
- Delete your browsing history.
- If your browser has a private browsing feature, use it.

There are also risks to using your own device if you are using it in a public place. Some precautions you can take when using your device in a public location include:

- Be aware of anyone attempting to shoulder surf.
- Install or apply a screen shield to prevent people from easily seeing what is on your screen.
- Connect only to secure wireless networks so that there is less chance of your data being intercepted.
- Turn off Bluetooth to prevent people from connecting to your device.
- Never leave your device unattended.

Guidelines for Performing Secure Web Browsing

Many people spend a good portion of their day online. You need to be aware of the risks when browsing the web and use common sense and available tools to make it as secure as possible.

To protect your own information and your organization's information, be sure to follow these guidelines:

- Make sure your browser is up to date. Security patches and updates fix any security holes that have been uncovered. Also, avoid using legacy browsers.
- Disable cookies and clear the browser cache and history to saved data whenever possible.

- When installing plug-ins and browser extensions, install only the ones required for your browsing. Disable any plug-ins, toolbars, and extensions that you are not using.
- If you access a site with an invalid certificate, be sure to close the page unless you are 100 percent positive that the page can be trusted.
- Avoid selecting suspicious links or banner ads. These are often the preferred method of attackers to gain access to your computer and data.
- Be aware of spoofed web pages that appear to be the web page of another company. The pages most likely to be spoofed are sites such as PayPal or financial institutions.
- If your browser has been infected with adware, be sure to clear the cache and cookies, reset passwords, and use your antivirus software to try to eradicate the infection. You might need to download additional software to deal with the adware infection.
- Be careful to protect your personally identifiable information including your Social Security number, driver's license number, financial account numbers, and log in credentials.
- If you are using a public workstation be sure to remove all traces of your activity when you are done using the workstation.

ACTIVITY 7-3

Securely Browsing the Web

Before You Begin

You have a connection to the Internet.

Scenario

You are continuing to work with the team that is creating the security policies document. Today you are working on the section regarding securely browsing the web. You want to make sure to include information about secure websites, digital certificates, how to recognize sites that might be malicious, and how to generally protect the user's browsing experience. You will try out the recommendations to see how they work.

---

1. **What recommendations would you make to include in the security policy regarding secure web browsing?**

2. Open Internet Explorer from the Windows 8 Start screen.
   a) If necessary, switch to the Windows 8 Start screen.
   b) On the Windows 8 Start screen, select the **Internet Explorer** tile.

3. Open an InPrivate tab.
   a) In the **Tabs** section of the window, select the **Tab tools** button.

   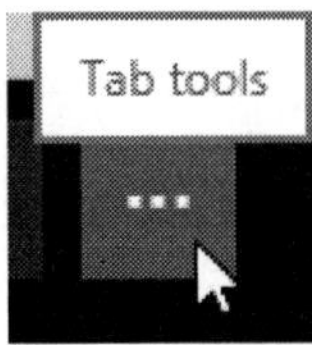

   b) Select **New InPrivate tab.**
   Notice that the left side of the address bar is now displayed InPrivate.
   c) Select the **InPrivate** button.

   A description of how InPrivate browsing helps keep your browsing experience secure is displayed.

4. Compare the address of secure and unsecured sites.
   a) In the address bar, type ***bing.com*** and press **Enter.**
   Notice that the address expands to **www.bing.com**.
   b) In the address bar, type ***google.com*** and press **Enter.**
   Notice that the address expands to **https://www.google.com**.

c) Select the **padlock** icon.

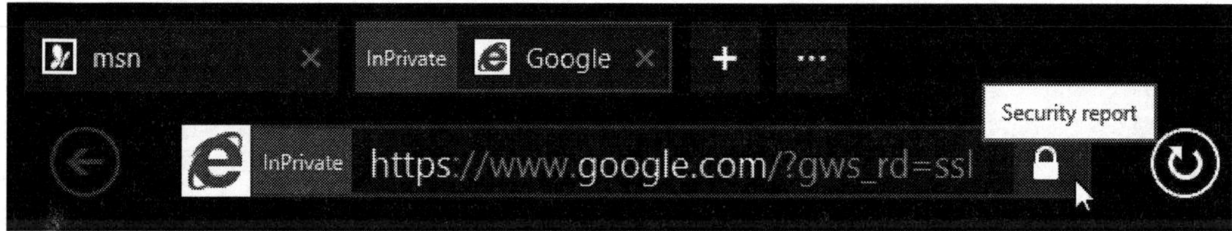

Information about the certificate for the secured site is displayed.

5. Clear data from the browser.
   a) Select the **Page tools** button, and then select **Options.**

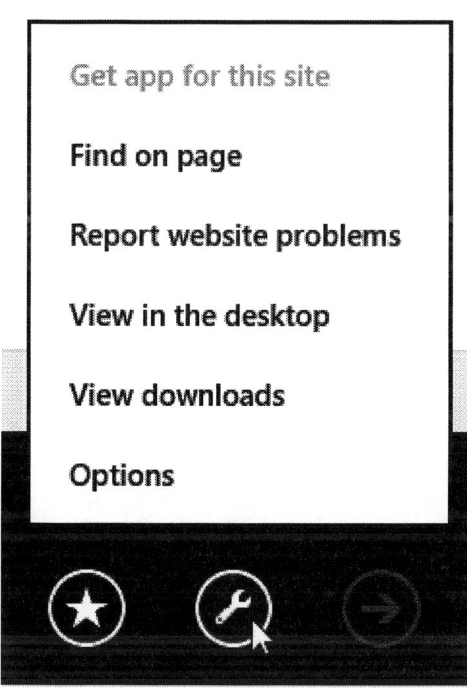

   b) Under the **History** section, select **Select.**
   c) Under **Delete these types of data** verify that **Cached images, Cookies** and **Browsing history** are checked.
   d) Select **Delete.**
   e) After the data has been deleted, select the **Back** button.
   f) Close Internet Explorer.

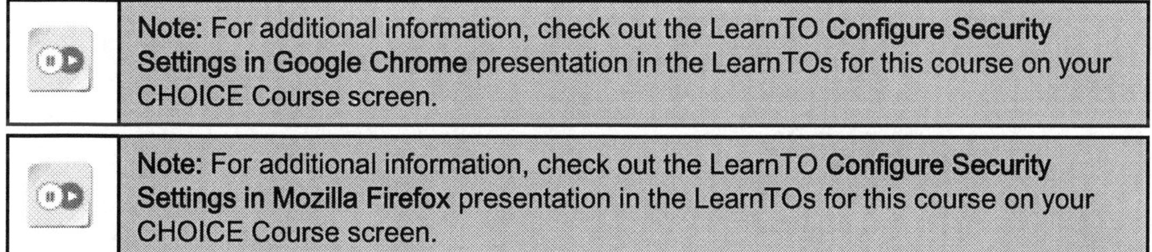

Note: For additional information, check out the LearnTO **Configure Security Settings in Google Chrome** presentation in the LearnTOs for this course on your CHOICE Course screen.

Note: For additional information, check out the LearnTO **Configure Security Settings in Mozilla Firefox** presentation in the LearnTOs for this course on your CHOICE Course screen.

Summary

In this lesson, you secured computing devices. By identifying security threats, applying security best practices, and performing secure web browsing, you can protect your computing systems and data from theft and unauthorized access.

What are the practices that might make your home or office computer vulnerable to social engineering exploits?

What security measures will you use to counteract possible social engineering attacks?

Note: Check your CHOICE Course screen for opportunities to interact with your classmates, peers, and the larger CHOICE online community about the topics covered in this course or other topics you are interested in. From the Course screen you can also access available resources for a more continuous learning experience.

8 Supporting Computers and Users

Lesson Time: 1 hour, 30 minutes

Lesson Objectives

In this lesson, you will support computers and users. You will:

- Describe the importance and impact of environmental and safety concerns.
- Back up and restore data.
- Manage software.
- Implement basic support measures.

Lesson Introduction

So far, you have built and configured a workstation, configured wireless devices, and identified some of the security risks involved with using computing devices. Now that you have a general understanding of how everything comes together, you can begin to explore ways to apply this knowledge to assist others. In this lesson, you will support computers and users.

Supporting computers and users involves many different sorts of tasks. From ensuring that people use their hardware safely and with minimal impact on the environment to protecting data by using backup and restore processes, managing software, and performing basic troubleshooting routines, the world of computer support can be exciting, sometimes frustrating, but ultimately rewarding.

TOPIC A

Environmental and Safety Concepts

Awareness of the latest trends in power-efficient technology combined with the support of energy-saving policies can help you ensure that you are getting the most life out of your equipment. However, most equipment eventually needs to be replaced after a certain amount of time. In this topic, you will describe the importance and impact of environmental and safety concerns.

It might seem harmless to throw away a single old laptop battery or monitor rather than go through the hassle of disposing of it properly. However, the effect of one million people each throwing an old monitor in the trash is the same as taking one million monitors and dumping them into a landfill. If each person decided not to do his or her part in recycling and disposing of unneeded materials responsibly, the effect on the environment would be disastrous. In addition, there are other environmental and basic safety concerns you need to be aware of as you begin to support computers and users.

Ergonomics

Ergonomics is the study of a person's efficiency at the workplace as it relates to his or her health, safety, and productivity. The Occupational Safety and Health Administration (OSHA) regulates ergonomic standards and guidelines for office situations. Chairs, workstations, keyboards, monitors, and other peripheral equipment (mouse, document holder, and so on) need to be adjustable so that they can be properly aligned or the individual users.

Figure 8-1: An ergonomically correct workstation.

Ergonomic Best Practices

Depending on the peripherals or components you work with, there are several ergonomic best practices you should follow:

- **Keyboard and mouse**: The keyboard and mouse should be directly in front of the person and within a comfortable reach. The placement of the keyboard and mouse is important to reduce repetitive stress injuries. To meet a user's abilities and working style, the keyboard and mouse should be adjustable and customized to his or her needs. For example, keyboards with a split layout offer a more natural hand placement. The ability to switch the primary mouse button for left-handed use is helpful. Additionally, the pressure required to tap the keys can vary among models and should be considered. Keyboard trays can be used to place the keyboard at the correct height. Wrist rests can provide additional support while typing. Many users now prefer to use a wireless keyboard and mouse as it gives them the freedom to place the devices anywhere on their desks.
- **Office furniture**: The height of the chair and the desk is critical for proper posture. Adjustable chairs are a must and should also provide lower-back support. Footstools might be necessary. For some, the ability to stand at the workstation helps to relieve lower-back pain. Another alternative to the standard office chair is balance ball chairs.
- **Monitor**: The top of the monitor needs to be at eye level to reduce eye and neck strain. Monitors should be adjustable both in angle and height. If necessary, place them on top of a stand to elevate them.

Note: For additional information, check out the LearnTO **Clean a Desktop Computer** presentation in the LearnTOs for this course on your CHOICE Course screen.

RoHS Guidelines

Restriction of Use of Hazardous Substances (RoHS) is a compliance directive launched in 2006 and enforced by the European Union that aims to restrict certain dangerous substances commonly used in electronic devices. These regulations limit or ban specific substances, including lead, cadmium, polybrominated biphenyls (PBB), mercury, hexavalent chromium, and polybrominated diphenyl ethers (PBDE) flame retardants, in new electronic and electric equipment.

The following table outlines the permitted amounts of materials restricted by RoHS guidelines.

Material	*Allowable Amount*
Lead	0.1% by weight at raw homogeneous materials level
Cadmium	< 0.01% by weight at raw homogeneous materials level
Mercury	100 parts per million (ppm) or less; not intentionally added
Hexavalent chromium	< 0.01% by weight at raw homogeneous materials level
Polybrominated biphenyls	0.1% by weight at raw homogeneous materials level
Polybrominated diphenyl ethers	0.1% by weight at raw homogeneous materials level

WEEE Directive

The Waste Electrical and Electronic Equipment (WEEE) is a directive launched in 2003 in Europe that serves a very similar purpose as the RoHS. It imposes the responsibility for the disposal of waste electrical and electronic equipment on the manufacturers of such equipment. It also requires companies that collect such waste to use it in an ecologically friendly manner, either by means of refurbishment or proper disposal.

Device Disposal Options

As equipment ages, it eventually reaches a point where repairing it or using it is no longer cost effective. There are a number of environmentally friendly alternatives to throwing out an old computer.

Disposal Option	Description
Donating	Rather than disposing of your computer, the best option for proper management of unneeded computer equipment is material recovery for all usable parts. If the equipment still functions, consider donating it to a local school or nonprofit organization.
Selling	Instead of throwing computers away, many companies have a retired equipment program in which desktops or laptops that are no longer supported by the company are sold to employees. Like donating, this ensures 100 percent reuse of materials and results in no waste. If you are looking to get rid of personal property, consider selling it at a garage sale or through an online auction site. Chances are good that there is a user who has lower demands of the hardware than you and will be content with it.
Bringing to recycling center	If you cannot find an individual or organization interested in your old computer or monitor, it is best to bring it to a location authorized in hardware recycling. This ensures that all hazardous components will be processed properly. Any useful components in the system may still be put to good use.
Shipping to vendors	Many computer manufacturers and computer hardware manufacturers also have their own recycling and/or trade-in programs. This information will likely be hosted on the website of the manufacturer.

Note: Before disposing of equipment, be sure that any storage devices have been removed or wiped clean to prevent data theft.

Disposing of Certain Devices

The following devices are common candidates for disposal, and you should observe proper environmental and safety precautions when disposing of them.

Device	Disposal Methods
CRT monitors	CRT monitors have a high concentration of lead, which could be a safety hazard if not disposed of properly. Some electronics retailers will accept your CRTs for recycling if you drop them off. If this isn't possible, you should contact your local sanitation department for instructions. You can also consult the Environmental Protection Agency's (EPA's) eCycle program. CRTs should never be thrown into the garbage.
Scanners	Like CRTs, some scanners contain toxic materials that, if thrown in the trash, may prove an environmental hazard. Donate the scanner to a manufacturer or retailer or contact a waste management authority.
Batteries	Manufacturers of alkaline batteries today have largely eliminated mercury from their products, so disposing of these batteries in the trash is safe. Keep in mind that this doesn't necessarily apply to older batteries, which you may need to dispose of as you would a scanner or CRT. Lithium-ion batteries used in laptops are also typically free of toxic materials and are safe to throw away normally. Due to a lack of cost-effectiveness, these batteries are typically not recycled at this point in time.

Device	Disposal Methods
Ink/toner	Different ink and toner manufacturers may include different materials in their product. Some, such as carbon black, may be carcinogenic to humans in large quantities. Many electronics retailers and manufacturers accept ink and toner cartridges for recycling, or even refilling. You should avoid throwing these cartridges in the trash.
Hard drives	Functioning hard drives are good candidates for donation or re-selling, but you should take care to wipe all data on the drive before giving it away. Malfunctioning or obsolete hard drives can usually be disposed of in the trash, as they do not normally contain toxic materials.

Device Placement

The environmental conditions in which you work can have an effect on the devices you work with. Computers operate best in environments that are protected against several different environmental hazards, as described in the following table.

Environmental Hazards	Description
Temperature	Extreme temperature conditions could cause computers to malfunction or break down. It is necessary to keep computers under normal temperature conditions. Airflow around a computer and its external devices helps to dissipate the heat generated, so make sure that the components have enough room around them to prevent overheating problems.
Humidity	Although too much moisture can be problematic and cause physical damage to equipment, low humidity can contribute to more electrostatic charge in the air. Computers function best in a relative humidity of 50 to 60 percent.
Dust	Dust can be a more subtle hazard as compared to humidity or temperature. The accumulation of dust particles over time can cause problems with different types of equipment. Excessive amounts of metallically conducive particles in the air can cause power supplies and other electronic components to shut down. Dusting equipment often can prevent these types of issues.
Electromagnetic interference (EMI)	EMI occurs when sources that output electromagnetic radiation interfere with your electronic devices. This interference can cause malfunctions in the affected equipment. Sources of interference can range from other electronic devices that operate in the electromagnetic spectrum, to natural causes such as rays of sunlight. You should therefore position your devices where they are less likely to conflict with other devices, and away from sunlight or other natural electromagnetic phenomena.

Ventilation Components

Ventilation components are essential to protect any electronic device from heat and dust.

Ventilation Component	Used To
Fans	Cool the internal components of a computer.
Ozone filters	Filter the ozone that is generated inside printers during the printing process.
Dust filters	Prevent dust from entering the critical components of a computer.

Power and Energy Efficiency

Reducing the amount of power and energy your electronics consume and output is a significant part of keeping your home or office environmentally friendly. What's more, power and energy efficiency can go a long way in saving you money on electric bills. As the technology used in computer devices evolves, the newer devices tend to be more efficient than their predecessors. For example:

- Liquid crystal display (LCD) flat-panel displays are a compact, lightweight alternative to traditional CRT displays. LCDs consume much less energy than CRTs and do not emit nearly as much electromagnetic radiation as CRTs do.
- A *solid state drive (SSD)* has no moving parts. This makes it more energy efficient than traditional hard drives. Also, mechanical failures and disk replacements are less likely.
- Because many companies cannot yet justify the high cost of solid state drives, there are now green Parallel Advanced Technology Attachment (PATA) hard drives that consume less power than regular hard drives. Advanced green hard drives can dynamically change their speed of operation depending on use, and they can power down sectors of the drive when data is not being sent or retrieved.
- A *network-attached storage (NAS)* device is used to supply file-based data storage services to other computers on the network. This may increase overall efficiency because the file serving is done by the NAS device and not by a file server, which is responsible for other processing.
- A Bluetooth version 4.0 wireless mouse or keyboard battery can last up to 5 or 10 years before needing to be replaced.

Energy Star

Energy Star is a U.S. government (Department of Energy and EPA) program to help individuals and businesses increase energy efficiency. One thing this program does is rate household products. Those products that meet Energy Star guidelines get to display the Energy Star logo. In addition, the EPA has systems for measuring and rating the efficiency of buildings.

The website **www.energystar.gov** contains information about the Energy Star specifications as well as product lists for a wide variety of categories, such as Electronics, Batteries, and Office Equipment. The Office Equipment category is categorized further into computers, displays, imaging equipment, small network equipment, and uninterruptible power supplies. For example, the monitors category lists both the Dell™ G2210t and Samsung™ SyncMaster 305T monitors.

Power Profiles

The **Power Options** in the **Control Panel** can be used to reduce the power consumed when the monitor and hard drive have not been active for a specific amount of time. You can adjust the settings so that the system uses less power when it has been idle for a certain amount of time, or you can enable hibernation. During Hibernate mode, the computer stores whatever it has in memory on the hard drive, and then powers down.

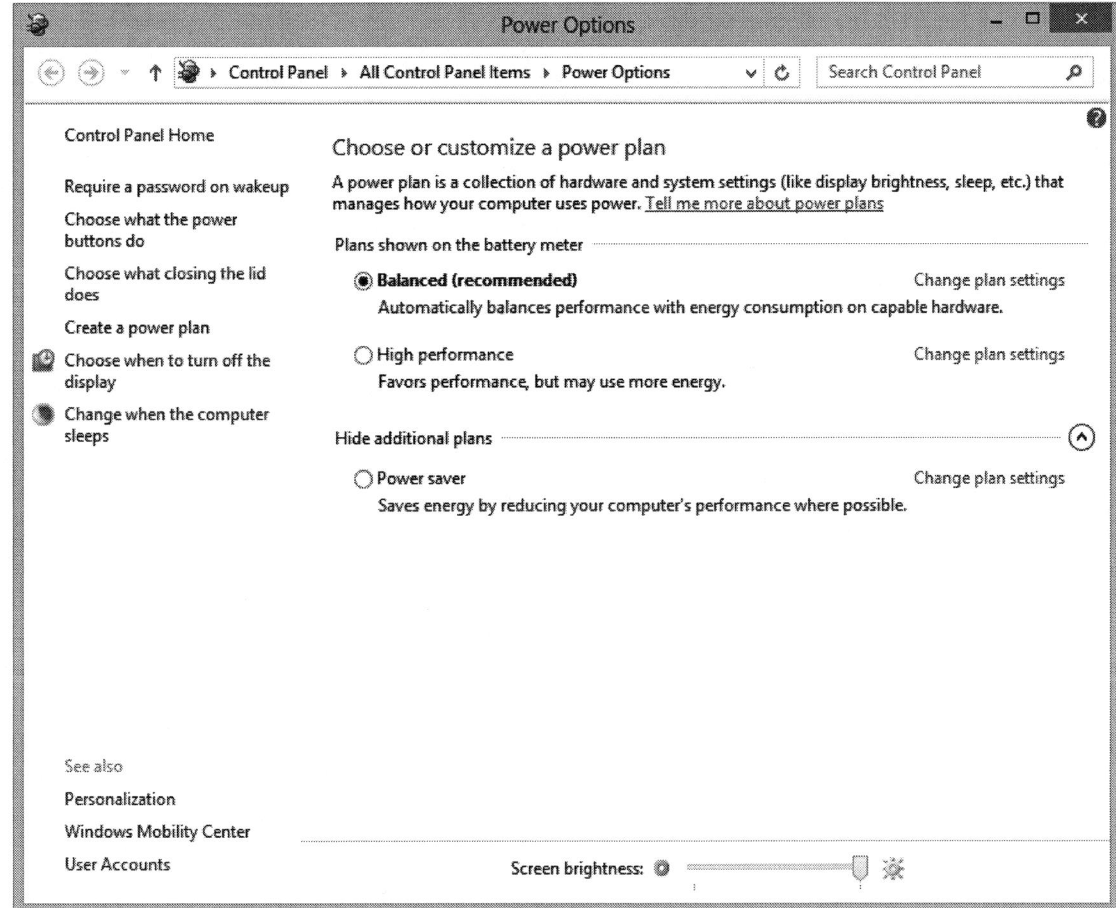

Figure 8-2: The Power Options dialog box.

To improve the power efficiency of your PC, there are standard recommendations for power management settings.

Function	*Setting*
Monitor/display sleep	After 15 minutes or less
Turn off hard drives/hard disk sleep	After 15 minutes or less
System standby/sleep	After 30 minutes or less

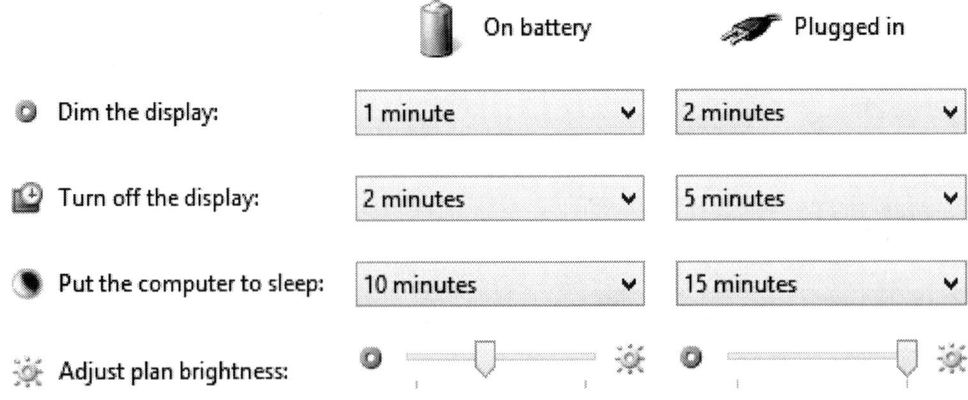

Figure 8-3: Power Saver plan options.

Power Supply Options

Appropriate power management is one of the most important maintenance techniques you can employ to maintain personal computer components. Use proper power devices.

- A *power strip* is a device that attaches to a power outlet in order to provide more outlets for you to use. This is convenient for providing power to multiple devices located in the same basic space. However, power strips alone do not provide any sort of protection against surges, outages, or any other anomalous electrical behavior.
- A *surge protector*, on the other hand, provides the additional outlets of a power strip with the added benefit of protecting connected devices from surges. A surge, or spike, is a quick change in voltage that can damage electronics. Surge protectors either block or divert unsafe voltage levels.
- An *uninterruptible power supply (UPS)* is able to provide power to connected devices in the event of a general power failure without interruption. It does this by storing a small amount of power in a reserve battery, which activates if there is no main power. This type of device is essential to server farms and data centers, as even a second of downtime could negatively impact business operations.

There are limitations to how much you can rely on any of the previously listed power devices. Although a UPS provides the best chance of keeping your systems from going down, there is still a very slight delay in crossing over from a wall outlet to the UPS. In most cases that delay will not result in your system going down, but not always. When purchasing a UPS, look at the rating for how long it will take to have the UPS take over supplying power. Remember that a power strip or surge protector will not supply any power if there is a power outage.

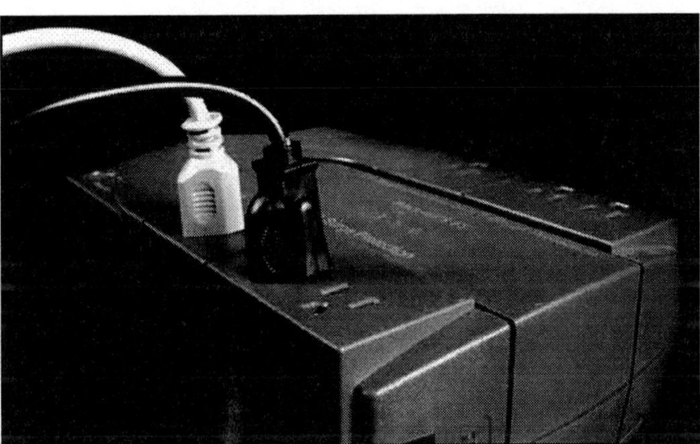

Figure 8-4: Power connectors connected to a UPS.

If you are traveling between countries, be sure that you have the appropriate power adapter for use with that country's power outlets. Kits can be purchased with appropriate adapter plugs for the United Kingdom, Europe, Asia, Australia, Africa, the Middle East, North America, and South America. In some locations, you will also need a voltage converter or transformer to step the power up or down as appropriate.

Note: For more information about the types of adapters used in various countries, visit rei.com/learn/expert-advice/world-electricity-guide.html.

The manual that comes with your device will include information about the power requirements and any limitations. Be sure to follow the manufacturer safety guidelines when using your device.

Electrostatic Discharge

Electrostatic discharge (ESD) occurs when a path is created that allows electrons to rush from a statically charged body to another with an unequal charge. The electricity is released with a spark. The charge follows the path of least resistance, so it can occur between an electrical ground, such as a doorknob or a computer chassis, and a charged body, such as a human hand. ESD can cause damage to people as well as sensitive computer equipment.

Antistatic Tools

The following table describes the common tools used in preventing ESD.

ESD Tool	Description
Antistatic strap	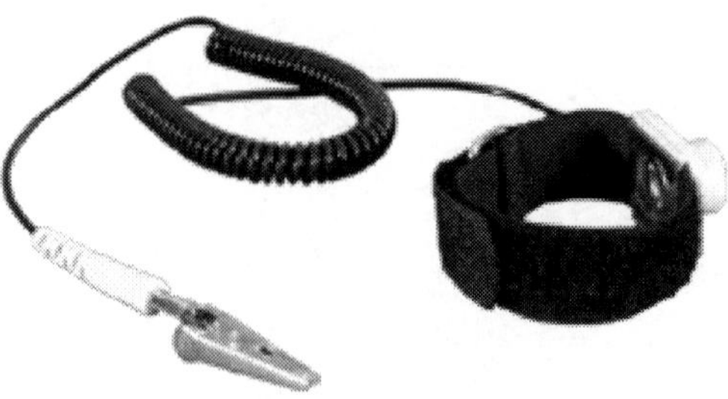 Antistatic straps are usually wrist straps made of stretchy fabric bound by a stainless steel clasp. A coiled retractable cable connects the wrist strap to ground. Antistatic straps can be worn by technicians to ground themselves. There are specially designed antistatic straps that can be worn on the legs. There are even antistatic garments.
Antistatic mat	 An antistatic mat is designed to carry static charges to ground from an electrical device. Grounded mats are usually used to cover the work surface and for the technician to stand on. The mats contain a snap that connects to a wrist or leg strap. It is very useful in protecting users and equipment from shock hazards.
Antistatic bag	 Antistatic bags are used for storing components but can be included in an ESD toolkit.

ESD Tool	Description
ESD smock	 An ESD smock, which covers from the waist up, can be helpful if the technician's clothing has the potential to produce static charges.

Note: Antistatic bags that are used for shipping components actually conduct electricity, so keep them away from equipment that is powered on.

Guidelines for Protecting Against ESD

Note: All of the Guidelines for this lesson are also available as checklists from the **Checklist** tile on the CHOICE Course screen.

You can work safely and efficiently on computer hardware devices if you protect yourself from potential hazards by taking the appropriate measures and precautions.

To ensure safety from electrical hazards:

- Unplug the device from its power supply before you start servicing it. Power supplies have a high voltage in them any time the device is plugged in, even if the device power is turned off. Before you start working inside the device cover, disconnect the power cord and press the power button to dissipate any remaining power in the system circuitry. Leave the power off until you are done servicing the unit.
- Perform only the work for which you have sufficient training.
- Do not attempt repair work when you are tired; you may make careless mistakes, and your primary diagnostic tool, deductive reasoning, will not be operating at full capacity.
- Do not assume anything without checking it out for yourself.
- Do not wear jewelry or other articles that could accidentally contact circuitry and conduct current.
- Plug wires and connectors into the appropriate sockets.
- Perform as many tests as possible with the power off.
- Suspend work during an electrical storm.
- Do not handle electrical equipment when your hands or feet are wet or when you are standing on a wet surface.
- Stand on a totally insulated rubber mat to increase the resistance of the path to ground and provide some protection for yourself. In some cases, workshops are located in areas with grounded floors and workbenches, so static electricity has a low-resistance, nondestructive path to ground.
- Employ proper ESD prevention measures.
- Power the device only after you ensure that it is completely dry.

- Label wires and connectors as you detach them, and ensure you plug them back into the proper sockets in the proper order.
- When you replace the device's cover, ensure that all the wires are inside. The cover may have sharp edges that can cut through exposed cables.
- Ensure that the appropriate power source and power protection is used. Information on this will be available in the device's documentation.
- Ensure that power cables and network connections are routed properly.
- Replace all faulty, damaged, and flayed wiring, insulation, and cords.
- Avoid powering the device from an overloaded circuit.
- Take special care when handling high voltage components.
- Maintain a dry work environment.

ACTIVITY 8–1
Discussing Environmental and Safety Concepts

Scenario

As an intern at Develetech working with the IT staff, you occasionally come across equipment that must be discarded. You have been given a number of items and were told that they must be disposed of, and you want to be sure you are making environmentally sound choices. Additionally, you have been tasked with identifying some of the technologies than can help reduce energy consumption.

---

1. **The Develetech staff has identified a dozen CRT monitors that are no longer going to be supported. What options should you consider as alternatives to throwing the monitors out? Which might you consider first?**

2. **Up until now, the location where you are working has been disposing of toner and ink cartridges by throwing them in the garbage. Why is this considered a hazard? What incentives exist to encourage users to recycle the cartridges?**

3. **True or False? If you shut a device off, it cannot draw any power from an outlet.**
   - ☐ True
   - ☐ False

4. **What characteristics of solid state drives allow them to be considered more "green" than typical hard drives? (Choose two.)**
   - ☐ They are physically smaller and consume less space within the enclosure.
   - ☐ There are no moving parts, which means less likelihood of failure and replacement.
   - ☐ Because all data is stored in solid state memory, information can be retrieved faster and with less power.
   - ☐ They are less expensive than a typical hard drive.

TOPIC B

Back Up and Restore Data

The most critical aspect of a computer system is the data stored within it. One part of computer maintenance tasks is to ensure the security of data. In this topic, you will back up and restore data.

The consequences of data loss can be devastating. Though there are many ways to recover data, it is best to restore it from backup files. Data backup and restoration ensures that your information is intact, even if there is data loss in the primary location.

Data Backups

A *data backup* is a type of information protection scheme that enables you to store copies of critical files and folders on another medium for safekeeping. Data backups can be local, or they can be network-based, where a network administrator backs up the data on network file servers and other network computers.

Figure 8-5: Data backup stores copies of files on another storage medium.

Importance of Data Backups

Backups protect against data loss due to disasters such as file corruption or hardware failure. In the event of a hard disk failure or loss of data, due to, say, a virus attack, you can still have your information intact if you have a backup of your files. You can recover the files without having to re-create them, thereby saving time and effort. Information backups are needed if the original source is no longer available for further reference.

Backup Methods

Data backups can be accomplished in several ways, including manually copying individual files and folders to another location, such as a CD-ROM, and using software specifically designed to assist you in backing up your data. Information that you back up is static, so if additional changes are made to a file after the backup, the backup copy will not include the changes.

Windows 8.1 comes with File History, which can be configured to automatically back up your files. To ensure your files are safely stored off of your computer, File History requires you to use an external storage device or a network drive. Once File History is turned on and your storage device is designated, it will run in the background, saving the different versions of your files from your libraries, Desktop, contacts, and favorites automatically. If you use an external storage device, you must leave it attached to your PC for File History to automatically back up your files. If you choose to, you can specify folders to exclude from your backup, specify how often backups are created, or begin a manual backup. File History is available as part of the Windows 8.1 **PC settings** app as well as a traditional Desktop app.

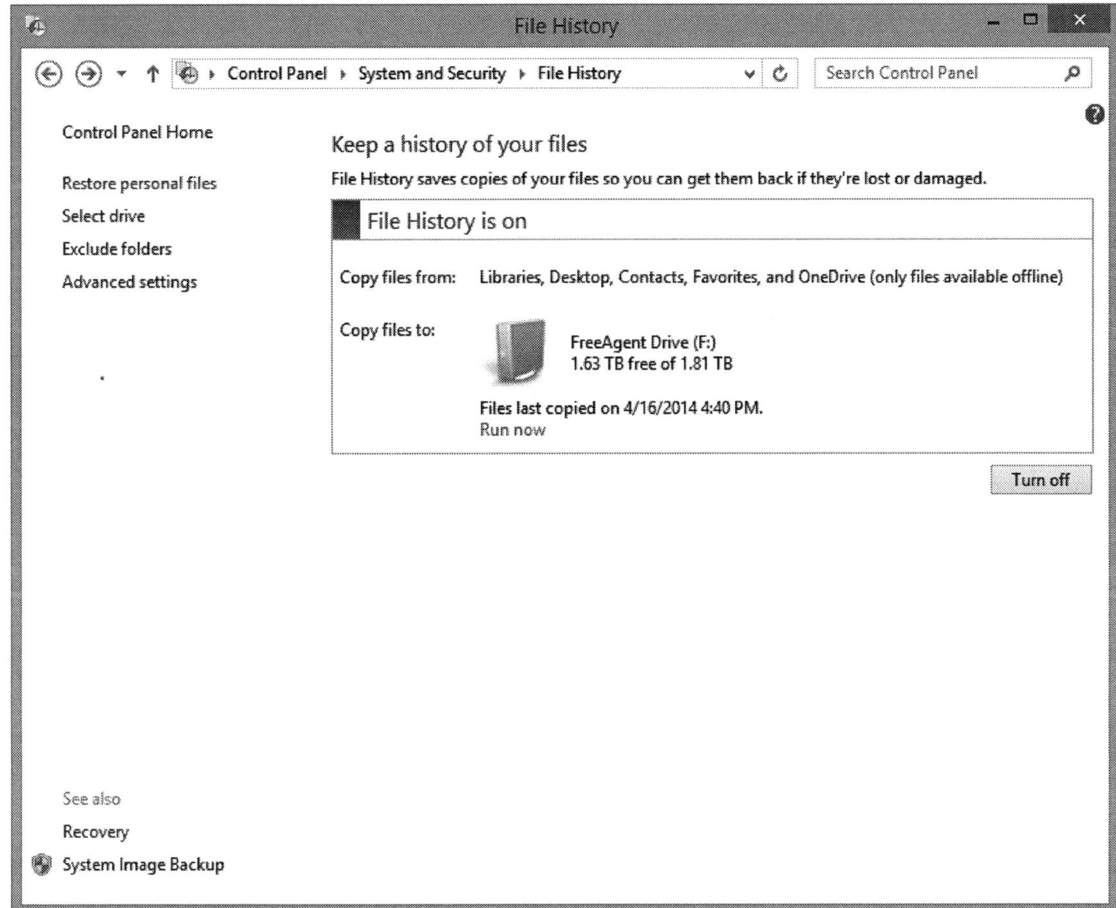

Figure 8-6: Using File History from the Desktop to back up data.

Backup Frequency and Schedules

Regular backups are necessary because a system failure can strike at any time. You may end up losing whatever changes you have made since the last time you created a backup, which could cost you time and money. That's why it's important to set your backups on a schedule. The actual scheduling frequency you choose will depend on the total size of your data, the number of files in that data, how sensitive that data is, how often the data changes, and how available and accessible that data must be to yourself and others. For example, you may back up the drives in your home office once a month, whereas a network administrator will likely implement real-time backing up of data on a network share that their employees use every day.

Backup Storage Media

There are different types of backup media on which you can store backed-up data. Aside from removable media such as USB thumb drives, DVD-ROMs, and so on, there are other storage media options, including:

- Locally attached storage, which refers to drives attached directly to workstations and servers through a connection such as Serial ATA (SATA). Although this is cost-effective for home or small-office use, it cannot match the speed and capabilities of other solutions.
- Offsite/cloud-based, in which you offload storage to a third party that takes over the burden of storing and maintaining your backups. This is an attractive option to companies that want to cut

costs or users who want to take advantage of powerful infrastructure that they cannot provide themselves. However, security is a major issue with cloud storage.

- Network-attached storage (NAS), which is a popular solution for small-to-mid-size companies that need to share network storage with dozens of employees in an efficient manner. This is a relatively inexpensive method of ensuring that you have multiple backups of your data, but it does require more expertise than locally attached storage to implement and maintain.

Backup Verification and Testing

Unless you routinely test your backups and verify that they are in an acceptable state, then your backup efforts may be in vain. This is especially true of data that is being backed up in real time—writing data to new storage always runs the risk of corrupting that data, and that risk increases over time. Without actually taking the time to test each backup medium, these corruption issues may go unreported. When a failure does occur, and you go to recover your data from a backup, you may find that it is unusable and your data may be lost.

Backup testing can be as simple as opening random files and folders on a backed up locally attached drive, or it can be a more complex process of accessing and restoring entire directories and drives periodically. However you go about it, testing your backups is an important part of protecting your data from loss.

Guidelines for Backing Up Data

To determine when and how to back up data, follow these guidelines:

- When you are determining what files to back up and how often to back them up, consider the costs of re-creating or replacing the information, and balance those costs against the costs of backing up data.
- Consider backing up your data or the entire system prior to installing new hardware or software, in case the installation does not proceed as smoothly as planned.
- Consult your organizational policies to determine if rules or guidelines for backups are included in them.
- Consider implementing a regular schedule for backups to protect your files.
- Consistently test your backups to verify that your data is intact and not corrupted.

ACTIVITY 8-2
Backing Up Data

Before You Begin

You will need a blank CD, DVD, or USB drive for this activity. You should have some files in your Documents folder.

Scenario

You will be responsible for backing up users' data before performing tasks such as installing updates, installing new software, or repairing hardware. You want to practice backing up data before you have to do it on a user's computer.

---

1. Insert a blank writable optical disc or plug in a USB drive to your computer.

2. Open the File History window.
   a) From the Windows 8 Start screen, display the **Charms** bar and select **Settings→Change PC Settings→Update and recovery→File History**.
   b) In the right pane, under **File History** slide the slider right to change the setting to **On.**

3. Open File History settings through Control Panel.
   a) Select the **Back** button to return to **PC settings.**
   b) Select **Control Panel.**
   c) In **Control Panel,** under **System and Security,** select **Save backup copies of your files with File History.**

4. Use the Advanced Settings to set scheduling options.
   a) Select **Advanced Settings.**
   b) From the **Save copies of files** drop-down list, select **Every 10 minutes.**

   Note: Normally, the default of every hour is sufficient; however, for class you'd like to be able to view the backup copies.

   c) Observe the size of the offline cache and how long versions will be saved. Accept the default settings.
   d) Select **Save Changes.**
   e) Select **Run now.**
   The backup will begin. When the backup is complete, the message will change to indicate the time of the last backup.

Data Restoration

Data restoration is a type of information protection scheme that enables you to recover stored copies of critical files and folders from another medium. A restore protects you against the loss of data due to disasters and goes hand in hand with data backups. Restored information will not include any changes made after the backed-up file was created. Data restoration can be local or network-based.

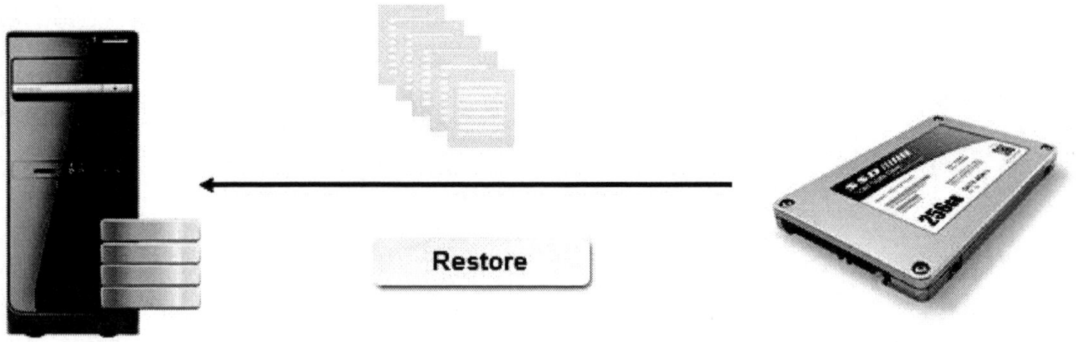

Figure 8-7: Data restoration restores backed up files.

Restoration Methods

Data restoration can be accomplished in several ways, including manually copying individual files and folders from another location, and using software specifically designed to assist you in restoring data. You can also restore a *system image*, or the entire state of an operating system and its corresponding software, by loading the image from a storage medium such as a DVD-ROM or USB thumb drive.

Microsoft® Windows® operating systems provide a variety of recovery tools. For example, Windows 8.1 includes **File History**, **System Restore**, and **Recovery**. Each of these is described in detail in the **Help and Support Center** for Windows 8.1.

Access the Checklist tile on your CHOICE Course screen for reference information and job aids on How to Back Up and Restore Data.

ACTIVITY 8-3
Restoring Data from Backup

Before You Begin

Your File History window contains at least one "event."

Scenario

You have backed up data by using File History and are ready to try restoring files from the backup. You want to see what was backed up to your removable media as well. You want to try replacing the file in its original location and restoring it to a different location.

---

1. Explore the files that were backed up.
   a) Open **File Explorer** from the Desktop.
   b) Navigate to the drive to which you backed up the files.
   c) Expand the folders under the folder **File History** to view what was backed up.

2. Restore files from the backup by using File History.
   a) Switch to the **File History** window.

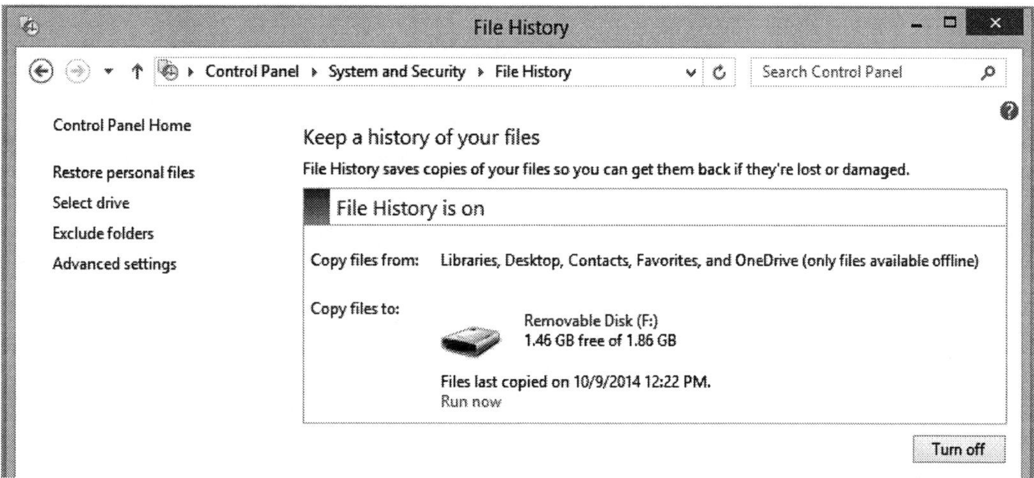

   b) Select **Restore personal files**.
   c) Expand the folders until you find some files.
   d) Select a file.
   e) Select the **Restore to original location** button.

   f) Close the **Replace or Skip Files** dialog box.
   g) Right-click the selected file and select **Restore to**.
   h) Select **Desktop** then select **Select Folder**.

i) Close all open windows on the desktop and verify that the file you restored to the **Desktop** is shown on the desktop.

TOPIC C

Manage Software

So far, you've examine environmental and safety concepts related to supporting computers and users, and you've backed up and restored data. Another important skill related to computer support is to administer the applications installed on computers. In this topic, you will manage software.

In the course of your work, you may come across people who desperately need to get a task done quickly and efficiently on their computers. These tasks may range from editing a picture to formatting a document. Many software applications are available to accomplish these tasks, and computers can end up with hundreds of applications installed. By managing software, you can ensure that applications are current, secure, and meet the needs of your users.

Software Management

Software management involves installing and updating operating system features, applications, and drivers, as well as obtaining the appropriate licenses. When considering what software to add or remove in your office environment, you should ask yourself the following questions:

- What applications do end users absolutely need to get their jobs done?
- What are the best products to fulfill this need?
- Can this product be easily uninstalled if necessary?
- What operating system features might be helpful to the end user?
- What operating system features might be beyond the scope of the end user's duties?
- Are these features easy to add and remove, if necessary?
- What drivers are available for the hardware that an end user uses?
- Are these drivers necessary, or are they optional?
- Will it be easy for you to roll back these drivers in case of incompatibility or other issues?

Software Versions

Versioning provides information about the iteration of the software you are using. Software versions are changed every time the software is upgraded or newer features have been added to it. Most vendors will clearly mark revisions to their products in sequential numbers, often with decimal points to indicate minor changes. For example, Windows 8.1 is a relatively minor update to the Windows 8 operating system. The "32" in Firefox version 32.0.3 indicates feature changes or major updates, whereas the two other numbers are usually reserved for minor bug fixes and security patches. The exact versioning scheme used by each piece of software may be different, but they tend to be similar.

Before installing software, you must consider compatibility issues to ensure that it works properly.

Compatibility Issue	Description
Hardware requirements	Hardware requirements vary with each piece of software, and a new version changes these requirements. Without the minimum hardware requirements, software will not function properly. The hardware requirements deal with central processing unit (CPU) specifications, random access memory (RAM) and hard disk space, display adapters, and peripherals.

Compatibility Issue	Description
Operating system compatibility	Software applications interact with the operating system to perform their tasks. Applications written for earlier versions of an operating system might not always work with your new operating system version, but you may be able to select an appropriate application compatibility mode for the application after you have upgraded the operating system.

Software Updates

A *software update* is the process of replacing a software application completely with a newer version. It can be done in two ways: either by replacing a few selected files only, or by completely overwriting the software. Software manufacturers release new software updates to make their software function better. Sometimes new features are included in a new release. Generally, you update software applications online by downloading the required files from the software manufacturer's website. Examples of *software upgrades* include a version change of an operating system, productivity applications, security utilities, or various other tools.

With many software products, especially operating systems, it's a good idea to keep its updates on a schedule. This way, you won't miss a crucial security fix and leave your system vulnerable to attack. *Automatic updates* is a feature of an operating system or a software application that enables updates to be downloaded and installed automatically on a system at a scheduled time or a certain frequency. After a manufacturer releases an update, it gets downloaded to your system the next time you connect to the Internet. You can configure the settings to allow for automatic installation of the updates the moment they are downloaded or to notify you of the downloaded update so that you can install it later. You can also disable automatic updates.

Risks Associated with Upgrading Software

As an IT technician, you will need to keep your system up to date with the latest software and hardware components to get the most out of your computer system. By upgrading a system, you are making changes to the parts of the system that can affect the functioning of the whole system. By identifying the risks associated with upgrading, you will know the things to consider before you make an upgrade to your system.

Software Licensing

software will often require that you purchase a license in order to legally confirm that you have the rights to use that piece of software. This license can extend to individual users on individual computers, or it may come in a multi-license (volume) form for enterprises that need many instances of software. Licenses typically entitle the licensee to a product or activation key, which you use to activate the software on a computer. Unactivated software may not function, or it may have limited functionality. This is why activating software, especially an operating system such as Microsoft Windows, is vital.

Because you may need to purchase and manage many different licenses for many different users, it's important to keep track of how licenses are used. There are some license management tools available, and you can also create a spreadsheet or database to map each license with its user or its computer. This way, no license will go unaccounted for, and you won't be forced to spend extra money to buy more.

Software Registration

It is always good practice to register the software you use. Registering your copy of a software application helps prevent software piracy. By registering the software, a user becomes eligible to receive regular updates, upgrades, and technical support.

Guidelines for Managing Software

Use the following guidelines when managing software:

- Identify which applications, operating system features, and drivers your users absolutely need to get their jobs done.
- Identify how easy it is to uninstall any of these pieces of software should issues arise.
- Identify the version numbers of the software you are looking to download.
- Identify any compatibility issues that these versions have with your hardware or operating system.
- Schedule a check for updates, such as through automatic updates, to keep your software at the most current version at all times.
- Obtain the necessary licenses and product keys for each piece of proprietary software.
- Manage and keep track of all licenses and product keys, mapping them to specific users and machines they are deployed to.

Access the Checklist tile on your CHOICE Course screen for reference information and job aids on How to Manage Software.

ACTIVITY 8-4
Managing Software Updates

Before You Begin

Notepad++ has been installed.

Scenario

One of your responsibilities as a Develetech intern will be to make sure that workstations are receiving updates to Windows 8.1 when they are available. You want to be able to review the updates before installing them, so you will modify the default to prevent automatically installing the updates. You also want to check to see if there are any updates for the Notepad++ application you installed previously.

---

1. Update the Windows operating system and related apps.
   a) From the **Charms** bar, select **Settings→Change PC settings.**
   b) Select **Update and recovery.**
   c) Select **Windows Update.**
   d) Select **View your update history.** Any updates that have been installed are listed.
   e) Select the **Back** button.
   f) Select **Choose how updates get installed.**
   g) Under **Important updates**, from the drop-down list, select **Download updates but let me choose whether to install them.**
   h) Verify that the check boxes under **Recommended Updates** and **Microsoft Update** are checked.
   i) Select **Apply.**
   j) Select the **Back** button.
   k) If necessary, select **Check now.** All available updates that haven't already been installed are listed.
   l) Select **View details.**
   m) Scroll through the list of updates. Notice that all of the updates in the **Important** category are checked by default. Other categories might be listed and the items might or might not be selected.
   n) Select **Install.**
   o) If prompted to restart, select **Restart now.** If you restarted the computer, log in again after the system has been restarted.

2. Check for updates for Notepad++.
   a) From the desktop, open **Notepad++.**
   b) From the menu, select **?→Update Notepad++.**
   c) If any updates are found, install them. If no updates are found, select **OK.**
   d) Close Notepad++.

TOPIC D

Implement Basic Support Measures

In the last topic, you managed software. The last main component of supporting users and computers is to perform basic troubleshooting skills. In this topic, you will implement basic support measures.

Problems in computer systems can happen at the most unexpected times. It is frustrating for the user when a computer system refuses to work and applications do not work properly. If you are considering an IT career, for example, as a computer support technician, your ability to quickly and effectively solve these problems will be essential in providing your users with the computing environments that they need to be able to perform their jobs.

General Troubleshooting Tips

Whenever you are attempting to resolve a problem, you need to keep some general points in mind. These are the basic troubleshooting steps you will want to take almost every time you face a device problem.

Tip	*Description*
Use common sense	Some solutions are very obvious if you examine the equipment. For example, a cable might be loose or disconnected. If a power strip is in use, is it turned on? Be sure to look for these obvious problems before delving too deeply into troubleshooting mode.
Check the physical connections	This might involve making sure the device is plugged in and connected to the computer, that it is connected to the right port, that an adapter card is fully seated in the slot, and so forth.
Check external issues	Make sure there are no loose cables or connections. Verify that the power is reaching the device: • Are indicator lights lit? • Is the power cord loose? • On a laptop, is the power cord securely connected to the transformer as well as the laptop and the outlet? Check for any physical damage. This is especially true for portable devices.
Check the adapter to which the device is connected	If you are having trouble with a device, it might not be a fault in the device. It might be a problem with the adapter or the adapter card to which it is connected. Be sure to troubleshoot the entire interface including the card, port, cable, and device.
Check **Device Manager**	An exclamation point (!) or X in red or yellow over a device indicates there is a problem. The **Properties** sheet of a device has a **Device Status** box that indicates whether the device is working properly. This box also contains a **Troubleshoot** button that accesses topics in the **Help and Support Center.**
Use the **Help and Support Center**	This Windows utility can guide you through the things you should check when troubleshooting a particular device problem.

Tip	Description
Check for a number of causes	Many times when you are troubleshooting a problem, you will find that there is more than one cause for the problem. In this case, you might need to combine several troubleshooting strategies to resolve the problem. Often, you will need to reboot to test whether your attempt to fix the problem has actually worked. If it did, great. If it did not, just keep trying to work your way through the rest of the list of possible solutions. If none of the solutions work for your problem, ask a colleague for help. Sometimes that second set of eyes sees the solution that you do not.

Common Operational Problems

You might encounter several problems when troubleshooting PC hardware.

Symptoms	Possible Problems	Possible Solutions
No input is sent when keys are pressed on a keyboard.	Keyboard unplugged. Keyboard plugged into mouse port. Keyboard interface contains bent or broken pins. User attempted to connect the keyboard by using a PS/2-to-USB adapter on a keyboard that does not support this translation. Keyboard port on the computer is damaged.	Physically check the connections and reseat cables if necessary. Make sure a PS/2 keyboard is not plugged into the PS/2 mouse port. For wireless keyboards, there may be connectivity issues, interference, or frequency conflicts from other nearby devices such as mobile phones, baby monitors, and so on. Wireless devices also require batteries, so you might need to replace the batteries. For USB devices on a hub, make sure the hub is plugged in and is supplying power. If other devices are using too much power, the USB hub or port might shut down.
Mouse is not working.	Mouse is not plugged in. Mouse is plugged into the keyboard port. Mouse was connected after the computer was started. Some pointing devices require special drivers and possibly additional software to function properly. Pointing device is not supported by the operating system. Driver for the pointing device is corrupted or outdated.	Physically check the pointing device connection. Use **Device Manager** to verify that the correct driver is installed. Check the pointing device's documentation to see if any additional software is required for it to function properly. Check the website of the device manufacturer to see if newer drivers or software should be installed.
Local network connection but no Internet connection.	The default gateway address might be configured incorrectly, the gateway might be down, or there might be a problem with the Internet Service Provider (ISP).	Check the default gateway address, verify that the default gateway is functioning, and contact the ISP to find out if there are any problem conditions.

Symptoms	Possible Problems	Possible Solutions
Unable to print.	Printer is not plugged in. Printer not supported by the operating system. Driver for the printer is missing, corrupted, or outdated.	Physically check the printer connection. Use **Device Manager** to verify that the correct driver is installed. Check the printer's documentation to see if any additional software is required for it to function properly. Check the website of the device manufacturer to see if newer drivers or software should be installed.
No network connectivity or connection lost.	This could indicate a physical problem such as a loose cable or a defective network adapter. On IP networks, check for a missing or incorrect IP address.	Check cables and connections and check for link lights on the network adapter. Reseat connections, replace cables, or reinstall/replace the adapter as necessary.
Hardware device not working properly.	The device driver is not compatible with the hardware. The driver software for the device is not installed. The latest driver has not been installed.	Open **Device Manager** and check the status of the device. Reinstall the device driver or download and install the latest device driver from the manufacturer's website.

Boot Issues

There are several errors that can occur during the boot process or Windows startup.

Issue	Description
POST errors	If there are errors during the Power On Self-Test (POST), the system might display a numeric error message. Typically, you can press **F1** to acknowledge the error and continue booting. For other POST errors, a series of audible beeps will tell you if a problem has been detected. The sequence of beeps is a code that indicates the type of problem.
Invalid boot disk	The most common cause of this is a non-bootable disk in a drive. If your system has floppy-disk drives, or bootable CD-ROM or thumb drives, check to see if you need to remove a disk from the drive. If this is not the case, there could be a hardware problem with the hard disk. Also verify that the complementary metal oxide semiconductor (CMOS) is set to boot from the hard drive. Most basic input/output systems (BIOSs) allow for the configuration of four or more boot devices as first, second, third, and so on. If one fails, it will automatically try the next in line. The only way this process will fail is if the boot devices are set to "None" or all the same (which many do not allow). Also, it cannot be assumed that the user will want the CMOS to be set to "boot from the hard drive," because many times there is a need to boot from CD, or even boot through the network.
Failure to boot	There might be a hardware problem with the hard disk or hard disk controller. Check hard drive and hard drive controller connections. You may also have a missing Boot.ini file. In this case, you need to use the Bootcfg.exe to rebuild the file.

Issue	Description
Missing operating system	If you receive an error message on boot up that states the operating system is missing, then this could be a sign that the hard disk is damaged. You should try connecting the disk to another machine to see if it boots up; if not, then you will need to replace the hard drive.
Missing dll message	On startup, if the device displays a "missing dll" message, then this can indicate an issue with one of the system files. A file may be disabled, damaged, or deleted completely. You should first boot to Safe Mode and run a virus scan on the computer to find any viruses that may have infected the system and remove them. The next step is to determine what files are missing. This can be a tedious task and in most cases a third party dll finder utility can be used. Once you determine the specific files needed, you can download them from the appropriate website or manufacturer and install them on the system.
System files fail to open or are missing	If NTOSKRNL.EXE is missing, you can copy it from the Windows installation CD-ROM. This error can also indicate a problem in the Advanced RISC Computing (ARC) path specifications in the Boot.ini file. If Bootsect.dos is missing on a dual-boot system, you will have to restore it from a backup file, as its contents are specific to a particular system. System files should not be deleted or become corrupt during normal system operation, so these errors are rare. They might indicate an underlying hardware problem, a disk error, or the presence of a computer virus.
Device or service fails to start	There might be a problem with a missing or corrupted device driver, or there could be hardware resource conflicts (although this is rare on a Plug and Play [PnP] system).
Boots to safe mode	There may be a drive problem if the computer continues to boot only into Safe Mode. Use the system BIOS utility to check drives and verify the boot order.
Device, or program in Registry, not found	A device driver or related file might be missing or damaged. You might need to reinstall the device.

CMOS Error Codes

In addition to the POST error codes, you might also see a CMOS error code. The following are examples of CMOS error codes that you might see displayed after the POST.

- The error `Display Type Mismatch` is displayed if the video settings do not match the monitor attached to the system.
- The error `Memory Size Mismatch` is displayed if the amount of RAM detected and the amount specified in CMOS do not match. This error is usually self-correcting, although you might need to reboot to fix it. Other devices such as hard drives can also generate mismatch errors. This generally happens when the physical device is different from what is specified in CMOS.

System Management Tools

Problems with a PC can occur with hardware and software. Some hardware problems can be fixed by using software tools provided by an operating system. Every operating system comes with a host of utilities designed to help you diagnose and troubleshoot problems and simplify tasks. If you are considering an IT career, for example, as a computer support technician, knowledge of these tools will help you troubleshoot the issues and maintain the operating system.

There are several important utilities you will use to manage the performance of Windows computers and correct errors. The following table lists each utility along with its description.

<table>
<tr><th>System Management Tool</th><th>Description</th></tr>
<tr><td>Device Manager</td><td>
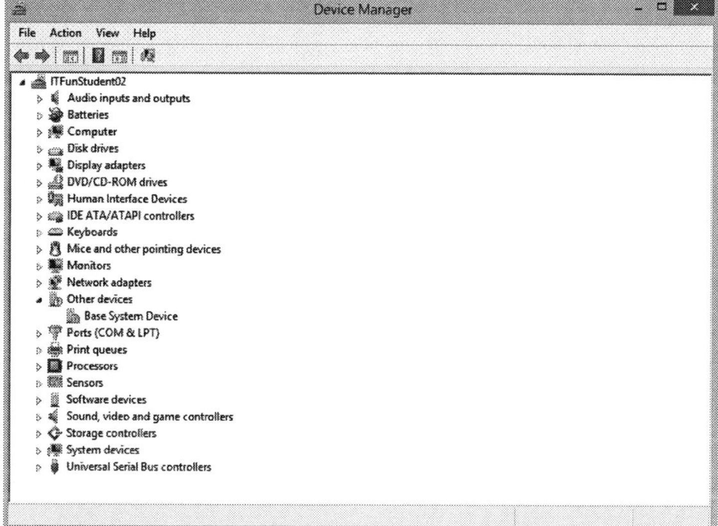

Device Manager is a useful tool used to manage and configure system devices. The default Device Manager view displays a categorized list of all devices attached to the system. You can use Device Manager to:
<ul>
<li>View the status of a device. An exclamation point means there is a problem with a device; a yellow question mark means the device has been detected but a driver is not installed, or there is a resource conflict.</li>
<li>Enable or disable a device. A disabled device appears with a red X.</li>
<li>Determine the device driver a device is using; upgrade a device driver; roll a device driver back to a previous version.</li>
<li>Uninstall or re-install devices.</li>
</ul>
Open Device Manager by using the Search charm to find it, through Control Panel, or through the Computer Management utility.
</td></tr>
</table>

System Management Tool	Description
Windows Task Manager	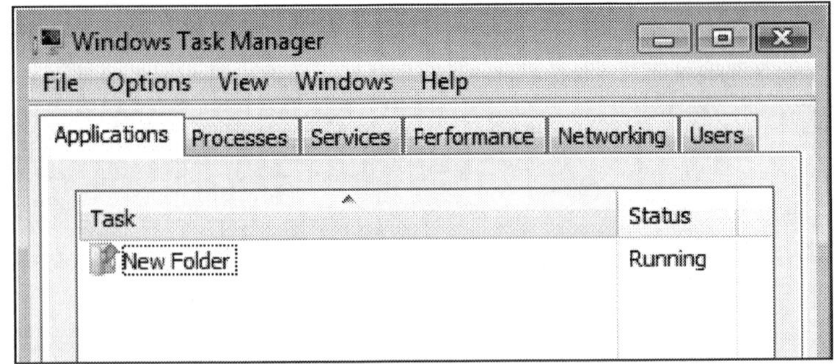 **Windows Task Manager** is a basic system-diagnostic and performance-monitoring tool. You can use **Windows Task Manager** to monitor or terminate applications and processes; view current CPU and memory usage statistics; monitor network connection utilization; set the priority of various processes if programs share resources; and manage logged-on local users. Run **Windows Task Manager** by right-clicking the taskbar and selecting **Task Manager,** or by pressing **Ctrl+Alt+Del** and selecting **Task Manager.**
System Information utility	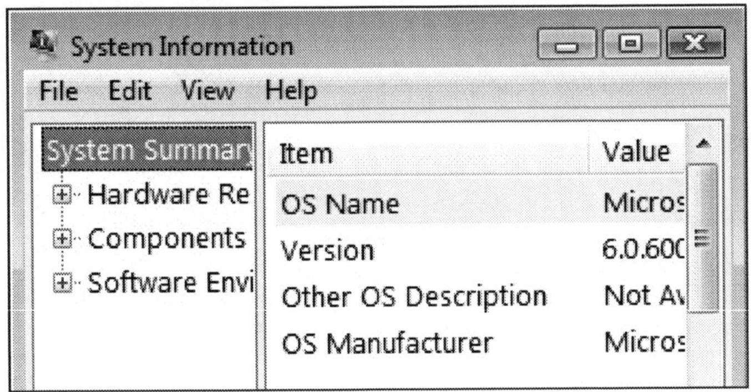 The **System Information** utility displays detailed information about the current system configuration, including a general summary of the system components, hardware resource assignments by category, installed hardware devices, the software environment, and Internet Explorer® settings. Open **System Information** by entering the following command into the **Search charm** or at a command prompt: ***msinfo32*** A subset of this information is available through **Settings→Change PC settings→PC and devices→PC info.**

System Management Tool	Description
Event Viewer	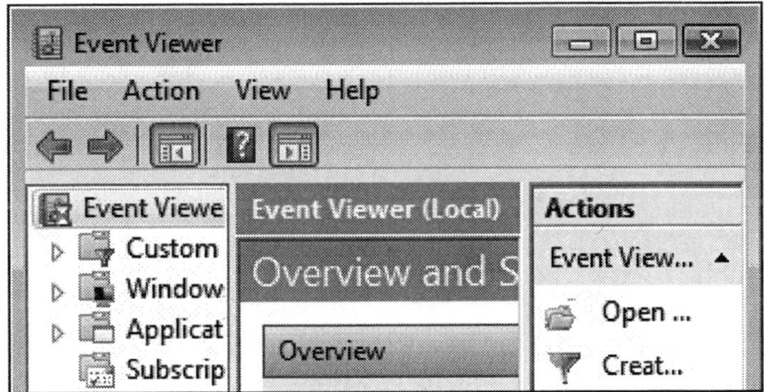 Use **Event Viewer** to view the contents of event logs, which are files that contain information about significant events that occur on your computer. You can access the **Event Viewer** by right-clicking the **Start screen** button on the Desktop and selecting **Event Viewer**.
Computer Management	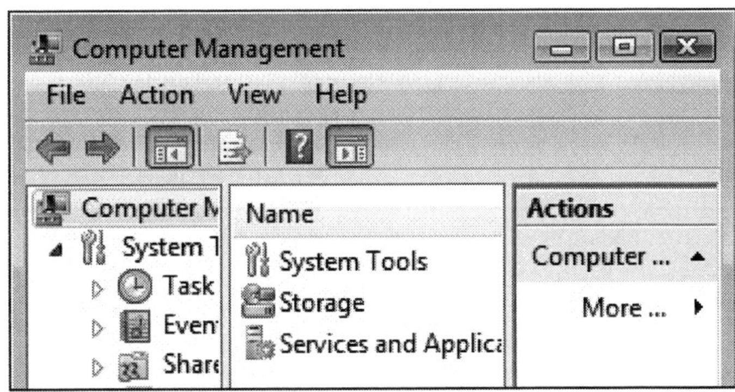 The **Computer Management** console serves as a veritable Swiss army knife of major system administration and information tools. Open the **Computer Management** console by right-clicking the **Start screen** button on the Desktop and selecting **Computer Management**.

Disk Management Tools

There are several command-line and graphical utilities you can use to perform disk management tasks in Windows. The following table lists each disk management tool used in Windows along with its description.

Disk Management Tool	Description
Disk Management	Manages disk drives as well as the partitions the drives contain. With **Disk Management,** you can: • Display the drives attached to the system. • Display, create, and remove partitions on the drives. • Assign drive letters to partitions. • Determine the amount of free space on a partition. • Reformat partitions. • Convert partitions from a file allocation table (FAT) or 32–bit file allocation table (FAT32) file system to an NT File System (NTFS).
Check Disk command (chkdsk.exe)	Verifies the logical integrity of a file system. With the `/f` switch, chkdsk can repair the file system data. Enter `chkdsk` *`drive letter:`* `/f` in the **Run** dialog box or at the command line. With the `/r` switch, chkdsk can locate bad sectors on the disk and recover any readable information.
Format command (format.exe)	Formats partitions to a selected file system. You can run the `format` command at the command line, or right-click a drive letter in Windows Explorer and choose **Format.**
Optimize Drives *(dfrgui.exe)*	Arranges stored data on a disk into contiguous blocks (defragmentation). Because individual files are stored on disks in multiple separate blocks, the used and empty storage areas on a disk can become fragmented and scattered. This can affect disk performance. Windows provides the **Optimize Drives** tool to reorganize the stored files. You can run **Optimize Drives** by issuing the command `dfrgui.exe` in the **Run** dialog box or at the command line.

Support Resources

As an IT technician, you cannot know everything, but your knowledge of available resources can go a long way.

- Research a specific topic or problem by using the **manufacturer's documentation**.
- Obtain software and device driver updates on **manufacturer's websites**.
- Connect with other users and specialists through online **technical user groups and communities**.
- Use an **Internet search engine** to find web pages containing information about a specific keyword or phrase.
- Contact **technical support** to obtain personal help from an IT specialist.

ACTIVITY 8-5
Implementing Basic Support Measures

Scenario

One of your main functions as an intern at Develetech will be assisting the help desk team to resolve customer problems. You want to get familiar with some of the tools included in Windows to help get information about the system and assist with troubleshooting.

---

1. Open Computer Management.
   a) From the **Desktop**, open **File Explorer.**
   b) In the **Navigation** pane, right-click **This PC** and then select **Manage.** The **Computer Management** window opens.

2. Examine Performance monitoring.
   a) Expand **System Tools→Performance→Monitoring Tools.**
   b) Select **Performance Monitor.**
   c) Select **Add.**
   d) In the **Add Counters** dialog box, select **Physical Disk** and then select **Add.**
   e) Select **Processor** and then select **Add.** Select **OK.**
   f) Open **File Explorer** and navigate to **Documents.**
   g) Create a new blank text document.
   h) Observe the graph in **Performance Monitor.** As you opened File Explorer, navigated, and created the file, activity spiked for each event.

3. Examine Device Manager.
   a) In the **Computer Management** window, in the left pane, select **Device Manager.**
   b) Expand various categories and verify that none of the items indicate any issues.
      A warning icon is a yellow triangle with an exclamation point indicating there is an issue. A red X indicates that the device is disabled.

4. Close **Computer Management** and **File Explorer.**

5. View PC info.
   a) From the **Charms** bar, select **Settings→Change PC settings.**
   b) Select **PC and devices.**
   c) Select **PC info.**
      Information such as the installed processor, the amount of RAM, the system type, and the Windows edition are shown. This information can be useful when troubleshooting an issue.
   d) Close the **PC Settings** window.

6. Close all open windows and shut down.

Summary

In this lesson, you supported computers and users. Knowing how to prevent and solve common issues makes you equipped to deal with common problems on a PC and prepares you for a career in the IT field as a computer support technician.

What types of problems have you encountered while working with computers? How have you addressed them on your own?

When disposing of unused or outdated equipment, do you follow the guidelines outlined in this lesson? How do you dispose of the items?

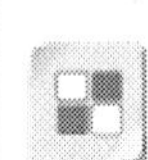

Note: Check your CHOICE Course screen for opportunities to interact with your classmates, peers, and the larger CHOICE online community about the topics covered in this course or other topics you are interested in. From the Course screen you can also access available resources for a more continuous learning experience.

Course Follow-Up

Congratulations! You have completed the *CompTIA® IT Fundamentals™ (Exam FC0-U51 or FC0-Z51)* course. You have gained the skills and information you will need to set up a basic workstation, including installing basic hardware and software, and establishing basic network connectivity; to identify and correct compatibility issues; to identify and prevent basic security risks; and to practice basic support techniques on computing devices.

You also covered the objectives that you will need to prepare for the CompTIA IT Fundamentals+ (Exam FC0-U51 or FC0-Z51) certification examination. If you combine this class experience with review, private study, and hands-on experience, you will be well prepared to demonstrate your expertise both through professional certification and with solid technical competence on the job.

What's Next?

Your next step after completing this course will probably be to prepare for and obtain your CompTIA IT Fundamentals+ certification. In addition, there are a number of other CompTIA courses and certifications that you might want to pursue following the *CompTIA® IT Fundamentals™ (Exam FC0-U51 or FC0-Z51)* course including *CompTIA® A+®: A Comprehensive Approach (Exams 220-801 and 220-802), CompTIA® Network+® (Exam N10-005),* and *CompTIA® Security+® (Exam SY0-401).* You might also wish to pursue further technology-specific training in operating system or network design, implementation and support, or in application development and implementation.

You are encouraged to explore computing device setup, support, and configuration further by actively participating in any of the social media forums set up by your instructor or training administrator through the **Social Media** tile on the CHOICE Course screen.

Mapping Course Content to the CompTIA® IT Fundamentals™ (Exam FC0-U51 or FC0-Z51) Certification Exam

Obtaining CompTIA IT Fundamentals certification requires candidates to pass exam FC0-U51 or FC0-Z51. This table describes where the objectives for CompTIA exam FC0-U51 or FC0-Z51 covered in this course.

Domain and Objective	*Covered In*
1.0 Software	
1.1 Compare and contrast common Operating Systems and their functions and features	Lesson 2, Topic A

• Types
  • Mobile
    • Apple iOS
    • Android
    • Windows Phone
    • BlackBerry
  • Workstation
    • Windows
    • Mac
    • Linux
    • Chrome OS
  • Open source vs. commercial
	Lesson 2, Topic A

• Software compatibility for different OS types and versions	Lesson 2, Topic A
• Awareness of hardware compatibility for OS support • 32bit vs. 64bit operating systems	Lesson 2, Topic A

Domain and Objective	Covered In

• Basic functions of an operating system
  • Interface between user and machine
  • Coordination of hardware components
  • Provides environment for software to function
  • Monitors system health and functionality
  • Displays structure / directories for data management
	Lesson 2, Topic A

1.2 Identify common programs, applications and their purpose
• Types
  • Productivity Software
    • Word processing
    • Spreadsheet software
    • Email software
    • Basic database software
    • PDF viewers/creators
    • Presentation software
    • Desktop publishing software
    • Personal Information Manager
    • Remote desktop software
  • Collaboration Software
    • Online workspace
    • Document storage/sharing
    • Screen sharing software
    • Video conferencing software
    • Instant messaging software
    • Email software
  • Utility Software
    • Anti-malware
    • Software firewalls
    • Diagnostic/maintenance software
    • Compression software
  • Specialized Software
    • CAD
    • Graphic design
    • Medical
    • Scientific
    • Financial
    • Gaming
    • Entertainment
  • Open source vs. commercial
	Lesson 2, Topic A;
	Lesson 2, Topic B

• Platforms
  • Mobile
  • Desktop
  • Web-based
	Lesson 2, Topic B

Domain and Objective	Covered In

• Common file types
  • Documents
    • txt
    • rtf
    • doc/docx
    • xls/xlsx
    • ppt/pptx
    • pdf
  • Audio
    • mp3
    • wav
    • flac
    • aac
    • m4a
  • Images
    • jpg
    • gif
    • tiff
    • png
    • bmp
  • Video
    • mpg
    • mp4
    • flv
    • wmv
    • avi
  • Executables
    • exe
    • msi
    • app
    • bat
    • scexe
  • Compression formats
    • rar
    • tar
    • zip
    • dmg
    • iso
    • 7zip / 7z
    • gzip / gz
    • jar
	Lesson 2, Topic B

1.3 Given a scenario, use software management best practices	Lesson 8, Topic C

Domain and Objective	Covered In
• Install / uninstall • OS features • Applications • Drivers	Lesson 8, Topic C
• Patching / updates for OS, drivers, applications and security software • Scheduling • Frequency • Automatic updates	Lesson 8, Topic C
• Software version identification and compatibility	Lesson 8, Topic C
• Licensing • Product keys • Single / multi-license	Lesson 8, Topic C
1.4 Identify the following alternative technologies and their purpose	Lesson 4, Topic C; Lesson 6, Topic B
• Virtualization • Physical machine vs. virtual machine	Lesson 4, Topic C
• Cloud Computing • Streaming media (audio/video)	Lesson 4, Topic C
• Web applications	Lesson 4, Topic C
• VoIP	Lesson 4, Topic C
• Telepresence	Lesson 4, Topic C
• Gesture-based interaction • Swiping • Pinch-to-zoom • Kinetics	Lesson 6, Topic B
1.5 Explain the basic software features and functions of wireless devices	Lesson 6, Topic A; Lesson 6, Topic B
• Unlocking / security	Lesson 6, Topic A
• Bluetooth pairing • Hands free • Data transfer	Lesson 6, Topic A
• Wireless connection setup • Verify wireless capabilities • Turn on WiFi • Locate SSID • Enter wireless password (if applicable) • Verify internet connection	Lesson 6, Topic A

Domain and Objective	Covered In

• Email configuration
  • POP3
  • IMAP
  • SMTP
	Lesson 6, Topic A

• Screen orientation	Lesson 6, Topic B
• Synchronization configuration	Lesson 6, Topic A
• Airplane mode	Lesson 6, Topic B
• Stores for mobile applications	Lesson 6, Topic A; Lesson 6, Topic B
2.0 Hardware	
2.1 Identify basic wired and wireless peripherals and their purpose	Lesson 1, Topic D

• Output devices
  • Printer
    • Laser
    • Inkjet
    • Thermal
  • Display devices
    • Flatscreen
    • CRT
    • Projector
  • Speakers
	Lesson 1, Topic D

• Input devices
  • Keyboard
  • Pointing devices
    • Mouse
    • Touchpad
    • Joystick
    • Stylus pen
    • Trackball
  • Scanner
  • Microphone
  • Webcam
	Lesson 1, Topic D

Domain and Objective	Covered In

• Input & Output devices
  • Fax
  • External storage devices
    • Flash drive
    • External hard drive
    • CD/DVD/Blu-ray
    • Network Attached Storage
    • Memory card
    • Mobile media players
    • Smart phone
  • Touchscreen display
	Lesson 1, Topic D

2.2 Compare and contrast common computer connector types	Lesson 1, Topic C

• Video
  • VGA
  • DVI
  • HDMI
  • Display port/Thunderbolt
  • USB
  • S-video
  • Component - RGB
	Lesson 1, Topic C

• FireWire	Lesson 1, Topic C
• eSATA	Lesson 1, Topic C
• Thunderbolt	Lesson 1, Topic C
• USB	Lesson 1, Topic C
• PS/2	Lesson 1, Topic C
• Parallel	Lesson 1, Topic C
• Serial	Lesson 1, Topic C
• RJ-45	Lesson 1, Topic C
• RJ-11	Lesson 1, Topic C
• Audio	Lesson 1, Topic C
• Power • AC/DC	Lesson 1, Topic C
2.3 Identify the purpose of internal computer components	Lesson 1, Topic B
• CPU	Lesson 1, Topic B
• Power Supply	Lesson 1, Topic B
• RAM	Lesson 1, Topic B

Domain and Objective	Covered In

• Storage
  • Optical drive
  • Hard drive
  • Solid state drive
	Lesson 1, Topic B

• Expansion cards
  • Video card
  • Audio card
  • Network card
  • Modem
	Lesson 1, Topic B

• Motherboard/mainboard	Lesson 1, Topic B

• System cooling
  • Case fans
  • CPU fans
  • Liquid cooling
	Lesson 1, Topic B

3.0 Security	
3.1 Define basic security threats	Lesson 7, Topic A

• Malware
  • Virus
  • Trojan
  • Spyware
  • Ransomware
	Lesson 7, Topic A

• Phishing	Lesson 7, Topic A
• Social engineering	Lesson 7, Topic A
• Spam	Lesson 7, Topic A
• Password cracking	Lesson 7, Topic A

• Physical security
  • Hardware theft
  • Software/license theft
  • Shoulder surfing
  • Dumpster diving
	Lesson 7, Topic A

3.2 Given a scenario, use security best practices	Lesson 7, Topic B

• Password management
  • Password complexity
  • Change default passwords
  • Password confidentiality
  • Password expiration
  • Password reuse
  • Awareness of Single Sign On
	Lesson 7, Topic B

Domain and Objective	Covered In

• Device hardening
  • Disable unused features
    • Disable Bluetooth
    • Disable NFC
  • Timeout / lock options
  • Enable security software/features
    • Software firewall
    • Anti-malware
  • Encryption options
	Lesson 7, Topic B

• Open WiFi vs. secure WiFi	Lesson 7, Topic B
• Multifactor authentication	Lesson 7, Topic B

• Suspicious emails
  • Attachments
  • Hyperlinks
	Lesson 7, Topic B

• Act on security software alerts	Lesson 7, Topic B
• Admin vs. user vs. guest account	Lesson 7, Topic B
3.3 Given a scenario, use web-browsing best practices	Lesson 7, Topic C

• Recognize a secure connection/website
  • https
  • lock symbol
	Lesson 7, Topic C

• Recognize invalid certificate warnings	Lesson 7, Topic C
• Recognize suspicious links	Lesson 7, Topic C
• Recognize suspicious banner ads	Lesson 7, Topic C

• Recognize adware symptoms
  • Constant pop-ups
  • Home page redirection
  • Search engine redirection
	Lesson 7, Topic C

• Limit the use of personal information (PII)	Lesson 7, Topic C
• Update browsers and plugins • Avoid use of legacy browsers	Lesson 7, Topic C
• Disable unneeded/suspicious browser plugins, toolbars and extensions	Lesson 7, Topic C
• Disable autofill forms/passwords	Lesson 7, Topic C
• Clear browser cache/history/cookies	Lesson 7, Topic C
• Recognize untrusted source warnings	Lesson 7, Topic C
• Risks of using public workstations	Lesson 7, Topic C
4.0 Networking	

Domain and Objective	Covered In
4.1 Given a scenario, set up and configure a basic SOHO router (wired / wireless)	Lesson 4, Topic B
• Verify wired connection, if applicable	Lesson 4, Topic B
• Set WEP vs. WPA vs. WPA2	Lesson 4, Topic B
• Change SSID from default	Lesson 4, Topic B
• Apply a new wireless password	Lesson 4, Topic B
• Change admin password for router	Lesson 4, Topic B
• Connect to the new network	Lesson 4, Topic B
• Verify internet connectivity	Lesson 4, Topic B
• Update firmware if necessary	Lesson 4, Topic B
4.2 Compare and contrast cellular, wireless and wired data connections	Lesson 4, Topic A
• High vs. low mobility	Lesson 4, Topic A
• High vs. low availability	Lesson 4, Topic A
• High vs. low throughput/bandwidth	Lesson 4, Topic A
• High vs. low reliability	Lesson 4, Topic A
• Connection delay	Lesson 4, Topic A
• Number of concurrent connections	Lesson 4, Topic A
• Levels of security	Lesson 4, Topic A
4.3 Compare and contrast different methods of sharing and storage	Lesson 4, Topic D
• HTTP vs. HTTPS • Browser-based file downloads	Lesson 4, Topic D
• FTP vs. FTPS vs. SFTP (Secure File Transfer Protocol)	Lesson 4, Topic D

• Local vs. hosted storage
  • Cloud-based services
    • Cloud-based collaborative applications
    • Cloud-based storage
  • File and print sharing
    • Workgroup
    • Homegroup
  • Network drives
  • Network attached storage
  • Direct attached storage
  • External hard drives
	Lesson 4, Topic D

Domain and Objective	Covered In

• Peer-to-peer
  • Local ad-hoc network
    • Bluetooth sharing
  • Direct link (PC-to-PC)
  • Online peer-to-peer network
	Lesson 4, Topic D

• Network vs. local printing
  • USB
  • Wireless / wired network
	Lesson 4, Topic D

5.0 Basic IT literacy	
5.1 Perform appropriate steps to set up a basic workstation	Lesson 3, Topic A; Lesson 3, Topic B; Lesson 3, Topic C
• Plug in cables	Lesson 3, Topic A
• Power on computer	Lesson 3, Topic A

• Follow initial operating system setup wizard
  • Localization settings
  • Screen resolution
  • Audio settings
	Lesson 3, Topic A;
	Lesson 3, Topic B

• Install security software	Lesson 3, Topic A; Lesson 3, Topic C
• Configure peripherals (if applicable)	Lesson 3, Topic A; Lesson 3, Topic B
• Uninstall unneeded software (if applicable)	Lesson 3, Topic A; Lesson 3, Topic C
• Configure and verify internet connection	Lesson 3, Topic A;
• Install additional software (if applicable)	Lesson 3, Topic A; Lesson 3, Topic C
• Run software and security updates	Lesson 3, Topic A; Lesson 3, Topic B; Lesson 3, Topic C
• Other user accounts (if applicable)	Lesson 3, Topic A; Lesson 3, Topic B
• Basic cable management	Lesson 3, Topic A

Domain and Objective	Covered In
5.2 Explain the basic methods of navigating an operating system	Lesson 3, Topic D; Lesson 5, Topic A; Lesson 5, Topic B; Lesson 5, Topic C; Lesson 5, Topic E
• Executing programs	Lesson 5, Topic A
• Difference between shortcuts and files	Lesson 5, Topic A

• Manipulating files
  • Open
  • Edit
  • Save
  • Move
  • Copy
  • Cut
  • Paste
  • Delete
  • Rename
	Lesson 5, Topic C

• Read-only vs. modifiable files	Lesson 5, Topic C
• Navigate a file structure	Lesson 5, Topic B
• Search, sort and display files	Lesson 5, Topic C
• Create screen captures	Lesson 5, Topic E
• Navigate with hot keys	Lesson 5, Topic B
• Folder and file size	Lesson 5, Topic C
• Accessibility options	Lesson 3, Topic D
• Folder and file permissions	Lesson 5, Topic A
5.3 Given a scenario, implement basic support concepts	Lesson 8, Topic D

• Check for external issues
  • Loose cables / connections
  • Power
  • Physical damage
	Lesson 8, Topic D

• Manufacturer documentation	Lesson 8, Topic D
• Manufacturer websites	Lesson 8, Topic D
• Technical community groups	Lesson 8, Topic D
• Internet search engine	Lesson 8, Topic D
• Contact technical support	Lesson 8, Topic D
5.4 Explain basic backup concepts	Lesson 8, Topic B

Domain and Objective	Covered In
• Importance of backups	Lesson 8, Topic B
• Scheduling	Lesson 8, Topic B
• Frequency	Lesson 8, Topic B

• Storage mediums
  • Locally attached storage
  • Offsite/cloud-based
  • Network attached storage
	Lesson 8, Topic B

• Backup verification and testing	Lesson 8, Topic B
5.5 Describe the importance and impact of various environmental and safety concepts	Lesson 8, Topic A

• Proper disposal methods
  • RoHS
  • CRT monitors
  • Scanners
  • Batteries
  • Ink/toner
  • Hard drives
	Lesson 8, Topic A

• Power
  • Energy efficient devices
  • Power profiles
    • Power options
    • Sleep / hibernation
  • UPS vs. surge protector vs. power strip
    • Power limitations
  • International power differences
	Lesson 8, Topic A

• Device placement
  • Airflow
  • Humidity
  • Temperature
  • Dust accumulation
  • EMI
	Lesson 8, Topic A

• Electrostatic discharge concepts	Lesson 8, Topic A

• Ergonomic concepts
  • Proper keyboard and mouse placement
  • Sitting positions
  • Monitor level placement
	Lesson 8, Topic A

• Follow manufacturer safety guidelines	Lesson 8, Topic A

Mastery Builders

Mastery Builders are provided for certain lessons as additional learning resources for this course. Mastery Builders are developed for selected lessons within a course in cases when they seem most instructionally useful as well as technically feasible. In general, Mastery Builders are supplemental, optional unguided practice and may or may not be performed as part of the classroom activities. Your instructor will consider setup requirements, classroom timing, and instructional needs to determine which Mastery Builders are appropriate for you to perform, and at what point during the class. If you do not perform the Mastery Builders in class, your instructor can tell you if you can perform them independently as self-study, and if there are any special setup requirements.

Mastery Builder 3-1

Configuring Workstation Settings

Activity Time: 15 minutes

Scenario

You are working for a small electronics store. You provide pre-purchase and post-purchase assistance to customers. On Saturday mornings, you are presenting a group class on how to perform some basic workstation configuration, including installing and uninstalling Windows Store apps. You will also show participants how to use the on-screen keyboard. Finally, you will show them how to create a new local child's account.

---

1. Install the app of your choice from the Windows store.
2. Open the app and verify that it functions as advertised in the Windows Store.
3. Uninstall the app you just installed.
4. Open the Ease of Access Center and turn on the on-screen keyboard.
5. Open Internet Explorer and use the on-screen keyboard to access google.com.
6. Close the on-screen keyboard.
7. Create a new local user configured as a child's account.
8. Log in with the new local user account.
9. Log out.

Mastery Builder 5-1

Working with Files and Folders

Activity Time: 15 minutes

Scenario

You are working for a small electronics store. You provide pre-purchase and post-purchase assistance to customers. On Saturday mornings you are presenting a group class on how to manage files and folders in Windows 8.1.

---

1. Log in with your student account.
2. Create files in **Paint** and **WordPad**, saving the files to each app's default locations. Name the files with names that begin with LabFile.
3. In File Explorer, open the **OneDrive** folder.
4. Create a folder named ***My Lab Files***
5. Copy the **Paint** file to the **My Lab Files** folder.
6. Move the **WordPad** file to the **My Lab Files** folder.
7. Create a compressed file of the **My Lab Files** folder.
8. Use the method of your choice to take a screen capture of **File Explorer** showing the compressed file.
9. Log out.

Mastery Builder 6-1

Configuring and Using Wireless Devices

Activity Time: 15 minutes

Scenario

You are working for a small electronics store. You provide pre-purchase and post-purchase assistance to customers. On Saturday mornings you are presenting a group class on how to configure and use smartphones and tablets.

---

1. Turn on your mobile device and if necessary, log in.
2. If available, connect your device to a wireless network.
3. Install the app of your choice from the app store for your mobile device operating system.
4. If available, connect your device to another device by using Bluetooth, and then transfer a file over your non-cellular connection.
5. Disconnect from the wireless network and the Bluetooth connection.

Solutions

ACTIVITY 1-1: Identifying Computing Devices

1. **Ariana is taking company sponsored training at the local college next semester. She has always used either work computers or public computers at the library. She sees the Windows® Surface™ advertisements everywhere and thinks this would be what she would like to get. The course she is taking uses Adobe® Photoshop® and some custom applications designed by the instructor. Ariana has saved up about $500 for her new computing device. What computing device would best meet her needs?**

   A: Answers will vary, but she should probably be looking at a lightweight laptop or notebook computer. Photoshop and the custom software might not work well on the Surface tablets available for under $500, although they should work on the more powerful Surface tablets that are out of her price range.

2. **Stephanie is getting ready to retire. At work, she performed data entry, prepared management reports by using Microsoft Office applications, and responded to customer inquiries by using email. She will be traveling with her spouse for six months each year, visiting family and various parks across the country. They will reside at their beach-side home the other six months of the year. She has only ever used a standard desktop computer at work and would like to purchase a device that can be used in their RV to help with directions to their destinations. She wonders if she should also purchase a portable computer for accessing email, writing about their travels, and possibly creating a book about their experiences. What advice would you give her?**

   A: Answers will vary, but a tablet with a detachable external keyboard might suit her needs. It would be small and light-weight for use by the RV passenger for route directions. If it has cellular connection, it could be used as a GPS unit that speaks the directions aloud. The keyboard would be helpful when she is accessing email and writing about their travels. Another choice might be a laptop or notebook computer. A desktop computer would not be as useful in this scenario.

3. **Douglas is a company sales rep. He travels about 75 percent of the time, traveling by air, train, and car. He needs to be able to show customers images of the new products he is promoting, maintain his contact database, find directions to the companies he is visiting, and reply to emails. What device would you recommend?**

   A: Answers will vary, but a tablet might suit his needs. It would be small and lightweight for use while traveling and meeting with customers. He may also want to attach an external keyboard to make typing easier.

ACTIVITY 1-2: Identifying Internal Computer Components

1. **Locate the motherboard and the CPU.**

   A: The motherboard is labeled E, and the CPU is labeled I.

2. **Locate the power supply.**

   A: The power supply is labeled A.

3. **Identify the memory installed on the motherboard.**

   A: The memory is labeled B.

4. **Identify the storage devices installed in the computer.**

   A: The hard drive is labeled C, and the CD-ROM drive is labeled D.

5. **Locate and identify each of the expansion cards installed in the computer.**

   A: The expansion card is labeled G, and it is probably a network interface card.

6. **Locate and identify each of the cooling strategies employed in the computer.**

   A: The CPU fan is labeled H, and the power supply fan is labeled J.

ACTIVITY 2-1: Comparing Functions and Features of Operating Systems

1. **Identify the functions of operating system software. (Choose three.)**

   ☑ Creates a working environment

   ☐ Performs specific tasks

   ☑ Sets rules for how a system and application work together

   ☑ Specifies how security is handled

2. **Which operating system from Microsoft is available for desktop and server use?**

   ○ Linux

   ○ Mac OS X

   ◉ Windows

   ○ Chrome

3. **Which operating system is freely available and comes in many distributions.**

   ◉ Linux

   ○ Mac OS X

   ○ Windows

   ○ Chrome

4. Which operating system distribution method is available by purchase only?

- ○ Open source
- ○ Freeware
- ○ Shareware
- ◉ Commercial
- ○ Copyleft

5. Which operating systems are for mobile devices, in particular, smartphones? (Choose two.)

- ☐ Linux
- ☐ Chrome OS
- ☑ Apple iOs
- ☐ Mac OS X
- ☑ Android OS

ACTIVITY 2-2: Identifying Application Software

1. Laura needs to use her personal computer to analyze tables of numbers. Which application software would you recommend?

- ○ Word processing
- ◉ Spreadsheet
- ○ Database
- ○ Web browsing

2. Daniel needs to display a series of images and text in a meeting with the sales reps. Which application software would you recommend?

- ○ Word processing
- ○ Database
- ◉ Presentation
- ○ Spreadsheet

3. Gary is creating a newsletter for his department. It will highlight many of the accomplishments achieved over the past quarter. He knows that some of the information is contained in an Access file and some is contained in Excel files. Some of the managers have given him Word documents containing information they would like him to include in the newsletter. He would like to send the newsletter electronically rather than printing it. Which types of applications will he need to access these files? What do you recommend that he use to create the newsletter?

A: He will need a database application to open the Access file and a spreadsheet application to open the Excel files. He will need a word processing document to open the Word documents. To send the newsletter electronically, he will need an email application. Depending on how fancy he wants to get with the newsletter, he could create a simple newsletter in the word processing application, or he could use a desktop publishing application to create a more polished looking newsletter.

4. Jordan works with an outside vendor that is constantly sending him files that have a .zip extension, or ZIP files. What type of application will he need to open these files?

- ◉ File compression software
- ○ Presentation software
- ○ Graphic design software
- ○ Spreadsheet software

5. **Josie has a USB drive with XLSX files on it. Which of the following applications should she use to open them?**
   - ○ Microsoft Paint
   - ○ Adobe Reader
   - ◉ Microsoft Excel
   - ○ Microsoft WordPad

ACTIVITY 4-1: Comparing Network Connection Types

1. **When would a WAN be used?**
   - ○ To share files among employees within an organization
   - ◉ To share files between computers in offices located in different countries
   - ○ To share a printer for printing documents
   - ○ To use resources present on a server

2. **Which tasks require the use of a network? (Choose three.)**
   - ☐ Creating a spreadsheet by using software that is installed on your computer
   - ☑ Printing a spreadsheet by using a printer that you share with the other members of your department
   - ☑ Sending an email to a group of coworkers regarding a department meeting
   - ☑ Saving a file so that others in your group can access the most updated copy of that file and make changes to it when needed

3. **Which of the following best describes Ethernet?**
   - ○ A network of computers that share a large geographic area
   - ○ A network that includes workstations and a server and supports a small geographic area
   - ◉ A LAN technology used for connecting computers and servers in the same building or campus
   - ○ A LAN in which computers communicate with a server without using wires, but through a wireless device attached to a computer

4. **The accounts payable department requires a great level of security and availability. Which network connection type would you recommend for this department?**

   A: A wired network would be the most ideal.

ACTIVITY 4-2: Installing and Configuring a SOHO Router

5. **If you were configuring an actual SOHO router, how would you confirm that the configuration meets your needs?**

   A: You could have users try to connect to the router and verify Internet connectivity. They could do this by opening a browser and performing a search.

ACTIVITY 4-3: Identifying Network and Alternative Technologies

1. **What is the benefit of a cloud computing infrastructure?**
   - ○ Companies have full control over the data that is hosted.
   - ◉ Companies need to pay for only the resources used.
   - ○ Companies can host all applications internally on their own servers.
   - ○ Companies do not need to worry about the security of hosted data.

2. **Why might you use virtualization?**
   - ◉ To host multiple operating systems on a single computer.
   - ○ To host a single operating system over multiple computers.
   - ○ To duplicate your system for redundancy.
   - ○ To set up multiple computers from a single virtual image.

3. **Why might your organization use web applications? (Choose two.)**
   - ☑ So you don't have to install the applications on each computer
   - ☐ So you don't need networks
   - ☑ So you can use the applications on any device with an Internet connection
   - ☐ To regulate how fast the user works

4. **What is VoIP, and why has it become popular?**

   A: VoIP is Voice over IP. It is voice communication over an IP network. It is popular because it saves companies money, doesn't incur long distance charges, and enables collaboration.

ACTIVITY 4-4: Comparing Methods for Sharing and Storing Information

1. **Which are examples of local storage? (Choose two.)**
   - ☑ An internal optical drive such as a DVD or Blu-ray drive
   - ☑ An external USB drive
   - ☐ A folder on OneDrive
   - ☐ A NAS device

2. **True or False? You cannot configure a wireless peer-to-peer network.**
   - ☐ True
   - ☑ False

3. **Which protocols are most commonly associated with browser-based file sharing? (Choose two.)**
   - ☑ HTTP
   - ☐ FTPS
   - ☐ FTP
   - ☑ HTTPS

4. **You can share data by using all of the devices and storage locations you examined in this topic. Which device or location is the most secure and the least secure? Why?**

   A: The most secure storage location would be OneDrive because it is accessible only through your Microsoft account. The printer would be the least secure because anyone walking by the printer could see what you printed. Removable storage devices can be secured by using encryption, but if they are not encrypted and you misplace the storage device, anyone could access the information stored on it.

ACTIVITY 7-1: Identifying Security Threats

1. **What should be included in the policy manual regarding virus protection?**

   A: Answers will vary, but all computing devices should have antivirus software installed and updated on a regular basis. Users should receive training about sites and email messages that are more likely to contain malware and how to avoid accessing these items.

2. **How can computing devices be secured while an employee is traveling to help prevent theft of the devices?**

   A: Answers will vary, but keeping the devices within the employee's sight is a good first step. If the employee will be leaving the devices in a hotel room, the device should be locked in a safe or secured to an immobile object with a security cable. The information on the device should be password protected and encrypted as well.

3. **Why should the organization be concerned about someone taking old equipment that was going to be recycled anyway?**

   A: Answers will vary, but unless the hard drives have been wiped, removed, or destroyed, it is possible that attackers could gain access to company information. This information might be used to steal business away from the company or to plan an attack on the company computers.

ACTIVITY 7-2: Applying Security Best Practices

1. **In this organization, some employees travel between sites. This group of users does not use laptop computers, but does use desktop computers at each of the sites they visit. Which type of user account should be created for these users and how can they be sure not to leave traces of their presence on the computers they use?**

   A: Answers will vary, but might include setting up Microsoft accounts that are synchronized between all of the computers they will be using. Clearing browser history will help prevent their browsing history information and related logins and passwords from being stored on the computer after they log out.

2. **Users who travel between sites have been using thumb drives to take their documents with them to other sites. You suggest that they use Microsoft OneDrive instead. What are pros and cons of using OneDrive versus a thumb drive?**

   A: Answers will vary, but thumb drives could easily be lost or misplaced, resulting in loss of data. If the data falls into the wrong hands, the organization's information could be breached depending on what was on the drive. By using a Microsoft Account, users would have access to their OneDrive content on each computer they accessed. However, if they lost connection to the Internet, they would not be able to access the files in their OneDrive accounts.

3. **Sales team members have smartphones, tablets, and laptops they take with them when they travel. What policies should be put in place to keep these items secure?**

   A: Answers will vary, but the employees should never leave their portable devices unattended. If they are using a wireless network, they should make sure it is a secured connection. A secure password should be required to sign in to the device.

ACTIVITY 7-3: Securely Browsing the Web

1. **What recommendations would you make to include in the security policy regarding secure web browsing?**

   A: Answers will vary, but might include making sure the browser has all updates and patches applied to fix any known security issues, enabling only the plug-ins and extensions that are needed, not accessing sites that have invalid digital certificates, recognizing suspicious web page components and symptoms of adware infections. It should also address being wary of untrusted sources, knowing how to protect PII, disabling automated forms, and knowing how to remove traces of your presence on public workstations.

ACTIVITY 8-1: Discussing Environmental and Safety Concepts

1. **The Develetech staff has identified a dozen CRT monitors that are no longer going to be supported. What options should you consider as alternatives to throwing the monitors out? Which might you consider first?**

   A: The most environmentally friendly options are to either donate the monitors to an organization, such as a school, or to sell them to employees or non-employees, as this allows for 100 percent reuse of materials. If you can't find someone to accept the monitors, then you should either bring them to a recycling facility or arrange to have them picked up by an organization that recycles them properly, even if this incurs a cost.

2. **Up until now, the location where you are working has been disposing of toner and ink cartridges by throwing them in the garbage. Why is this considered a hazard? What incentives exist to encourage users to recycle the cartridges?**

   A: Throwing toner and ink cartridges away is hazardous to the environment because the chemicals are capable of seeping into the soil in the landfill and leaking into underground water. In addition, the cartridges are not biodegradable; they will sit in a landfill for years and years. Many retailers and cartridge manufacturers offer a store credit or rebate for the return of empty ink and toner cartridges, which can often be refilled and reused.

3. **True or False? If you shut a device off, it cannot draw any power from an outlet.**

   ☐ True

   ☑ False

4. **What characteristics of solid state drives allow them to be considered more "green" than typical hard drives? (Choose two.)**

   ☐ They are physically smaller and consume less space within the enclosure.

   ☑ There are no moving parts, which means less likelihood of failure and replacement.

   ☑ Because all data is stored in solid state memory, information can be retrieved faster and with less power.

   ☐ They are less expensive than a typical hard drive.

Glossary

802.11
The most recent encryption standard that provides improved encryption for wireless networking.

802.11i
A complete wireless standard that adds strong encryption and authentication security to 802.11 and relies on 802.1x as the authentication mechanism. Also referred to as WPA2.

accelerometer
Mobile technology that can determine the orientation of a device with a sensor that measures the acceleration of the device direction.

accessibility
The use of assistive technology to make computers available and easier to use.

adapter card
A printed circuit board that you install into a slot on the computer's system board to expand the functionality of the computer. Also referred to as an expansion card, I/O card, add-in, add-on, or board.

adaptive technology
Tools that are designed to ensure that people with disabilities are able to use software applications.

Address Bar
A File Explorer component that is located below the ribbon and displays the address of an object.

adware
Malicious code that enters the computer system while installing some software applications, and is usually distributed through freeware.

AES
(Advanced Encryption Standard) A feature of WPA2 that provides cipher-based Counter Mode with Cipher Block Chaining Message Authentication Code Protocol (CCMP) encryption for even greater security and to replace TKIP.

airplane mode
A mobile device setting that you can use to quickly disconnect the mobile device from Wi-Fi and cellular connections, as well as disable the ability to send and receive calls, email, and text messages.

all-in-one computer
A computer that has the monitor and the computing components all built into one physical device.

Android
A layered environment built on the Linux kernel foundation that includes not only the OS, but middleware, which provides additional software for the OS, and additional built-in applications.

application software
A program that provides specific functionality such as word processing, graphics creation, or database management.

attacker
A term for a user who gains unauthorized access to computers and networks for malicious purposes. See "cracker."

audio card
An adapter card that enables you to connect speakers, a microphone, and headphones to a computer.

automatic update
A feature of an operating system or a software application that enables updates to be downloaded and installed automatically on a system at a scheduled time.

Berg connector
A power connector used to supply power to floppy disk drives and some tape drives.

bit
The smallest unit of information in a computer system. Short for "binary digit," bits are represented either as 1 or 0.

black hat
A hacker who exposes vulnerabilities for financial gain or for some malicious purpose.

bloatware
A slang term that describes software that has lots of features and requires considerable disk space and RAM to install and run.

bluejacking
A method used by attackers to send out unwanted Bluetooth signals from mobile phones and laptops to other Bluetooth-enabled devices.

bluesnarfing
A method in which attackers gain access to unauthorized information on a wireless device by using a Bluetooth connection within the 30-foot Bluetooth transmission limit.

Bluetooth
A wireless technology that facilitates short-range wireless communication between devices.

BNC connector
(Bayonet Neill-Concelman connector) A connector that is used with coaxial cable to carry radio frequencies to and from devices.

brute force attack
A password attack in which the attacker uses password-cracking software to attempt every possible alphanumeric password combination.

BS
(base station) A transceiver on a cellular network. Also referred to as a cell site.

bundled applications
Software programs that are sold together as a set or suite, or that are sold with an operating system or with a new computer.

byte
A unit of computer storage equal to approximately one character.

CCFL
(cold cathode fluorescent lamp) The backlight source used by LCD monitors.

cellular network
A radio network that consists of different areas called cells. Also referred to as a mobile network.

chromebook
A laptop computer that comes pre-installed with the Chrome OS.

cloud computing
A computing infrastructure in which resources, such as storage and applications, are hosted in a distributed fashion by a third party over the Internet.

coaxial cable
A type of copper cable that features a central conducting copper core surrounded

by an insulator and braided or foil shielding.

commercial
A software licensing scheme that is intended to meet commercial needs. Many commercial software publishers ask their users to register their copies within a specified period of time. This type of software does not allow users to access the source code or modify it.

component/RGB connectors
Video connectors that transmit analog video information as two or more separate signals.

composite video
The format of an analog (picture only) signal before it is combined with a sound signal and modulated onto a radio frequency (RF) carrier.

computer connection
A physical access point that enables a computer to communicate with internal or external devices.

computer network
A group of computers that are connected together to communicate and share network resources such as files, applications, and devices.

computing device
An electronic machine that uses binary data to automatically perform calculations.

Contents pane
A File Explorer component that displays a list of files and subfolders within a folder.

cookie
A text file that is created by a website and placed on a computer's hard drive to store information that is used to identify users and, possibly, to prepare customized web pages for them.

copyleft
A method of ensuring that all original work, and all the derivative works created from it, are kept free and open.

CPU
(central processing unit) A computer chip where most of the computing calculations take place. Also referred to as the microprocessor or processor.

cracker
The term preferred by the hacker community for a user who gains unauthorized access to computers and networks for malicious purposes.

CRT
(cathode ray tube) A type of display device that uses electron beams within a vacuum tube to create images on a fluorescent screen.

data backup
A type of information protection scheme that enables you to store copies of critical files and folders on another medium for safekeeping.

data restoration
A type of information protection scheme that enables you to recover stored copies of critical files and folders from another medium.

data synchronization
The process of automatically merging and updating common data that is stored on multiple devices.

data wiping
A method used to remove any sensitive data from a mobile device and permanently delete it.

DB-15 connector
A high-density video graphics array (VGA) connector that was the most common cable used for LCD monitors.

desktop computer
A computing device designed to be placed on or near a user's desk.

Details pane
A File Explorer component that displays the file properties such as file name, file type, author, last modified, size, and other properties.

device hardening
A collection of security tasks used to reduce the scope of the device's vulnerability and attack surface.

dictionary attack
An automated password attack that involves guessing by comparing encrypted passwords against a predetermined list of possible password values.

digital certificate
An electronic document that provides for the secure exchange of information over a network.

directory
A container object that can store your files in an organized manner. Often referred to as a folder.

discovery mode
A Bluetooth device mode that will transmit a friendly signal to another device in close proximity.

DisplayPort
A digital display standard that aims to replace the DVI and VGA standards.

driver
Specialized software that controls a device attached to a computer.

dust filter
A ventilation component that prevents dust from entering the critical components of a computer.

DVI connector
(digital video interface connector) A digital interface that is used to connect a video source (for example, a display controller to a display device) such as a computer monitor.

EAS
(Exchange ActiveSync) Microsoft's synchronization protocol that enables mobile devices to connect to an Exchange Server to access mail, calendar, and contacts.

eBook reader
A device used to read electronic books, or eBooks.

EMI
(electromagnetic interference) A situation that arises when sources that output electromagnetic radiation interfere with your electronic devices.

encryption
The process of converting data into a form that is not easily recognized or understood by anyone who is not authorized to access the data.

ergonomics
The study of a person's efficiency at the workplace as it relates to his or her health, safety, and productivity.

ESD
(electrostatic discharge) A situation that occurs when electrons rush from a statically charged body to another unequally charged body.

Ethernet
A set of networking technologies and media access methods specified for LANs.

expansion card
A printed circuit board that is install into a slot on the computer's system board to expand the functionality of the computer.

fan
A ventilation component that cools the internal components of a computer.

file
An object that stores information on a computer.

file attribute
A characteristic that can be associated with a file or folder that provides the operating system with important information about the file or folder and how it is intended to be used by system users.

file compression
The process of reducing the size of a file.

file encryption
A type of file protection that disguises the data within a file or message so that the specific information included within the file or message cannot be read or understood by unauthorized users.

File Explorer
A Microsoft Windows tool that offers a single view of all the resources and information that you can access from a computer.

file extension
A series of characters at the end of a file name; used by an OS to identify the software application that is associated with a file.

file extraction
The process of restoring a compressed file to its original size.

firewall
A device or group of devices that connect and control access between networks.

FireWire connection
A computer connection that provides a high-speed interface for peripheral devices that are designed to use the IEEE 1394 standard.

firmware
Specialized software that is stored on a hardware device's read-only memory (ROM) whether or not the device is powered.

flash drive
A solid state storage device that typically connects to a USB port on your computer.

flashing
The process of overwriting existing firmware.

folder
A container object that can store your files in an organized manner. Also referred to as a directory.

freeware
Applications that you can download from the Internet directly and use without any restrictions.

FTP
(File Transfer Protocol) The set of rules used to transfer files across a TCP/IP network, such as the Internet.

FTP over SSH
(File Transfer Protocol over Secure Shell) A secure version of FTP that uses an SSH tunnel as an encryption method to transfer, access, and manage files. Also referred to as Secure FTP.

FTP-SSL
(File Transfer Protocol-Secure Sockets Layer) Same as FTPS.

FTPS
(File Transfer Protocol Secure) FTP with additional support for SSL/TLS. Also referred to as FTP-SSL.

GPRS
(Global Packet Radio Service) A mobile data service that promises data rates from 56 up to 114 Kbps and continuous connection to the Internet for mobile phone and computer users.

graphics tablet
A tablet surface typically used by artists and computer-aided design (CAD) designers to draw image and pictures by using a stylus the same way you would draw the image on paper, but instead, you draw on the tablet.

guessing attack
The simplest type of password attack and involves an individual making repeated attempts to guess a password by entering different common password values, such as the user's name, a spouse's name, or a significant date.

gyroscope
Mobile technology that changes the orientation of the device by reading the x and y coordinates of the device's position.

hacker
A user who excels at programming or managing and configuring computer systems, and has the skills to gain access to computer systems through unauthorized or unapproved means.

HDD
(hard disk drive) A storage device that is used to store digital data in a computer.

HDMI connector
(high definition multimedia interface connector) The first industry-supported, uncompressed, all-digital audio/video interface; it has largely superseded DVI and is compatible with the DVI standard.

heat sink
A cooling device that is metal, usually formed into ridges, and installed on components to increase the surface area that can be cooled by fans or liquid cooling systems.

hoax
Any message containing incorrect or misleading information that is disseminated to multiple users through unofficial channels.

homegroup
A Microsoft Windows–based peer-to-peer network that is typically implemented in a SOHO environment and that usually requires users to input a user name and password when they join the homegroup.

hosted storage
Storage media that places data on specialized devices that serve files to clients in a network based on each client's need.

hotfix
A patch that is often issued on an emergency basis to address a specific security flaw.

HTTP
(Hypertext Transfer Protocol) The TCP/IP service that enables clients, such as a web browser application, to connect and interact with websites.

HTTPS
(Hypertext Transfer Protocol Secure) A secure version of HTTP that supports web commerce by providing a secure connection between web browsers and servers.

hub
A networking device that connects multiple computers to form a LAN.

hybrid password attack
A password attack in which multiple attack vectors, including dictionary, brute-force, and other attack methodologies, are used to try to crack a password.

IEEE
(Institute of Electrical and Electronic Engineers) Pronounced "I-triple-E." An organization of scientists, engineers, and students of electronics and related fields whose technical and standards committees develop, publish, and revise computing and telecommunications standards.

IMAP4
(Internet Mail Access Protocol version 4) A protocol used to retrieve email messages and folders from a mail server.

impersonation
An approach in which an attacker pretends to be someone he or she is not, typically an average user in distress, or a help-desk representative.

inkjet printer
A printer that forms images by spraying liquid ink from an ink cartridge out of nozzles aimed carefully on the printer.

Internet cache
A local storage area that holds the files saved by a web browser to decrease the time it takes to reload a web page.

iOS
The base software that allows all other applications to run on an iPhone, iPod touch, or iPad.

joystick
A pivoting stick or lever attached to a base that is used to control movement on a device.

kinetics
The study of human movement.

LAN
(local area network) A group of computers and associated devices that share the resources of a single processor or server within a small geographic area.

laptop
A complete computer system that is small, compact, lightweight, and portable.

laser printer
A printer that uses a laser beam to form images and toner to print the images on a printing medium, such as paper or photo paper.

LCD
(liquid crystal display) A flat-panel display device that is a compact, lightweight alternative to traditional CRT displays.

LED
(light emitting diode) A display device that uses either dynamic RGB light-emitting diodes or white edge–light-emitting diodes as the light source.

Linux
An OS that is an open-standards UNIX derivative originally developed and released by a Finnish computer science student named Linus Torvalds.

Linux distribution
A complete Linux implementation, including kernel, shell, applications, utilities, and installation media, that is packaged, distributed, and supported by a software vendor.

liquid cooling system
A system that uses tubes filled with a coolant connected to a radiator and a pump to circulate the liquid coolant through the inside of your computer case, along with fans to move air across the tubes to decrease the temperature within the case.

local storage
Any storage media that is directly attached to the computer that uses it.

logic bomb
A piece of code that sits dormant on a target computer until it is triggered by a specific event

mainframe
A large computer that might serve a large organization to process and store information for many users at once.

malware
A type of computer code that, often without manifesting itself to the targeted user, performs actions that cause undesirable results.

memory
A computer component that provides the temporary workspace for a processor.

MFD
(multifunction device) A piece of office equipment that performs the functions of a number of other specialized devices, such as a printer, scanner, fax machine, and copier.

Mini-HDMI connector
(mini–high definition multimedia interface connector) An HDMI connector that is specified for use with portable devices.

mobile app
A compact software program that is developed to perform a predefined function on a smartphone or a handheld mobile device such as a mobile phone, tablet, or feature phone.

modem
An adapter card that enables you to connect to other computers and the Internet by using an analog phone line.

molex connector
A power connector that is used to supply power to Parallel Advanced Technology Attachment (PATA) drives, optical drives, and SCSI drives.

motherboard
The personal computer component that acts as the backbone for the entire computer system. Also referred to as a system board.

mouse
A small object that runs across a flat surface and has at least one, but typically two or three, buttons that send electronic signals to the graphical user interface (GUI).

multicore processor
A central processing unit (CPU) that has two or more individual CPUs mounted in a single chip, working in parallel.

multifactor authentication
An authentication scheme that requires validation of two or more authentication factors.

multimedia player
A handheld device that enables you to play digitally recorded audio, video, and combination audio/video files.

NAS
(network-attached storage) A storage device that is directly attached to the network and is used to supply file-based storage services to other computers on the network.

Navigation pane
A File Explorer component that is located in the left pane of the File Explorer window; it enables you to scroll and directly access folders on your PC, your OneDrive files and folders, drives and devices connected to your computer, or other computers on the network.

network card
An adapter card that enables you to connect to other computers over a wired or wireless connection. Also referred to as NIC (network interface card).

network printer
A shared printing device that can be used simultaneously by multiple users on a network.

NFC
(Near Field Communication) A standard of communication between mobile devices such as smartphones and tablets in very close proximity, usually when touching or being only a few inches apart from each other.

notebook
A full-featured computer that is smaller and lighter than a laptop.

OLED
(organic light emitting diode) A type of LED flat panel display device that uses organic compounds that emit light when subjected to an electric current.

Open Handset Alliance
Developer of the Android OS.

open source
A software licensing scheme that enables users to access its source code and gives them the right to modify it.

optical disk
A personal computer storage device, such as a CD, DVD, or Blu-ray disc, that stores data optically, rather than magnetically.

OS
(operating system) A software package that enables a computer to function. It performs basic tasks, such as recognizing the input from a keyboard, sending the output to a display screen or monitor, and controlling peripheral devices such as disk drives and printers.

OS X
An OS developed by Apple Computing, Inc., for use on Macintosh computers.

ozone filter
A ventilation component that removes the ozone that is generated inside printers during the printing process.

pairing
The process by which Bluetooth mobile devices can establish a connection.

parallel connection
A computer connection that transfers data eight or more bits at a time over eight or more wires.

password
A case-sensitive string of alphanumeric characters that must be typed before a user can access a computer.

password attack
Any type of attack in which the attacker attempts to obtain and make use of passwords illegitimately.

patch
A small unit of supplemental code meant to address either a security problem or a functionality flaw in a software package or operating system.

PDA
(personal digital assistant) A mobile hand-held device that provides computing, information storage, and information retrieval capabilities for personal or business use.

peer-to-peer network
A network in which resource sharing, processing, and communications control are completely decentralized.

peripheral
A device that connects to a computer to expand the computer's functionality. This includes devices that enable the user to input, output, store, and share data.

permissions
Security properties that determine access to resources such as files and printers.

personal computer
(PC) A computing device designed to be used by one person at a time.

pharming
A form of phishing that redirects a request for a website, typically an e-commerce site, to a similar-looking, but fake, website.

phishing
A type of email-based social engineering attack in which the attacker sends email from a spoofed source, such as a bank, to try to elicit private information from the victim.

piconet
A connection of two to eight Bluetooth-enabled devices.

PII
(personally identifiable information) Any information that can be used to determine who a person is.

plasma display
A type of display device that uses xenon and neon rays and a flat panel of glass to provide visuals with high contrast, brightness, and vibrant colors that can be viewed from a multitude of angles.

plug-in
A piece of software that enables a web browser to process specific types of content.

POP3
(Post Office Protocol version 3) A protocol used to retrieve email from a mailbox on a mail server.

port
A hardware interface that you can use to connect devices to a computer.

power strip
A device that attaches to a power outlet in order to provide more outlets for you to use.

power supply
An internal computer component that converts line voltage alternating current (AC) power from an electrical outlet to the low-voltage direct current (DC) power needed by system components.

Preview pane
A File Explorer component that displays a preview of files such as documents, presentation slides, and images without opening them in an application.

printer
A device that transfers text and images from electronic content onto physical media such as paper, photo paper, and labels.

PS/2 port
A round 6-pin port commonly used to connect keyboards and mice to computers. Also referred to as a mini-Din port.

RAM
(random access memory) Volatile memory that requires a constant source of electricity to keep track of the data stored in it.

ransomware
Malicious software that prevents you from using your computer and demands payment before your access will be restored.

RCA connector
A connector that carries audio and video transmissions to and from a variety devices,

such as TVs, digital cameras, and gaming systems.

Recycle Bin
A container object located on the Windows desktop that temporarily stores deleted files.

redundancy
An alternate way in which to keep the network operating.

resilience
The ability of any network to survive disaster or avoid it in the first place.

ribbon
A File Explorer component that is displayed below the title bar and shows a list of common tasks depending upon the selected object or objects.

rights
Security settings that control what system-wide actions users can perform on a computer.

RJ-11 connector
A six-position connector that uses just one pair of wires. It is used in telephone system connections.

RJ-45 connector
An eight-position connector that uses all four pairs of wires. It is usually used for network connectivity.

RoHS
(Restriction of Use of Hazardous Substances) A compliance directive launched in 2006 and enforced by the European Union that aims to restrict certain dangerous substances commonly used in electronic devices.

rollup
A collection of previously issued patches and hotfixes, usually meant to be applied to one component of a system, such as the web browser or a particular service.

rootkit
Malicious code that is designed to hide the existence of processes or programs from normal detection methods and to gain continuous privileged access to a computer system.

router
A networking device used to send data among multiple networks that use the same protocol.

S-video connector
A video connector that carries S-Video, which is an analog video signal that carries the video data as two separate signals (brightness and color).

SATA power connector
(Serial ATA power connector) A power connector that is used to supply power to SATA drives.

scanner
A peripheral device that takes a photo-identical copy (scan) of a physical hard copy of any kind of document, such as a piece of paper or a photo, and creates a digital-format copy of the document.

Secure FTP
(Secure File Transfer Protocol) Same as FTP over SSH.

serial connection
A personal computer connection that transfers data one bit at a time over a single wire.

server
A network computer that shares resources with and responds to requests from computers, devices, and other servers on the network.

Service Pack
A larger compilation of system updates that can include functionality enhancements, new features, and typically all patches, updates, and hotfixes issued up to the point of the service pack release.

SFTP
(Simple File Transfer Protocol) An early, unsecured file transfer protocol that has since been declared obsolete.

shareware
Free applications that a user can download from the Internet directly. The only difference

between a freeware and shareware application is that the shareware is usually provided on a trial basis.

shortcut
A link or pointer to a program, file, or folder that is represented by a small icon.

shoulder surfing
A method of gaining information by simply viewing the information as the user enters it.

smartphone
High-end mobile device that provides users with a wide range of functions, such as a portable media player, video camera, GPS, high-resolution touchscreen, high-speed Wi-Fi, web browser, and mobile broadband, along with phone service.

SMTP
(Simple Mail Transfer Protocol) A communications protocol used to send email from a client to a server or between servers.

social engineering attack
A type of attack that uses deception and trickery to convince unsuspecting users to provide sensitive data or to violate security guidelines.

software management
The practice of installing and updating operating system features, applications, and drivers, as well as obtaining the appropriate licenses.

software updates
Software programs or code intended to address security flaws and performance issues in an existing version of software.

software upgrade
The process of replacing a software application completely with a newer version.

SOHO network
(small office home office network) A network that provides connectivity and resource sharing for a small office or home office.

soldering
A means of securing electronic components to a circuit board by using a combination of lead, tin, and silver (solder) and a tool called a soldering iron.

solid state storage
A personal computer storage device that stores data in non-volatile special types of memory instead of on disks or tape.

spam
A message or email that is sent indiscriminately to many people around the world.

spear phishing
See "whaling."

spim
An IM-based attack similar to spam that is propagated through instant messaging instead of through email.

spoofing
A human-based or software-based attack in which the goal is to pretend to be someone else for the purpose of identity concealment. Spoofing can occur in IP addresses, MAC addresses, and email.

spyware
Malicious software designed to intercept or take control of a computer's operation without consent.

SSD
(solid state drive) A storage device that uses solid state memory to store data, and is an alternative to using a hard disk drive in a computer.

SSID
(Service Set Identifier) A 32-bit alphanumeric string that identifies a wireless access point (WAP) and all the devices attached to it.

SSL
(Secure Sockets Layer) A security protocol that provides secure communications over the Internet.

SSL/TLS
(Secure Sockets Layer/Transport Layer Security) A data encryption method used by HTTPS.

SSO
(single sign-on) An access control property that you can use to provide users with one-time authentication to multiple resources, servers, or sites.

streaming
An example of a cloud service in which media files are transmitted by a provider over the Internet and viewed by the end user in real time.

stylus pen
An input device that absorbs electricity for use on modern smartphones, tablets, and other capacitive touchscreens.

supercomputer
The fastest and the most expensive computer among all types of computers; often used to complete a single, specialized task.

surge protector
A device that provides the additional outlets of a power strip with the added benefit of protecting connected devices from surges.

switch
A small network hardware device that joins multiple computers together within the same LAN.

system board
The personal computer component that acts as the backbone for the entire computer system. Often referred to as a motherboard.

system image
A data restoration option that restores the entire state of an operating system and its corresponding software, by loading the image from a storage medium such as a DVD-ROM or USB thumb drive.

tablet
A computing device similar to a laptop in size and function, but does not include an integrated keyboard.

tape drive
A personal computer storage device that stores data magnetically on a tape enclosed in a removable tape cartridge.

telepresence
The technology that allows a person to feel as though they are present in a location different from the one they are in by including stimuli to encourage that feeling of presence.

terminal
A typewriter-style keyboard and a display screen, or monitor, that is used to access the information stored on mainframes.

thermal paper
Special paper that contains chemicals designed to react and change color as it is heated by the heating element within the printer to create images.

thermal printer
A printer that uses a heating element to create the image on the paper with dye, ink from ribbons, or directly with pins while the feed assembly moves the media through the printer.

throughput
A measurement of how much data can actually pass through the network channel in a given time period.

Thunderbolt connection
An input/output connection developed by Apple and Intel that carries data and display signals on a single cable.

TKIP
(Temporal Key Integrity Protocol) A security protocol created by the IEEE 802.11i task group to replace WEP.

touchpad
A small, touch-sensitive pad that enables you run to your finger across its surface, which sends electronic signals to the computer to control the pointer on the screen.

touchscreen
A device that enables input by touching images on the screen, while the screen acts as the display for the computing device.

trackball
A mouse-like pointing device in which the ball is mounted on the top of the case.

trackpoint
A small button located in the center of laptop keypads that responds to user force in all directions in order to move the cursor on screen.

trojan
A malicious program that masquerades itself as a harmless application.

UPS
(uninterruptible power supply) A device that provides power without interruption of service to connected devices in the event of a general power failure.

USB connection
(universal serial bus connection) A computer connection that enables you to connect multiple peripherals to a single port with high performance and minimal device configuration.

USB drive
(universal serial bus drive) A small solid-state device, such as a "thumb" drive, or other drives that can be connected to the computer by using a USB connection.

user account
An information profile that uniquely identifies a user on a computer.

user authentication
A network security measure in which a computer user or some other network component proves its identity in order to gain access to network resources.

user name
A unique name identifying a user account on a computer.

versioning
Information about the iteration of the software you are using.

VGA
(video graphics array) A video connector that, until recently, was the primary way of connecting a display device to a computer.

video card
An adapter card that enables you to connect display devices to your computer, and that typically has its own bank of memory to improve the rate at which the images on screen can be updated.

virtual machine
A software implementation or emulation of a host machine, which is created by virtualization software, and runs independently from the host on which it is installed.

virtualization
The process of creating a logical (virtual) version of a computer environment by separating the elements of the computing environment from each other and from the physical hardware it runs on via an additional software layer.

virus
A computer program that spreads into a computer system by inserting copies of itself.

vishing
A human-based attack where the goal is to extract personal, financial, or confidential information from the victim by using services such as the telephone system and IP-based voice messaging services (VoIP) as the communication medium. Also referred to as voice phishing.

voice phishing
See "vishing."

VoIP
(voice over IP) The transmission of voice communications over IP networks such as the Internet.

WAN
(wide area network) A network of computers that are spread across a large geographic area.

WAP
(wireless access point) A network device that provides a connection between wireless devices and that can also connect to wired networks.

web application
A software application that is installed on a web server and delivered to users through the Internet.

web browser
A software application used to display web pages.

webcam
A peripheral device that sends periodic images or continuous frames to a website for display.

WEP
(Wired Equivalent Privacy) A security protocol for wireless local area networks (WLANs).

whaling
A form of phishing that targets individuals who are known or are believed to be wealthy. Also referred to as spear phishing.

white hat
A hacker who exposes security flaws in applications and operating systems so manufacturers can fix them before they become widespread problems.

Wi-Fi
The most common wireless computer networking protocol, which is a LAN technology used by many different kinds of devices.

wireless adapter
A device that converts digital data into radio waves and also receives radio waves and converts them into digital data.

wireless computer network
A network in which computers use wireless connections to link with other computers.

wireless encryption
An encryption method that conceals and protects data during transmission so that if the data were accessed during transmission it could not be read.

wireless router
A device that connects a computer to multiple networks through a wireless connection.

workgroup
A Microsoft Windows–based peer-to-peer network that is typically implemented in a SOHO environment and that usually contains fewer than 20 peers.

worm
A parasitic program that replicates itself and exploits a computer's file transmission capabilities.

WPA
(Wi-Fi Protected Access) A security protocol that provides a significantly stronger encryption scheme than WEP, and can use a shared private key, which are unique keys assigned to each user.

WPA2
(Wi-Fi Protected Access version 2) A complete wireless standard that adds strong encryption and authentication security to 802.11 and relies on 802.1x as the authentication mechanism. Also referred to as 802.11i.

Index

D

E

F

G

H

I

K

L

M

R

S

T

093004S rev 1.1
ISBN-13 978-1-4246-2286-3
ISBN-10 1-4246-2286-7